Valcamonica

Maiden Castle

Stonehenge

Carnac

Avebury

Tarxien

Skara Brae

Borremose

12,000 B.C. | 10,000 B.C. | 8,000 B.C. | 6,000 B.C. | 4,000 B.C. | 2,000 B.C. | A.D. 1

Newgrange

Biskupin

Hochdorf

Entremont

PLACES IN TIME

Exploring Prehistoric Europe

PLACES IN TIME

Series editors Brian M. Fagan and Chris Scarre

PLACES IN TIME

Exploring Prehistoric Europe

Chris Scarre

NEW YORK OXFORD
OXFORD UNIVERSITY PRESS

1998

Oxford University Press

Oxford New York

Athens Auckland Bangkok Bogotá Bombay
Buenos Aires Calcutta Cape Town Dar es Salaam
Delhi Florence Hong Kong Istanbul Karachi
Kuala Lumpur Madras Madrid Melbourne
Mexico City Nairobi Paris Singapore
Taipei Tokyo Toronto Warsaw
and associated companies in
Berlin Ibadan

Published by Oxford University Press, Inc.
198 Madison Avenue, New York, New York 10016-4314

Library of Congress Cataloging-in-Publication Data

Scarre, Christopher.
Exploring prehistoric Europe / Chris Scarre.
p. cm. — (Places in time)
Includes bibliographical references and index.
ISBN 0-19-510323-8
1. Prehistoric peoples—Europe. 2. Megalithic monuments—Europe. 3. Antiquities, Prehistoric—Europe. I. Title. II. Series.
GN803.S25 1998
936—dc21 98-17387

9 8 7 6 5 4 3 2 1

Printed in Hong Kong on acid-free paper
Designed by Diane Gleba Hall

Contents

Preface

Stonehenge, Lascaux, Carnac . . . there is no question that Europe has some of the most spectacular archaeological sites in the world, many of them household names. Who of us has not puzzled over how prehistoric communities were able to drag huge stones across miles of countryside and set them upright? Or still more puzzling, why they did it? And almost every book on Western art begins with images of bulls or bison from the famous painted caves of France and Spain, again evoking feelings of wonder and excitement.

With the opportunities for travel presented by the late twentieth century, "archaeological tourism" has become a rapidly growing field. In years gone by, most individuals with an interest in the past had to content themselves with what they could discover about it and its remains in books or articles. Travel —even in Europe—was a lengthy, hazardous, and expensive business. Only the fortunate few had the time and resources to visit the sites themselves. Nowadays, however, travel is both easy and relatively cheap. Almost anybody with an interest in archaeology can go to see the places where major discoveries have been made and walk over the ground themselves. Thousands of people do it every year and find it a rewarding experience, for in so doing, they gain a sense of place that provides them with a direct link to the past.

The present book aims to provide essential background for one selective series of explorations, a kind of "Grand Tour" of European prehistory. It takes Europe—mainly western Europe—as its geographical canvas and provides insights into its prehistory through an account of fifteen key sites, setting them in their prehistoric context. It isn't, strictly speaking, a guidebook. Plans and descriptions have been included to assist the visitor, and we envisage some of our readers holding the book open in their hands as they peer at the Valcamonica carvings or wander the ruins of Entremont. But many more of our readers will be settled in their armchairs. For it is more an attempt to show what can be learned, and what has been learned, about European prehistory from the individual sites. Yet we hope, above all, that the book will encourage visitors to look around themselves and to think about the meaning of what they see. In a famous passage by Sir Arthur Conan Doyle, the detective Sherlock Holmes admonishes his colleague Dr. Watson: "You see, but you do not observe." It is part of the aim here to take visitors beyond merely "seeing" the art of Lascaux or the stones of Stonehenge, so that they can begin to pick out what is of interest or significance, and to gain insight into its meaning.

What we have in this book are fifteen case studies, covering some of the most famous prehistoric monuments in Europe. The chapters lead the reader around the remains as they appear at the present day. These are not mere descriptions, however, for every opportunity is taken to show what these remains can tell us, and to explore what they might mean. We consider also what these places originally looked like and how they were used.

In prehistory there are no written records, and we don't know the names of the individual owners and builders, the people who carved the art or were buried in the tombs. That doesn't detract from the interest of these sites, however, for we can still seek to understand them as the work of people like ourselves, prehistoric individuals with hopes and fears similar to our own, going about their varied daily lives with the habits and beliefs that these sites begin to reveal.

The Selection

Fifteen is a small selection from among the countless thousands of prehistoric sites archaeologists have discovered in Europe. It was in Europe, in fact, that archaeology can properly be said to have begun, and early explorations are a repeated theme in several of the chapters that follow.

Before going further, however, a word must be said about the reasons for this particular selection of sites. How were they chosen?

Here I must confess that the list continued to develop from the very beginning of the project until almost the last minute, with a number of difficult decisions en route. No such selection could hope to please everyone, and every European specialist, if asked to draw up such a list, would most probably arrive at a different conclusion. A measure of arbitrariness is unavoidable. But to explain the final outcome—the fifteen sites presented here—it may be helpful to set out some of the guiding principles that were brought to bear.

- The aim of the Places in Time series as a whole is to describe sites that are open and accessible to the public. The choice was therefore made not from among all European prehistoric sites, but from that much smaller group where there is still something significant to be seen—not simply the trace of an excavation, long since abandoned or filled in, but the remains or ramparts or walls, or images carved or painted on rock.

  All the sites described here accordingly have significant visible remains. Many other sites important to the study of prehistoric Europe—many famous names—have been judged unsuitable for inclusion, because they are not visitable, or because there is nothing to been seen at the site today.

- This criterion of visitability has not only governed the kinds of sites presented here, it has also affected the geographical coverage. Countries that have good visitor arrangements, such as France and Britain, are relatively well represented. On the other hand, the countries of eastern Europe, where tourist facilities are less well developed, are represented by fewer sites.

  Every effort has nonetheless been made, within these limitations, to ensure a good geographical balance in the selection of featured sites. To achieve this, several sites that might have been obvious candidates for inclusion have been omitted in order to avoid undue emphasis on already well-covered areas.

  One area that has been omitted altogether is the Aegean—Greece, Crete, and the islands. The reason for this is simple: we plan that a future Places in Time volume will be devoted exclusively to the Aegean region, and it will include coverage of prehistoric sites alongside the more famous Classical remains.

- The concern to achieve balance applies equally to different periods of prehistory and different types of sites. Our choice of sites covers the entire range of European prehistory. We can think of them as stepping stones, leading us across the vast expanse of time from the first arrival of humans in Europe over a million years ago, to the beginnings of history (and the end of prehistory) as the Roman Empire absorbed much of Europe during the first centuries B.C. and A.D. The earliest of the sites described here—the Paleolithic encampment at Terra Amata on the Mediterranean coast of France—dates to around 380,000 years ago. One of the most recent—the hillfort of Maiden Castle in England—was attacked and destroyed by the conquering Romans in A.D. 43.

In choosing different types of sites, too, efforts have also been made to avoid duplication. So, for example, there are hundreds of Neolithic chambered tombs in northern and western Europe, not a few of them open or accessible to the public. But here we have restricted coverage to just one—Newgrange in Ireland (though chambered tombs do feature alongside other monuments in the chapters devoted to Carnac and Avebury). The same policy applies in the choice of painted caves. Archaeologists have recorded around three hundred decorated caves in southern France and northern Spain, and several of them are visitable, but we decided here to concentrate on the single most famous example, Lascaux.

The individual site treatments form the core of the present volume. In each of them, the aim has been to use the site itself as the peg from which to hang a discussion of a whole class of monument or a whole period of time. This is a further reason why duplication has been avoided. Stonehenge and Avebury are, however, special cases. Both are included, though both of them are stone circles, built at approximately the same period in the same region of southern Britain. But Avebury is presented here not as a single monument but as an entire complex, including the West Kennet long barrow, the causewayed enclosure of Windmill Hill, and the enigmatic Silbury Hill, as well as the great circle of Avebury itself.

And Stonehenge could hardly be omitted from a book of this kind. It is, in truth, probably the most famous prehistoric monument in Europe. Stonehenge has also taken on a new interest with the recent publication of a major reanalysis. This has substantially modified our knowledge of when and in what order its various parts were built. The chapter on Stonehenge in this book is one of the first general accounts to incorporate the results of this new assessment.

Another "first" for the present volume is the coverage of the open-air Paleolithic art in the Côa valley of northern Portugal. Whereas the existence of Stonehenge has been known for many centuries (it was first referred to in Henry of Huntingdon's history of England around 1130), the Côa engravings were only "discovered" in 1992 and were not publicly announced until 1994. The story of their survival, and the battle that was fought to save them from dam-builders, is told in the third chapter.

In each of the descriptions an attempt has been made to evoke a sense of place, both in words and pictures. As we have already explained, this is not intended as a guidebook, but a way of telling Europe's prehistory through the medium of fifteen key places. We hope it provides a lucid and engaging account of these sites—some of them famous already, others less so, but all without exception providing windows onto the past. Our further hope is that through reading these chapters, more and more people will be inspired with an interest in prehistory and will wish to see these places for themselves.

A Note on Further Reading

Suggestions for further reading have been included at the end of each chapter. These describe the literature that is available on that particular site, as well as works of broader coverage that might be helpful to the general reader. In most cases, some reference has been made to the relevant specialist literature, for those who wish to delve deeper or to explore particular aspects of a site. The literature on these sites is in many languages, however, and often obscure. In a number of cases, the descriptions given in these chapters are the only ones yet available in English, save for short summary notices.

A site without its associated finds is a mere skeleton. It is the artifacts and food remains found at a site that enable the archaeologist to bring it to life. Where relevant, therefore, a note has been included, indicating where the objects from the individual sites may now be seen on display. In some cases, this will be an on-site museum. In others, it will be the major regional or national museum. A third possibility is that the finds will be split between two or more museums. We have tried to indicate this in each case, so that those readers who want to use the book as a basis for archaeological itineraries may take in the relevant museums on their travels.

We should remember, however, that most archaeological sites yield thousands—if not tens or hundreds of thousands—of objects. In nineteenth-century excavations, or even twentieth-century excavations, many of these finds would be thrown away. Today, most will be put in storage. Either way, what is displayed in a museum is likely to be only a small selection—the edited highlights—of what the archaeologists discovered.

Acknowledgments

A book of this kind covers more ground in time and space than can ever be within the grasp of a single scholar. My indebtedness to friends and colleagues is accordingly all the greater for their information and advice, and for supplying up-to-date material and unpublished results. To all of them I owe an enormous debt of thanks.

Particular thanks are owed my wife, Judith, who painstakingly read through the chapters at their various stages and added comments and suggestions. I am also grateful to all the following who helped me with individual chapters or with the choice of sites: Professor Emmanuel Anati, Dr. Paul Bahn, Dr. Jörg Biel, Dr. Serge Cassen, Dr. John Coles, Dr. Gabriel Cooney, Professor Barry Cunliffe, Ms. Corinne Duhig, Professor Paul Mellars, Dr. Colin Richards, Dr. Marie-Louise Sørensen, Dr. Alasdair Whittle, Ms. Hanna Zawadzka, and Dr. João Zilhão.

Last but not least, I would like to express my thanks to Professor Brian Fagan, coeditor of the Places in Time series, and to the staff of Oxford University Press's New York office, especially Liza Ewell, Liz Sonneborn, Mary Kay Linge, and Hannah Borgeson, for their unfailing support and advice throughout the project.

Chris Scarre
Cambridge, England

Introduction

The fifteen sites featured in this volume are drawn from the rich and varied panorama that is European prehistory. They are hence widely scattered in space and time. Each of them can be thought of as a snapshot, a brief glimpse into the European past. Another way to think of them is as pegs—on each we seek to hang some account of the major changes that European societies underwent during this lengthy period. For, above all, it is human societies and the individuals who composed them that are the heart of archaeology. But to understand the particular sites that form the basis of the following chapters, some preliminary explanation is called for. This falls into two parts: a brief introduction to the methods archaeologists use in studying the past, with particular attention to chronology, and a short outline of European prehistory, to help show how the individual sites fit into an overall pattern.

Studying the Past

Time is of the essence in prehistoric studies. We cannot possibly hope to understand European prehistory without having at least an outline of the overall time frame. But time is also an elusive entity, difficult to pin down. For this reason, archaeologists have devised a number of ways to approach it.

First there is the concept of time *periods*. Back in the nineteenth century, antiquaries and archaeologists came to realize that even without knowing precise dates, it was possible to organize prehistoric material into separate periods that followed one another. The earliest of these periods they called the "Stone Age," when tools were made of stone and metals were unknown. Next came the Bronze Age, characterized by the manufacture of objects made of bronze, an alloy of copper and tin. These in their turn were replaced by more efficient tools of iron in the Iron Age. The Iron Age ended with the beginning of history, when written records first became available. Over much of Europe, this end to prehistory coincided with incorporation of regions into the Roman Empire.

The sequence of Stone, Bronze, and Iron Ages is known as the "Three-Age System" and was for many years the cornerstone of prehistoric chronologies. Its invention is generally attributed to Christian Jurgensen Thomsen, the son of a Copenhagen merchant who became curator of the Danish National Museum in 1816. Thomsen reorganized the displays in his museum in a sequence depending on whether they had cutting tools of stone, bronze, or iron, and in his *Guide to Northern Archaeology* he published an account of this chronological scheme that had wide influence and was rapidly translated into German, English, and other European languages.

At first no one was sure how long these ages of Stone, Bronze, and Iron had lasted. But soon archaeologists began to see separate divisions or phases within them. The Stone Age was the first of the three ages to be subdivided, on the basis of the distinction between polished stone tools and those that were merely chipped and flaked. The polished stone tools were assigned to the Neolithic ("New Stone Age"), along with pottery and farming. The earlier part of the Stone Age, before the Neolithic, was then itself subdivided into the Paleolithic ("Old Stone Age"), corresponding to the period of the Ice Ages, and the post–Ice Age Mesolithic ("Middle Stone Age"). These terms—Paleolithic, Mesolithic, Neolithic, Bronze Age, and Iron Age—though crude chronological markers, are still widely used as shorthand for the main divisions of European prehistory.

On their own, however, they don't tell us very clearly or precisely *when* an individual structure or artifact was made or used. For this archaeologists had to wait until after the Second World War, when a whole new series of scientific dating methods became available as a by-product of research into nuclear physics.

ESTABLISHING AN ACCURATE TIMESCALE

Since the Second World War, the dating of archaeological sites has been revolutionized by the invention of absolute dating techniques. These make it possible to go beyond labeling things "Early Neolithic" or "Late Bronze Age" and give them instead an accurate age expressed in calendar years. The most famous of these new dating methods is radiocarbon dating, based on the decay of the radiocarbon isotope carbon-14. Any material that contains carbon, such as wood, bone, or charcoal, can be dated by this means. Since its invention in the late 1940s, the method has undergone a series of refinements. One of them takes account of the discovery that the amount of naturally occurring carbon-14 in the atmosphere varies from time to time in response to fluctuations in solar radiation. This means that "crude" radiocarbon dates have to be "corrected" in order to arrive at accurate calendar ages. All the radiocarbon dates quoted in this book have been corrected in that way, except those relating to the Paleolithic (over 10,000 years ago), for which no correction has yet been devised.

RADIOCARBON DATING

The invention of radiocarbon dating—one of the most important tools in prehistoric archaeology—came about in the late 1940s and is associated with American chemist Willard F. Libby. The basis of the method is that cosmic rays bombard earth's atmosphere, causing some of the nitrogen in the atmosphere to convert to a radioactive form of carbon: carbon-14 or radiocarbon. The carbon-14 is unstable and decays steadily, at a rate of 50 percent in 5,730 years. In the atmosphere, new carbon-14 is continually being created; the radiocarbon pool is constantly being topped up. But where carbon is ingested by living things—through eating plants that contain carbon dioxide—the accumulation of carbon-14 ceases at death. After death, the radiocarbon begins to decay. Thus measuring the amount that has decayed gives a direct estimate of the length of time since that individual plant or animal died.

As so often in science, however, there are complications. The most important is the discovery that production of carbon-14 in the atmosphere has not always been constant. This means that radiocarbon dates have to be "corrected" or "calibrated" in order to arrive at a true age. These corrections can make a difference of several hundred years.

Radiocarbon dating can be used to date any organic material, such as wood, plant fiber, animal bones, or even seashells. All that is required is that enough carbon-14 survives to be accurately measured. This means that samples have to be of a certain size. In the past, 5 grams of pure carbon were needed, but the new methods of AMS (accelerator mass spectrometry) dating have reduced this to as little as 5–10 milligrams. This advance makes it possible for the first time to date materials containing only tiny amounts of charcoal. One notable beneficiary has been the study of Paleolithic cave art. AMS dating can date tiny fractions of charcoal scraped off the cave wall, without significantly damaging the art itself. French specialists have dated some of the charcoal drawings in the Grotte Chauvet to between 30,000 and 32,000 B.P. by this means.

A second problem is precision. Corrected radiocarbon dates are generally accurate—they point to the right place on the timescale—but they are by nature imprecise—they don't give an individual year date, but a time bracket. Some of the early radiocarbon dates had ranges extending over hundreds of years, but most recent dates are precise to within a century or so. It still happens, however, that radiocarbon dates for events that are known to be successive can overlap, owing to their imprecision. The imprecision becomes greater the further back in time we go, until around 40,000 years ago when radiocarbon dating reaches its upper limit. For earlier sites, other methods such as potassium-argon or thorium-uranium dating must be used. They are based on similar principles of radioactive decay, but are much less widely applicable than radiocarbon dating, which is based on carbon, an ingredient in all living things and one of the earth's most abundant elements.

In favorable circumstances, even more powerful dating techniques than radiocarbon can be employed. The most useful is dendrochronology, based on annual variations in the width of tree-rings. This technique only works where substantial timbers have survived relatively intact, which is rarely the case at prehistoric sites, though it can happen where they are waterlogged. An example in the present volume is Biskupin in Poland, dated by dendrochronology to 737 B.C. As we see here, the method often gives spectacular precision. To take just one other example, we know that the Sweet Track, a timber trackway across wetlands in southwest Britain, was built with timbers felled in the winter of 3807–3806 B.C.—an amazing chronological fix for a short event almost six thousand years ago.

At the other extreme are those sites that remain difficult to date despite all the techniques modern science can offer. Perhaps most notorious are rock carvings and engravings. There is hope here for the future, as new methods are developed. Until recently, for example, nobody would have predicted that it would become possible to date the famous Paleolithic cave paintings of France and Spain through the minute quantities of carbon in the charcoal outlines. But for rock art in the open air, where the coloring material has not survived, satisfactory methods of dating have yet to be devised. We shall meet this problem when we consider the heated debate on the dating of the Côa valley art.

PREHISTORIC LIFESTYLES

To say when a site was occupied is one thing. To determine how its occupants lived is an altogether different question, but just as important. What clothes did they wear? What foods did they eat? How long could they expect to live? What beliefs did they have? All are questions of prime importance if we are ever truly to understand the past, and archaeologists have assembled a wide range of techniques and approaches to answer them.

One of the biggest divisions is between the hunter-gatherers of early prehistory, who followed a mobile, peripatetic lifestyle and depended on wild foods, and the farmers and stock-breeders of later prehistory, who lived all year round in permanent settlements. The transition to farming was a gradual process, beginning in southwest Asia and spreading to southeast Europe some nine thousand years ago. It reached the northern and western fringes of the continent a few thousand years later. In conventional wisdom, the beginning of farming is linked to the onset of the Neolithic period, though it would be wrong to assume that all Neolithic communities had the same subsistence base.

The obvious way to find out what people gathered and hunted or tended and cultivated is to study their food remains. On prehistoric sites, archaeologists look first to the surviving bones of the animals whose meat they consumed.

Wild species are characteristic of hunter-gatherer communities, while domestic animals, such as cattle, sheep, and pig, become increasingly common from Neolithic times onward. By analyzing the cut marks on bones and the proportions of different species and age groups in the animal populations, archaeologists can show just how prehistoric communities planned their hunting or managed their herds. Plant foods also played a major role throughout prehistory, but they are intrinsically more perishable and hence more difficult to study. Impressions of cereal grains such as wheat and barley sometimes survive in pottery vessels, but we know from other evidence (such as the food remains preserved in the stomachs of Danish bog bodies) that a wide range of plants was eaten, including some that today are regarded as weeds. We mustn't imagine that prehistoric diet was rich in taste, though recent research is throwing new light on the consumption of alcoholic drinks and the use of narcotics such as hemp. Prehistoric Europeans weren't necessarily dour teetotalers!

Alongside subsistence are key questions relating to environmental conditions and landscapes. We see prehistoric sites in essentially modern landscape settings. Very little survives of the original European vegetation; most areas have been radically altered by human interference. Early farmers themselves deforested large areas of arable land, leaving them open to the skies and vulnerable to erosion and degradation. But today's landscape is not even the landscape of the Neolithic, but a palimpsest, a gradual accumulation of changes both small and large that have built up over the centuries. In most cases, the greatest changes of all have been those of the last hundred years, as mechanized farming replaced traditional practices. Obviously, archaeologists have an uphill task in seeking to understand prehistoric sites in their original settings. But they do find evidence of ancient pollen and snails, and sometimes old soils buried under later monuments, to tell them about the vegetation and climate. From this evidence, wherever it is available, archaeologists can discover what grew around a particular site at the time it was occupied, how much forest and field there was, and how early human communities—especially farming communities—used the land.

Some of the best evidence of prehistoric lifestyles is provided by settlements themselves. Mobile hunter-gatherers lived generally in small camps that might have been occupied for only a few days or weeks at a time. This was probably the case at Terra Amata, for example, though people returned to the site many times over the years. In many areas of Europe, these mobile lifestyles continued long after the beginnings of cultivation. Farming villages, however, generally have much more substantial remains, as we might expect of settlements occupied all year round for decades or centuries, or even millennia in some cases. By late prehistoric times, many areas of Europe had large villages. Some of them, especially in the south of Europe, even had towns built on the Greek or Roman model.

Planned towns of this kind are a far cry from simple hunting sites. The reader has only to compare Entremont and Terra Amata to appreciate the huge range and variety in the sites and societies that fall within the broad time frame of prehistoric Europe.

An Outline of European Prehistory

We have explained above some of the ways by which archaeologists have arrived at a prehistoric chronology and an understanding of prehistoric lifestyles and economies. The results form the basis of our knowledge of European prehistory. To do the subject justice would require a book of its own and is not the purpose of the present volume. So for those wishing to know more, a brief reading list is given at the end of this chapter. The purpose of the present section is simply to provide an outline narrative of European prehistory, linking together the fifteen sites described in the chapters that follow. We begin this narrative at the beginning, with the early hominids who were the first to colonize Europe and hence earn the label the first Europeans.

THE FIRST EUROPEANS

Imagine Europe at the height of the last Ice Age. Glaciers and snowfields blanket the northern regions, and temperatures are as much as 10°C lower than those of the present day. Much of the continent is covered by cold steppe and tundra, and temperate forests—typical of recent centuries—are confined to the Mediterranean littoral in the south. Hardly an inviting prospect. Yet it was in just these conditions, between 30,000 and 15,000 years ago, that the famous cave art was produced. Clearly our Paleolithic ancestors, like many more recent populations, had the ability to thrive amid great adversity.

The people who inhabited Europe 20,000 years ago were modern humans, biologically similar to ourselves. That they were mentally and psychologically similar, too, is suggested by the art they created and by their sophisticated hunting strategies. They were able to track and trap even the largest of the great open-country herbivores, such as mammoth and bison. Such species roamed the tundra during the last Ice Age, but became extinct when temperatures rose around 10,000 years ago.

These cave artists and big-game hunters belong to the period known as the "Upper Paleolithic"—the last of the three main stages into which the European Paleolithic or "Old Stone Age" is conventionally divided. The Upper Paleolithic begins around 40,000 B.C. with the appearance in Europe of the first anatomically modern humans. They came from Africa and the Levant, spreading across Europe from the east. They weren't, however, the first humans to inhabit Europe. For those we must go back hundreds of thousands of years to the first stage of the Paleolithic, the so-called Lower Paleolithic.

Archaeologists disagree as to when humans first came to Europe. There have been claims for humanly worked tools over two million years old in southern France, but many archaeologists remain skeptical. More persuasive

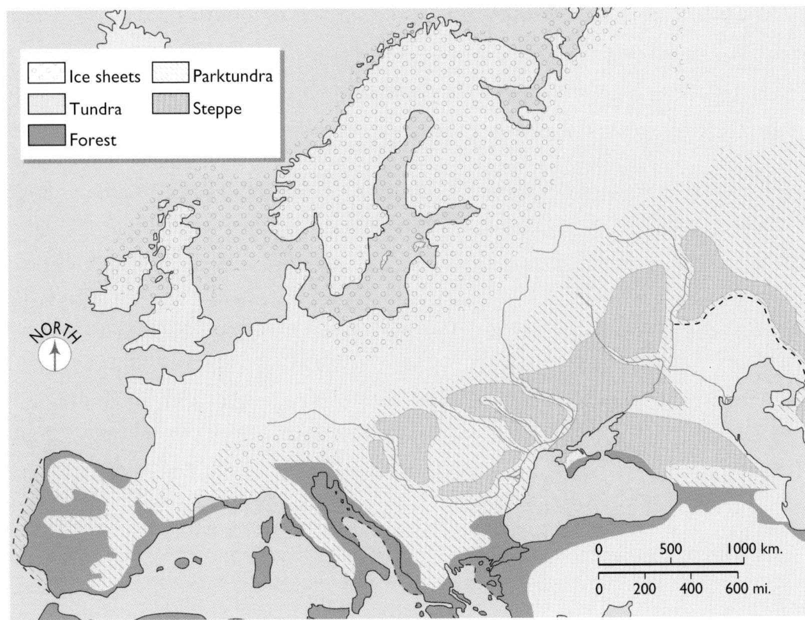

Europe at the height of the last Ice Age, around 20,000 years ago. Ice sheets covered Scandinavia and northern Britain, while forest was restricted to the Mediterranean margins. The quantity of water locked up in the ice sheets led to a fall in sea level, so that Britain and Ireland were joined to the Continent and the Black Sea was separated from the Mediterranean. When the ice sheets eventually melted and sea level rose again, large areas of coastal plain were lost to human settlement, and many early sites lie buried on the sea bed.

are recent finds from southern Spain that are more than one million years old. The earliest signs of human presence on which all can agree, however, date to around 800,000 years ago. These include the earliest human fossils from Europe, those recently discovered at Atapuerca in northern Spain.

We must piece together what we know about Europe's early human inhabitants from the stone tools and bones. The first point to bear in mind is that they had more limited mental abilities than modern humans. Much effort has been expended in arguing just what this might mean for the behavior of these first European populations. Anthropologists generally cast doubt, for example, on the idea that early humans had a well-developed language. But that doesn't mean they couldn't communicate, and they were able to make sophisticated stone tools, such as the impressive symmetrical hand-axes of flint, which are one of the hallmarks of the European early Paleolithic.

These first inhabitants of Europe spread into the continent from Africa, where the earliest hominids—the Australopithecines—had emerged some four million years before. In their origin and in their biology, humans are tropical animals. All the more remarkable, then, that they have been able to colonize cooler regions of the world such as Europe. They owe this success not so much to major changes in their physiology, such as a greater natural ability to withstand the cold, as to the development of clothing, fire, and shelter, which enabled them to survive even in harsh Ice Age conditions. There are few traces of early clothing, but archaeologists do occasionally find evidence of fire and shelter. Terra Amata is one site where French archaeologists claim to have found remains of large oval shelters and hearths dating back 380,000 years, though as we shall see, others dispute this interpretation.

Fire, clothing, and shelter would have been especially crucial during the periods of intense cold commonly referred to as the Ice Ages. Within the last million years or so, at intervals of around every hundred thousand years, temperatures have fallen and ice sheets spread over northern latitudes. During these Ice Ages, much of Europe was uninhabitable and the rest unpleasantly cold. Yet humans hung on, at first withdrawing to sheltered niches along the Mediterranean coast (or perhaps abandoning the contintent altogether), but later learning how to survive in the cold as their skills and abilities developed. And whenever the warmth returned, human societies spread out from their Ice Age refuges to cover virtually the entire continent. It is important to remember that these successive fluctuations of climate were not short episodes, but lasted tens of thousands of years. Our own period, the optimistically named "postglacial," has lasted little longer than previous warm interglacials. There is no saying exactly when cold conditions might return, or whether they have been forestalled by the modern and much-discussed phenomenon of global warming.

THE HUMAN REVOLUTION

The earliest inhabitants of Europe, for all their evident success, were biologically different from ourselves. They belong to a species labeled *Homo heidelbergensis*, with smaller brains and generally smaller physiques than modern humans. As time passed, however, these European populations developed new physical features and greater mental capacity. By 130,000 years ago, this had resulted in the emergence of a distinct type of human known as "Neanderthal," named after the first discovery of its remains in the Neander valley of western Germany in 1856. Remains of Neanderthals have only been found in Europe and western Asia. They had brains as large, or even slightly larger, than those of modern humans, but the rest of the body was much more massively built, to cope perhaps with the rigors of a harsh and demanding lifestyle. The Neanderthals were big-game hunters, roaming the cold landscapes of Ice Age Europe in search of their prey.

For all the Neanderthals' large brain size, archaeologists agree that in key respects they were less capable than fully modern humans. This must be the reason why modern humans eventually replaced the Neanderthals in Europe. Modern humans developed first in Africa over 100,000 years ago, but only began to colonize Europe around 40,000 B.C. The appearance of modern human culture marks the beginning of the Upper Paleolithic. By 35,000 years ago, modern humans had spread as far west as France and Spain, replacing the earlier Neanderthal populations. We don't quite know how the process occurred, but it may well be that they simply drove the Neanderthals to extinction. There are, after all, plenty of recent examples of modern humans' capacity for ruthless genocide.

The arrival of modern humans was much more than a simple biological change. With modern humans came a whole new range of human activity, including the famous cave art. It was modern humans who were responsible for the decorated caves of southern France and northern Spain. The earliest cave art, in the recently discovered Grotte Chauvet, is dated to around 32,000 years ago, but people continued to decorate caves for another 20,000 years. It is salutary to reflect that almost as much time separates the Grotte Chauvet art from the famous Lascaux paintings (c. 15,000 B.C.) as separates Lascaux from us. The spans of time involved are immense.

Lascaux justifiably takes pride of place in the present volume, but it is only one of three hundred or so known decorated caves from this region of western Europe. Most of the sites are much less spectacular, but the symbols and figures carved or painted on the cave walls, together with other evidence from their tools, campsites, and burials, show us that these were mentally sophisticated people, in no way inferior to us in terms of intellectual capacity. It is this change, from Neanderthals to modern humans, that has been called the "human revolution." From this point on, we can assume that these were human communities with fully developed language, and with aspirations, feelings, and beliefs in most respects similar to our own.

The polychrome figures of painted caves such as Lascaux and Altamira are without question the most dramatic evidence of this human revolution. But new discoveries in Spain and Portugal have just begun to show that Paleolithic art was far from limited to caves. The third of our featured sites shows this well: the Côa valley is the richest collection of open air Paleolithic art yet discovered in Europe. Not only does it reveal a whole new area of Paleolithic activity, it directs attention away from individual sites to entire landscapes and the meanings these held for the communities who lived there.

AFTER THE ICE

Around 10,000 years ago, temperatures rose and the last Ice Age came to an end. Sea levels rose as the ice sheets melted, gradually drowning out coastal lowlands. Land areas too underwent major changes as forest spread northward over most of Europe, replacing the cold steppe and tundra.

Bereft of their natural environment, mammoth became extinct and other large herbivores, such as reindeer and bison, were increasingly confined to northern latitudes. In their place came forest-dwelling species such as red deer and wild boar, along with the still widespread wild ox, the aurochs.

This was a much richer environment than any that had prevailed for the previous 100,000 years, and not surprisingly, human communities were quick to take advantage of it. First they spread northward along with the plants and animals on which they depended, colonizing regions that had been impossible to settle during the last Ice Age. With this geographical expansion, in the second place, came a steady increase in numbers—a prehistoric population boom. Third, the new environment placed new demands and opportunities at the door of these prehistoric communities. They devised new strategies for hunting and gathering, and new relationships with their environment and resources.

One significant change that puzzled earlier generations of archaeologists was the demise of cave art. The end of the Ice Age radically altered both the natural environment and the ritual practices of the hunter-gatherer communities. As Upper Paleolithic gave way to Mesolithic (its postglacial continuation), the deep caves fell into disuse. But this did not mean an impoverishment of either economy or human experience. Mesolithic communities simply followed different practices and chose different modes of expressing their beliefs. Most of them have left little material trace.

Mesolithic people, like their Paleolithic forebears, were hunter-gatherers dependent on the collection of wild plants and the hunting of animals. In the richly forested landscape of postglacial Europe, these people prospered and multiplied, developing new patterns of life and more complex types of social organization. Against this background an entirely novel economy began to spread across the continent—farming.

THE TRANSITION TO FARMING

The origins of farming lie outside Europe, in the Near East. It was there over 10,000 years ago that groups of hunter-gatherers began to experiment with the local wild cereals, eventually planting them in fields. Breaking the ground and then tending and harvesting the crop was laborious work, but it made

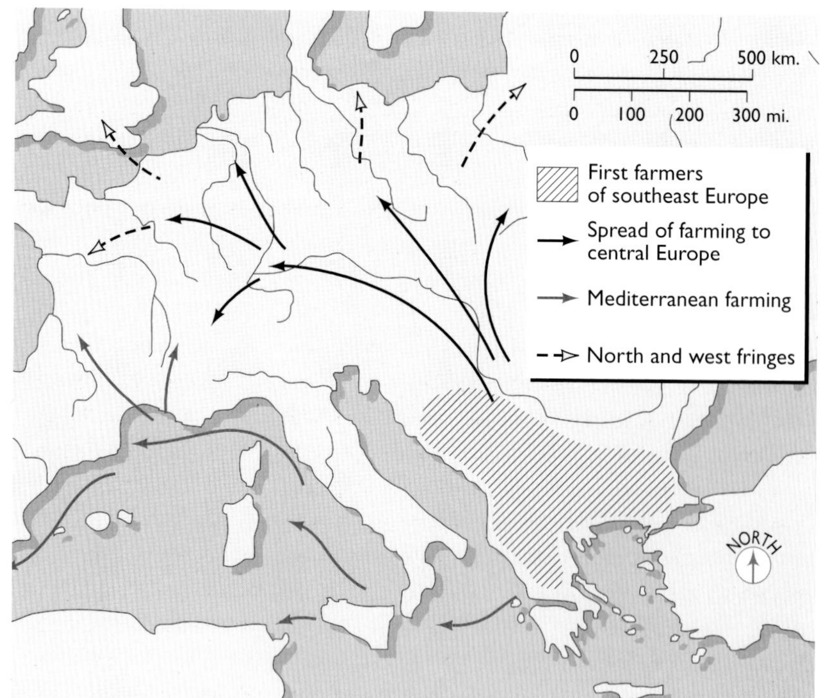

Based on cereals and domestic livestock of Near Eastern origin, farming first became established in southeast Europe around 7000 B.C. From 5500 B.C., mobile communities introduced a forest-farming lifestyle to large areas of central Europe. In the Mediterranean and in northern and western Europe, the spread of farming was more complex, with selective adoption of pottery, cereals, and domestic animals by indigenous groups. The scarcity of fixed farming settlements in northern and western Europe has led to much debate in recent years as to the nature of the transformation, and many archaeologists believe that changes in ideology or society were as important as economic innovations.

possible the production of more food than had ever been available through hunting and gathering. As gathering gave way to crop cultivation, so hunting was supplemented and then largely supplanted by herding of livestock such as cattle, sheep, goat, and pig, which were domesticated from the wild.

One key consequence of these new resources was that people could stay in the same place year-round, storing the produce of one harvest to tide them over until the next. It also became easier for larger groups of people to live together. As the use of the new resources intensified, so villages were formed, and later, as populations further burgeoned, towns and cities.

Farming was never an easy option, and its spread through Europe was slow and gradual, dependent on particular sets of local circumstances—a famine, perhaps, or a temporary need—to gain acceptance. It was not a sudden change, however, and hunting, gathering, and seasonal mobility continued to play a major role in many parts of Europe long after domesticated plants and animals had been introduced.

As we have seen, farming spread to Europe from the Near East, and was largely dependent on plants and animals of Near Eastern origins—wheat and barley, sheep and goat. Cattle and pig were native to Europe as well as the Near East, so they could have been locally domesticated, but the other species were intentionally introduced from outside. The process began in southeast Europe, where villages first appeared around 7000 B.C. From here, contacts between coastal communities carried domestic plants and animals to the central and western Mediterranean during the course of the sixth millennium B.C. At about the same time, communities spread westward and northward along the river valleys of central Europe, carrying a forest-farming way of life to Germany, the Low Countries, and eastern France. One tangible sign of this change was the establishment of substantial settlements, be they villages or simple farmsteads. Along with the adoption of crops and livestock went another key innovation much beloved of archaeologists: pottery. The shapes and decoration of pottery vessels henceforth provide an easy means of dating sites and assigning them to particular cultures or traditions.

MEGALITHS AND MONUMENTS

Northwest Europe was one of the latest areas to accept domesticated plants and animals, and the transition seems to have been more gradual and piecemeal than in the center or southeast of the continent. In Britain, for example, domestic plants and animals made their appearance before 4000 B.C., but there is little evidence of permanent farmsteads or villages for well over a thousand years. The new elements of the economy seem to have been integrated in a lifestyle that was still partly mobile in character. Gradually, however, as the centuries passed, farmsteads and villages did begin to appear in most of the British Isles. Built mainly of timber, they have generally left little trace beyond a scatter of artifacts, pits, and post-holes. But there are exceptions, espe-

Shaded areas represent the distribution of monumental tombs and megalithic monuments in western Europe during the fourth millennium B.C. The coastal emphasis suggests that maritime links may have been important, but if so these have left little direct trace. Evidence for contact between Britain and France, for example, is extremely limited, though parallels in the development of megalithic art imply there must have been some interchange of ideas.

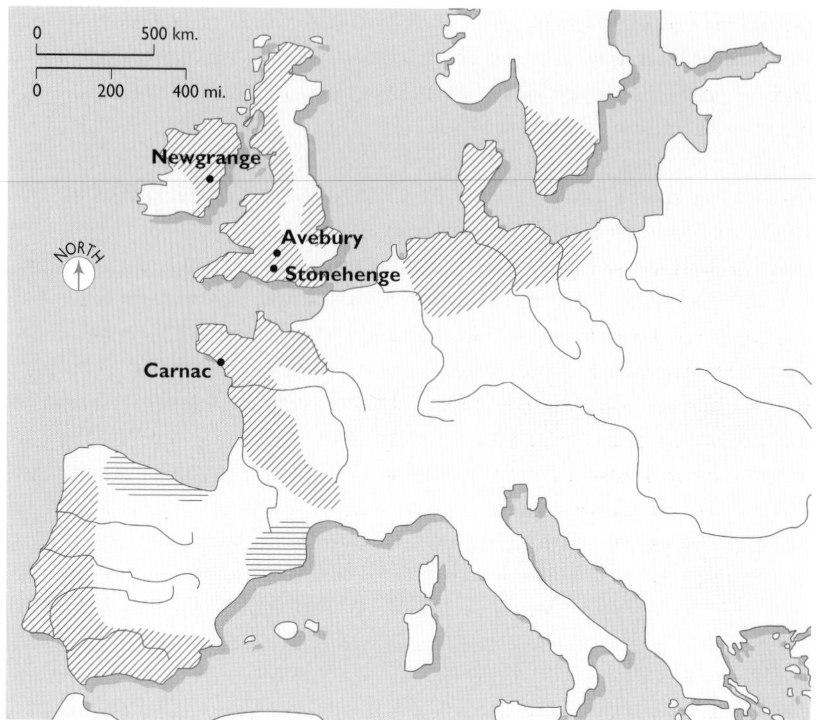

cially where timber was not available and more durable building materials were used. Such is the case at the northern margins of Britain, and it is there that we find the best-preserved Neolithic village in western Europe—the famous site of Skara Brae in the Orkney Islands. The still-standing houses of this early farming community, perched on the very edge of the European world, face out across the stormy waters of the Atlantic Ocean.

Western Europe may be short of Neolithic settlements, but it is rich in Neolithic monuments. These, as much as the changing economy, characterize the period. They include both impressive stone circles and numerous burial mounds of various shapes and sizes, many of them containing stone-built chambered tombs. Some of Europe's most famous prehistoric monuments belong to this tradition and were built at this time. In northwestern France there is the major center of Carnac, beside the Gulf of Morbihan, a complex of stone rows, long mounds, passage graves, and standing stones (now broken or reused). In southern Britain are the famous stone circles of Stonehenge and Avebury. And in Ireland we find one of the most spectacular of all megalithic tombs, the decorated passage grave of Newgrange. Long the subject of antiquarian interest, these sites have continued to draw the attention of archaeologists, and our knowledge of them and their surroundings is constantly being revised. New work at Carnac and Avebury, and a reassessment of earlier excavations at Stonehenge, are all included in this volume.

Before leaving the subject of Neolithic monuments, we must not forget one of the most interesting groups of all: the megalithic temples on the tiny islands of Malta and Gozo, in the middle of the Mediterranean between Sicily and Africa. The clues provided at Tarxien and elsewhere by statues and other ritual equipment give a rare insight into the rituals of these early island communities. They share some features of the mainland European monuments, for example the use of large stones ("megaliths"), but the Maltese temples are a distinct and idiosyncratic island tradition.

By the time the latest of these Neolithic monuments were being built, almost the whole of Europe had been brought under a more intensive farming economy. This now relied not only on the labor of human hands but also on plows drawn by oxen or horse. Wheeled vehicles, too, had been brought into use in many areas, though in the absence of proper roads their utility must inevitably have been limited. One of the most significant innovations of all, in terms of its long-term impact, was, however, unrelated to the plants and animals. It owed more to a developing knowledge of raw materials and pyrotechnology, gained from experience in sophisticated pottery firing. This innovation was the discovery and exploitation of metals.

NEW MATERIALS AND SOCIETIES

We saw earlier how the nineteenth-century scheme for European prehistory divided it into a sequence of ages based on the material used for cutting tools —first stone, then bronze, then iron. Archaeologists today realize that while these can be useful divisions, they don't necessarily correspond to major changes in the way prehistoric people lived or prehistoric communities functioned.

So the introduction of metals was not a radical transition with a sudden and immediate impact. It was part of a gradual change, beginning around 5000 B.C. when villagers in the Balkans began to experiment with new materials. They had already devised elaborate kilns for firing their pottery at very high temperatures. This was just the technology they needed to exploit copper. We don't know how they first discovered that copper-bearing rocks could be made to yield up their metal if processed in the right way. But by 4500 B.C. they were already making tools and ornaments of copper, and driving mines deep into copper-bearing deposits in quest of the valuable metal.

The mention of ornaments here deserves particular attention. For copper is not a particularly hard metal and wouldn't have been greatly superior to stone as a material for cutting tools. What was it, then, that people wanted it for? The answer seems to be personal display. Copper tools and ornaments were the fashion accessories of the rich and powerful, a visible sign that some sections of the community were more important than others. The message is brought home even more dramatically by the early use of gold, which was still less functional than copper but was worked into spectacular items for body ornamentation and status symbols.

From this it emerges that the discovery and exploitation of metals was closely linked to the development of new types of society. Gone were the societies of hunter-gatherers and early farmers, where divisions of wealth and status were few and weren't usually inherited across generations. In their place we now find stratified societies dominated by leading families who fueled the new demand for metal objects.

European copper metallurgy began in southeast Europe around 5000 B.C. Around 2500 B.C., societies in western Europe, too, started to use copper and gold. Within a short time, they and their eastern counterparts began to alloy the copper with tin to produce bronze (usually in the proportions 10% tin to 90% copper). This marks the formal beginning of the Bronze Age.

EUROPEAN SOCIETIES OF THE BRONZE AND IRON AGES

European societies of the Bronze Age, and of the Iron Age that followed it around 800 B.C., seem to have been dominated by powerful clans and clan leaders whose role increasingly included warfare. This wasn't the first time that conflict made its impact on the European scene; there is evidence of violent death from flint arrowheads as early as the Mesolithic period, and a number of Neolithic settlements were enclosed by protective walls for greater security. But the evidence of warfare becomes steadily more prominent as the Bronze Age proceeds, and weapons form one of the leading categories of bronze objects. By the Late Bronze Age, around 1200 B.C., powerful individuals in some regions were arming themselves with long bronze swords and wearing bronze breastplates and helmets for protection.

The artists of Valcamonica in northern Italy have left us with visual testimony of these changes. Their carvings on the exposed rock faces span hundreds of years and reflect changes in society and technology. In the third millennium B.C., they carved images of copper daggers with distinctive broad triangular blades. These daggers were the leading status symbols of the period. By the beginning of the Iron Age, the Valcamonica artists were showing not individual weapons but armed warriors on horseback, complete with helmets and spears. These weren't full-time warriors, however, but more likely ordinary homesteaders who engaged in occasional conflict and who were increasingly attracted by the prestige of the male-warrior image.

Settlements, too, show the growing preoccupation with security. Why else build a township such as Biskupin in such an uncomfortable and inaccessible location, on a marshy promontory jutting into a lake? Why also construct such an elaborate defensive perimeter, unless to ward off attack? These places may have been local centers of power, with perimeter walls built partly to express the prestige of the local community. But the timber defenses of Biskupin weren't simply decoration, especially if the original excavators of Biskupin were right in arguing that the settlement had been burned down by enemy action not long after it was built.

We don't see direct evidence of a ruling elite at Biskupin. The regimented layout and the fact that all the houses were of similar size suggest there must have been some central authority (whether an individual or a community assembly), but no richly furnished burials of local rulers have yet been found. Far different is the case in southern Germany some 250 years later, for here archaeologists have found a whole series of princely burials, with lavish grave furnishings including imports from the Classical world. These are the princely burials of the Early Iron Age, and the most famous of them is Hochdorf. It is significant, however, that the Hochdorf chieftain was not buried with weapons of war but with luxury items evoking a more peaceful image of Iron Age society.

By the sixth century B.C., the date of the Hochdorf burial, Europe was divided into a series of zones, each developing in its own way. In the south, the Mediterranean zone was the scene of major changes, with the rise of the Classical city-states in Greece and the Aegean. But these first European cities were not restricted to the Aegean, for the Greeks soon began to send out colonists to Sicily and southern Italy and the west Mediterranean. There they came into competition (and often open conflict) with the Phoenician traders and colonists who were also seeking to populate the Mediterranean coast of southwest Europe. Greek and Phoenician colonies such as Massalia (Marseille) and Gades (Cadiz) were keen to trade with the native populations of the interior. In general, Greek and Phoenician manufactures were exchanged for valuable raw materials. The links were not purely economic, however, for contacts with the Classical world brought new kinds of luxury goods to eastern

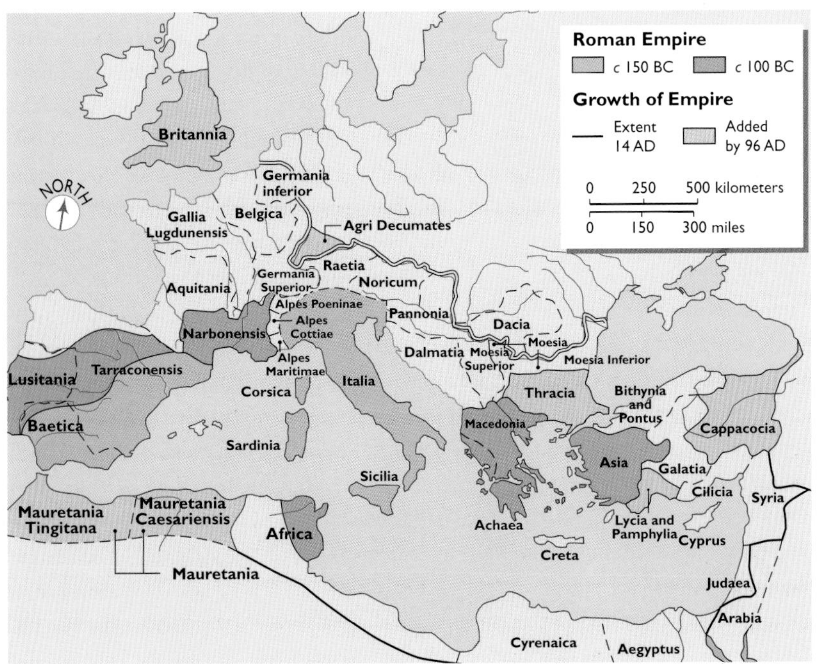

The expansion of the Roman Empire. By the end of the first century A.D., the whole of western and southern Europe (together with North Africa and much of the Near East) had been absorbed within the empire.

France, the Rhineland, and the Danube basin, and stimulated a taste for wine. They may also have been instrumental in the formation of the Celtic art style known as "La Tène," which was born in the fifth century B.C. in Germany and eastern France and survived into the early Middle Ages in the British Isles.

According to most Greek and Roman writers, the native peoples of western Europe were warlike and quarrelsome. These writers looked down on them as uncouth "barbarians." The warlike image is borne out by sites such as Maiden Castle in southern Britain, a hilltop fortress with an incredible complexity of defenses. Whether these were merely to impress—or a real sign of hostility and insecurity—it is difficult to be sure. Yet they were also resourceful people, organized along tribal lines, with a rich culture and tradition, though one that was not written down and of which little has survived. What we read about them in the Classical histories is clearly only half the picture.

THE END OF PREHISTORY

The mention of historians brings us close to the end of prehistory, for history begins when written records become available. In truth, the division is not so sharp, since early written records give often a very partial and incomplete picture, and archaeology often continues to provide the main source of information. Nor does archaeology cease to be of use when written documents become more abundant. There is much to be learned from archaeology about the Middle Ages or even the Industrial Revolution. But prehistory (as distinct from archaeology) ends with written records.

In western Europe, the earliest written records are those of the Etruscan cities of central Italy and the Greek and Phoenician colonies established along the Mediterranean coast in the eighth and seventh centuries B.C. In geographical terms, however, these cities are marginal to Europe as a whole, and prehistory ends only in the very last centuries B.C., with the spread of the Roman Empire. During the second century B.C. the Romans conquered most of the Iberian peninsula (building on Carthaginian—Phoenician—foundations). In 122 B.C., they found a pretext to take control of southern France, turning it into a Roman province ("provincia," from which the French region of Provence takes its name).

One casualty of the Roman conquest of Provence was the intriguing site of Entremont. This was a native township, belonging to a local people known as the Salluvians, but in building it they copied many features from their near neighbors, the Greek colonists at Marseille. It had stone buildings, a solid fortification wall with towers, and grid-plan streets. But in 124 B.C. the Roman army captured and destroyed the place, founding a new city at Aquae Sextiae (Aix-en-Provence) nearby. Seventy years later, Julius Caesar brought the remainder of Gaul under Roman rule, and in A.D. 43 Roman armies added Britain to their possessions. The mutilated bodies in the War Cemetery at Maiden Castle might be direct evidence of that campaign—the last stand of the natives against the invaders—though not all archaeologists are convinced that that is the correct interpretation of those graves.

In mainland Europe, the Roman frontier ran along the course of the River Rhine, and then struck out across mountainous terrain to the upper reaches of the Danube and followed the latter eastward to the Black Sea. Beyond the Roman frontier lay large expanses of Europe that never came directly under their control, and that remained technically "prehistoric" until the Viking period in the ninth century A.D. Here in northern Germany and Denmark we find some of the best-studied Iron Age settlements north of the Alps—small farmsteads or villages of timber long-houses with rows of cattle stalls an integral part of the houseplan. Borremose in Jutland is one such settlement, exceptional in being defended by a bank and ditch. It is also exceptional in being close to the site at which the Gundestrup cauldron—one of the most famous objects in European prehistory—was found just over a hundred years ago.

The great richness of European prehistory will be apparent even from this necessarily brief overview. From Paleolithic camp sites to silver cauldrons, from hillforts to painted caves, all throw light on the changing nature of European society and on the beliefs and activities of ordinary people. It is the aim of the following chapters to delve deeper and show just how individual sites, which are open to the public today, can provide windows onto this past.

Further Reading

The best general account of European prehistory is the *Oxford Illustrated Prehistory of Europe*, edited by Barry Cunliffe (New York: Oxford University Press, 1994). For more detail on particular periods, two volumes published by Cambridge University Press are especially useful: *The Palaeolithic Settlement of Europe* by Clive Gamble (New York, 1986) and *Europe in the Neolithic: The Creation of New Worlds* by Alasdair Whittle (New York, 1996). Less up-to-date but still useful is *The European Iron Age* by John Collis (New York: Schocken Books, 1984). The total available literature on European prehistory is more than any individual could hope to master in a lifetime. Among recent books that can be recommended to both specialists and nonspecialists are *Towns, Villages and Countryside of Celtic Europe* by Françoise Audouze and Olivier Büchsenschütz (Bloomington: University of Indiana Press, 1992); *Journey Through the Ice Age* by Paul Bahn and Jean Vertut (Berkeley: University of California Press, 1997); and *Symbols of Power at the Time of Stonehenge* by David Clarke, Trevor Cowie, and Andrew Foxon (Edinburgh: HMSO, 1985).

CHAPTER

ONE

Terra Amata

c. 380,000 *years ago*

Early settlers

in southern France

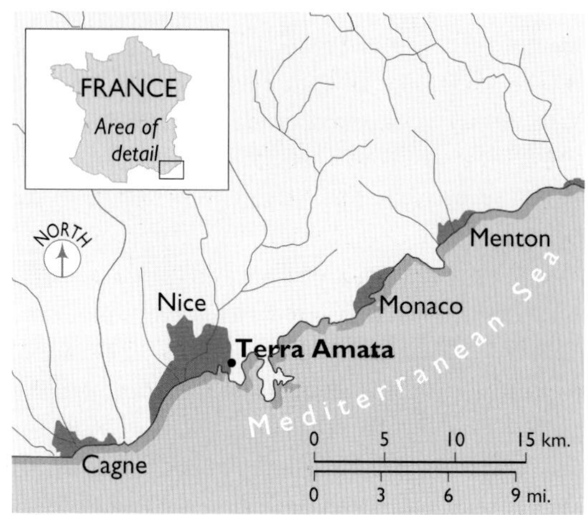

Some 380,000 years ago, a group of hunter-gatherers set up their temporary camp on a Mediterranean beach, at the spot where the modern town of Nice would later rise. Gathering together a collection of brushwood and timber poles, they constructed a roughly made oval shelter against the cooler night breezes, which can blow even in spring and summer. The wooden poles were driven into the beach sand in pairs, and then simply leaned or tied together at their tops to provide a kind of pitched roof. In the middle, a couple of larger branches were erected to support the midline of the roof. Leaves or skins may have been thrown over this framework to keep out the rain. Finally, around the base of the structure, stones were placed for extra stability, to hold the walls in place or hold down the covering skins.

This, at least, is the story deciphered from the remains by French archaeologists who excavated at Terra Amata in the 1960s. If true, it would be a remarkable discovery: the oldest known humanly made shelter in Europe. In recent years, however, Terra Amata has become the focus of controversy, as specialists have come to doubt much of the original interpretation. Were early humans, 400,000 years ago, really capable of building even such rudimentary structures as these? Or are we projecting our own ideas and assumptions back onto the past, looking for hearths and dwellings that are familiar from later periods but that early hominids hadn't yet begun to use? For the people who settled at Terra Amata were not anatomically modern humans like ourselves. They had smaller brains and larger jaws and belonged to a species known as *Homo heidelbergensis*. They may have communicated by sounds or gestures, but they had not yet developed a full spoken language. But whatever their limitations, they had been successful in spreading out from their original African homeland.

The people who stopped over at Terra Amata were not the first humans to arrive in Europe. We still aren't sure when Europe was first settled. One leading school of thought claims that stone tools from sites such as Chilhac and Saint Eble, in the Massif Central region of France, date back two million or more years ago. If this is correct, then hominids must have begun to spread from Africa long before they learned to use fire or build shelters. Other archaeologists claim that the colonization of Europe took place around a million years ago. They point to crudely worked chopping tools from the Vallonnet cave near Monaco, not far from Terra Amata, that have been dated to 900,000 years ago. The claim has received a boost from recent discoveries in northern Spain, where early human skeletal remains have been found in the cave of Gran Dolina at Atapuerca. These are dated to around 780,000 years ago. Stone tools thought to be well over a million years old have also been found at Orce, near Granada, in southern Spain.

The problem remains that many of these early sites are difficult to date with confidence. This means that alongside those archaeologists who believe in an early colonization of Europe there are others, more cautious, who favor a later arrival. But even the most determined skeptics accept that humans were present in Europe by 500,000 years ago. They had even reached northern parts of the continent. In December 1993, archaeologists found a shinbone at Boxgrove near the south coast of England. It was followed by the discovery of a pair of front teeth eighteen months later. All three finds are believed to be around half a million years old.

THERMOLUMINESCENCE DATING

The technique of thermoluminescence dating relies on the way that, in ancient deposits, electrons are gradually displaced from their usual positions through the action of natural radioactive decay. These electrons can then become trapped in the crystal lattice of crystalline materials such as flint or quartz. The process is cumulative, with more and more electrons becoming trapped as time elapses. The electrons can ultimately be released from the crystal lattice by heat, and as they are freed, energy is emitted in the form of light. By measuring the intensity of the light and comparing it with the natural radioactivity of the deposit we can calculate the amount of time elapsed since the material was last heated. Heating the material sets the electron clock back to zero. The thermoluminescence method is thus particularly suitable for the dating of materials such as flints that have been accidentally burned (as at Terra Amata), or quartz inclusions in fired pottery.

Whatever date we go for, the colonization of Europe represents a major human achievement. We don't know whether these first Europeans had hairy coats, like their closest primate relatives, but the Mediterranean would have been colder than their tropical African homeland. Humans are, in origin, a tropical species, and in order to colonize cooler climates they have used their technological skills to protect themselves from the environment. This protection has three separate components: an immediate covering for the human body (clothing), a place to keep warm and sleep (shelter), and a controllable source of heat (fire). There is no direct evidence of clothing at Terra Amata, but the excavators did discover what they thought were traces of fire and shelter.

The Original Setting

Looking at Terra Amata today, it is difficult to imagine the site as it was 380,000 years ago. For one thing, it is now enclosed in the museum located in the basement of the block that was built over it when the excavations were finished. For another, it finds itself near the center of modern Nice, only 300 yards (275 meters) from the town's commercial harbor. These are humanly induced changes, but the natural landscape too has been transformed. The early humans camped on a beach, only a little way back from the sea's edge. Today, the level of the Mediterranean lies 80 feet (25 meters) lower, leaving Terra Amata high and dry on the slopes of Mont Boron.

From geology and vegetation we are able to reconstruct the original setting of the Terra Amata site in some detail. The archaeological remains were in fact not those of a single occupation, but of a whole series of short stays in this limited area over a period of perhaps tens of thousands of years. What was it that made the site so attractive?

In the first place, it was a sheltered location, on the edge of a small cove that the sea had carved into the limestone slopes of Mont Boron. The cove opened to the south and so provided shelter from the cool northerly and easterly winds. But the cove also had an additional attraction: a small freshwater spring to supply the inhabitants' drinking needs. The springwater flowed into the cove in a small stream colonized by water lilies and other plants. The proximity of the sea, too, may have encouraged the choice of this location. Archaeologists found fishbones and shells of turtles, oysters, mussels, and limpets among the stone tools and other debris.

The climate was probably not much different from that of today. The site at Terra Amata falls within one of the milder periods between successive Ice Ages. One of them finished around 450,000 years ago; another began around 380,000 years ago. We can date these precisely from analysis of marine shells in cores recovered from the floor of the Pacific Ocean. This climate is broadly confirmed by the pollen contained in coprolites recovered from the site, which shows that Aleppo pine and holm oak grew on the neighboring mountain slopes. Conditions may perhaps have been a little cooler than they are in

Mediterranean France today, but if so, a more tropical feel was provided by the local fauna, which included elephant and rhinoceros alongside red deer and aurochs (wild cattle).

The age of the site was confirmed by thermoluminescence analysis (see page 19) of some of the flint tools that had been burnt. These gave a precise date of 380,000 years before the present.

The shoreline itself was constantly changing while the hunter-gatherers came and went from decade to decade. The first occupations were set up on ridges of pebbles thrown up by the waves and must have been very close to the active sea edge. During the period of human occupation the sea gradually retreated, however, and the shingle beach was covered by wind-blown sand. The last occupations were established on this sand, and their remains were eventually covered by it.

Discovery and Excavation

Like so many important archaeological sites, Terra Amata was discovered by accident. French prehistorians began finding Paleolithic stone tools in the late 1950s as the Nice shipyard was developed. It was a commercial building project on the nearby slopes of Mont Boron that led to the discovery of the site. In October 1965, terraces were being cut for a new building, the Palais Carnot. They laid bare a sandy deposit rich in Paleolithic tools, and archaeologists were called in to mount a rescue excavation. From 28 January to 5 July 1966 they toiled away under the direction of Henry de Lumley, removing 270 cubic yards (200 cubic meters) of deposit and revealing no fewer than twenty-one living floors in an excavated area of 175 square yards (144 square meters).

Considerable imagination is needed to envisage the lifestyle at Terra Amata 380,000 years ago. Two special finds do help us, however, to bridge the divide. The first is the discovery of a human footprint, remarkably preserved in the sand during all these millennia. The impression is indistinct, but the big toe can still be made out, and suggests the individual concerned was walking barefoot, not wearing a sandal or moccasin. The length of the footprint, 9.5 inches (24 centimeters), suggests he or she was approximately 5 feet 1 inch (1.56 meters) tall, though this calculation is based on measures devised for the later Neanderthal skeletons and may not be accurate in the case of the earlier Terra Amata humans.

The second direct trace is less savory but no less interesting: remains of human coprolites (feces). Careful to note that these were found near, rather than on, the prehistoric living areas, de Lumley took this to mean that the inhabitants of Terra Amata lived and slept in their shelters but went outside to defecate. Specialists who have studied the coprolites have found they contain pollen from many local plants, including trees that cannot possibly have formed part of the diet. Most likely they became mixed into the food accidentally.

THE FIRST EUROPEANS

We know about the first human occupants from their tools and the scarce remains of the living sites and activity areas, but for many observers the most evocative testimony comes from the fossil bones themselves. Only a handful of sites have yielded human remains more than 100,000 years old. One of the most recent, and most spectacular, is the growing collection from the site of Atapuerca in northern Spain.

Atapuerca is a complex of collapsed limestone caves that were inhabited by early human communities over several hundred thousand years. The oldest remains come from the Gran Dolina cave—skull and jaw fragments from at least five or six individuals. They have been dated by a method known as paleomagnetism. Geologists have discovered that from time to time, the direction of the earth's magnetic polarity is reversed. The last such reversal (which can be measured in volcanic rocks) took place 780,000 years ago. The Gran Dolina human remains come from a layer some 2 feet (0.6 meters) below this magnetic reversal. They are therefore at least 780,000 years old—in truth, somewhat older than this, though exactly how much time is represented by the overlying deposit we cannot say.

Anthropologists haven't yet decided upon a species name for the Gran Dolina hominids. But this isn't the only fossil-bearing cave at Atapuerca. Even more remarkable are discoveries in the Sima de los Huesos, the "Pit of Bones." This lies deep within the cave known as the Cueva Mayor and is a natural shaft 50 feet (15 meters) deep. Over 1,600 human bones, between 400,000 and 200,000 years old, have been found here—many more than in the rest of Europe combined. They belong to an early species known as *Homo heidelbergensis*, and seem to be immediate precursors to the larger-brained Neanderthals. The Spanish archaeologist in charge of the work, Juan Luís Arsuaga, believes that the bodies were intentionally dropped into the Sima de los Huesos by groups of humans living in the vicinity. If so, then this is Europe's oldest known cemetery.

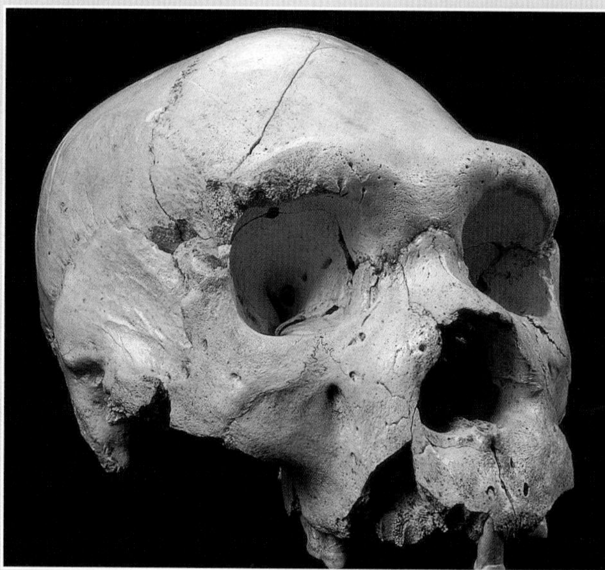

Skull of *Homo heidelbergensis* from the "Pit of Bones" (Sima de los Huesos) at Atapuerca in northern Spain. This skull was part of a collection of over 1,600 human bones dating to between 400,000 and 200,000 years old. They probably slipped or were washed into this deep pit through natural processes, though Spanish anthropologists have suggested that they might have been deposited there intentionally in what amounts to an early form of burial. Even older remains have come from an adjacent site at Atapuerca, the Gran Dolina. Indeed, dating o around 800,000 years old, the human skeletal remains from the Gran Dolina are the oldest yet known from Europe, but they are still over a million years younger than the oldest remains from Africa attributed to the genus *Homo*.

Sadly, the coprolites don't tell us much about what they actually did eat, and we therefore have to turn to the animal remains for any clues. The bones include those of several species that could have been hunted and eaten. Red deer bones were particularly abundant, but there were also large species such as elephant and rhinoceros, and small game including rabbits and rodents. Some of these may have been hunted, others must have been trapped, and a few were probably scavenged after they had died a natural death or been killed by other predators.

In addition to food, mammals were also an important source of skins for clothing, bedding, and shelter. It is here that we once again find controversy. We don't know for certain that the inhabitants of Terra Amata wore clothes. Terra Amata may have been a summer season camp, but it is hard to imagine its residents surviving the winter, even in the south of France, without some kind of body covering. Impressions preserved in the sand suggested that they did indeed have animal skins. More precisely, de Lumley thought these early humans had placed animal skins on the sand before sitting down to flake their stone tools. And the rough wooden shelters, if real, might also have had skins draped over them to provide cover from rain and wind.

The Shelters

The Terra Amata shelters are so remarkable that some archaeologists consider them too sophisticated to have been built by such early humans. A few go so far as to suggest the shelters are entirely illusory, the result of wishful thinking on the part of prehistorians anxious to provide homes for our early human ancestors. Yet protection against the elements must have been essential for the colonization of more northerly latitudes—and Mediterranean winters can be cold and inclement. In any case, the Terra Amata shelters must have been fairly rudimentary structures. They were after all made to be occupied only for a few days, so they had to be easy and quick to erect. They were probably equally quick to fall down, and all that survived for the excavators

Reconstruction of one of the shelters from Terra Amata. This follows the interpretation of the excavator, Henry de Lumley, who envisaged these shelters as carefully constructed huts. The artist has even included a smoke hole in the roof, though this would hardly be necessary unless the structures were sealed by clay or covered in animal hides.

Reconstruction of one of the shelters excavated at Terra Amata. This reconstruction gives the impression of a sophisticated structure of branches that have been carefully cut, shaped, and fitted together. Some archaeologists doubt whether the hominids who camped at Terra Amata some 380,000 years ago were capable of building such a complex structure. They envisage a more rough and ready shelter, but the recent discovery of long wooden hunting spears at Schöningen in Germany, around 400,000 years old, serves to warn us against being too dismissive of the technical abilities of early European hominids.

to find were traces they interpreted as living floors, fringed by a line of stake-holes and stones.

Twenty-one of these living floors were identified by de Lumley and his team; each, in their view, marked the site of an oval hut. The living floors represent successive settlements stretching probably over a period of hundreds if not thousands (or even tens of thousands) of years. According to de Lumley, the huts varied in size from 22 to 50 feet (7 to 15 meters) in length and 13 to 20 feet (4 to 6 meters) in width. But 50 by 20 feet is an enormous roof span for a simple shelter and gives rise to legitimate doubts about the conventional interpretation. The larger arrangements must at most have been windbreaks, rather than roofed dwellings. Yet careful study of the stake-holes around the perimeter did lead the excavators to argue that the stakes had been cut to form a point before they were pushed into the soft sand. A peculiarity of the construction was that the stake-holes were often in pairs, side by side.

Based on his findings, de Lumley argued that the inhabitants of Terra Amata had reinforced the rings of stakes by piling beach stones against the base. The stakes themselves have long since decayed, leaving only their impressions in the sand, but the stones survive, and oval arrangements of stones were one key feature of the site.

Within the living floors, the principal feature was the hearth. In the earlier huts, the only traces were scatters of ash and cinders, but de Lumley and his team found what they thought were well-preserved fireplaces in some of the later huts. These were located near the center of the living space and sometimes consisted of a shallow pit dug into the sand, up to 9 inches (24 centimeters) across and 6 inches (15 centimeters) deep. On the northwest side, the inhabitants built a low screen of stones or pebbles. This was always on the northwest side, and must have been made to shelter the hearth from winds blowing from this direction. That it was necessary at all suggests that the "huts" cannot have been windproof.

We don't know what the covering consisted of, and here imagination rather than hard evidence completely takes over. At one extreme are those archaeologists who dismiss the huts altogether, and argue that what we have at Terra Amata are the remains of a series of small-scale, transitory occupations, mixed in with scatters of beach pebbles and root holes. Others see the Terra Amata "huts" as crude brushwood shelters, affording little protection against the elements. What de Lumley himself prefers, however, is to envisage a rather neater construction, with a smoke hole in the roof. If the inhabitants had really wanted a weatherproof structure they would have had to cover the framework with skins or pack the crevices with leaves or mud. There isn't any evidence that they went to these lengths, but we can't be sure. If anything, skins are perhaps likeliest, since they could have lifted them off and carried them to their next camp site when they moved on.

Bones and Stones

To see what the inhabitants had been doing there, de Lumley and his team were especially careful to record details of the living floors. They even made casts of many of the floors. Apart from the hearths, they found a litter of stone tools and animal bones, but this was not evenly spread and the excavators

The excavated floor of one of the Terra Amata shelters, showing a scatter of debris from flint-working. The empty zone beyond and to the left of the string intersection has been interpreted as the place where the flint-worker sat.

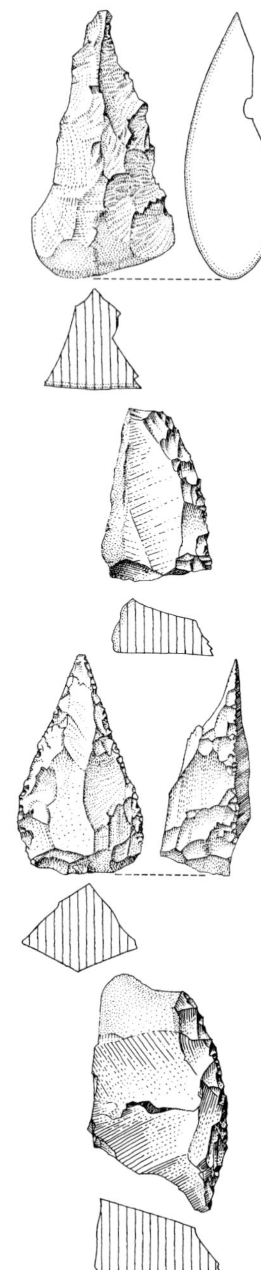

Stone tools from Terra Amata. These were used for a range of tasks, including woodworking and cutting and processing vegetable foods, as well as cutting up meat, scraping animal hides, and smashing bones to extract the marrow.

thought they could make out separate activity areas. In some huts, there seemed to be a workshop area, where stone tools had been flaked. In the middle there is a gap, perhaps marking the place where the toolmaker sat while he or she worked away at the flint, quartz, or limestone cobbles collected from the nearby beach.

The stone tools are of relatively unsophisticated type. Many of them were made quite simply by striking one or two flakes off a beach pebble, to give a sharp edge. These are known as choppers (if the flakes have been removed from one side) or chopping tools (if the flaker has worked from both sides to produce an edge). More sophisticated were the occasional bifaces (worked from both sides to give a pointed end) and cleavers (with a straight, chisel-like cutting edge at one end). There were also smaller stone tools, such as scrapers (perhaps for removing flesh from animal hides) and points (which could have been attached to spears or javelins). Some of these tools might have been used in hunting, while others may have been for cutting up meat or smashing bones to extract the marrow. But we shouldn't assume that the diet consisted mainly of meat. Plant foods were also important, and stone tools may have been used for digging up edible roots and cutting leaves and stalks. Stone tools must also have played a part in the cutting of brushwood for the huts themselves.

The people of Terra Amata must have had tools made from perishable materials. In one place the excavators noticed a rounded depression in a living floor and wondered whether a wooden bowl had been placed there. Some of the animal bones had been worked into useful points; they may have been used for stitching skins together. And we needn't imagine the inhabitants as colorless individuals: a few pieces of red ochre were found, and they might have been used for coloring skins or even for body-painting.

A Nomadic Lifestyle

Most of the stone tools at Terra Amata had been made at the site from local materials. Some, however, had been brought from elsewhere, and one of these was especially interesting since it was made of volcanic rock from Estérel, 30 miles (50 kilometers) west of Nice. It suggests that the people who stopped at Terra Amata had also passed through Estérel at some period during the year. As we have seen, the successive occupations at Terra Amata all seem to have been very brief, probably a few days at most. We can't say that the same group of people came back here every year, though there is one intriguing piece of information from the coprolites: the pollen they contained was all from plants that shed their pollen in late spring or early summer. It seems that this was the time of year when early humans came to Terra Amata.

The rest of the year they moved steadily around the surrounding area, following the cycle of the seasons, exploiting particular plants and animals as they became available. We don't know how far they traveled or whether they ever left the coast and explored the higher land behind. But we do know that in late spring or early summer, on at least twenty-one separate occasions, they came down to the beach at Terra Amata for a few days, perhaps building a shelter and lighting a fire, certainly gathering beach cobbles for their tools and hunting or scavenging for their food. We know this from the record they left at Terra Amata, providing a remarkable glimpse into everyday life in southern France almost 400,000 years ago.

Further Reading

The most accessible account of Terra Amata is given by the director of the excavation, Henry de Lumley, in his 1969 article in *Scientific American*: "A Paleolithic Camp at Nice" (*Scientific American* 220, pp.42–50). For a longer and more technical discussion, see de Lumley's chapter entitled "Cultural Evolution in France in Its Paleoecological Setting During the Middle Pleistocene," in K. W. Butzer and G. L. Isaac, editors, *After the Australopithecines* (The Hague: Mouton, 1975, pp. 745–808). For the broad background, the best general book on the European Palaeolithic period is Clive Gamble's *The Palaeolithic Settlement of Europe* (New York: Cambridge University Press, 1986). Useful up-to-date accounts of the earliest human fossils from Europe, including the recent Atapuerca discoveries, can be found in the January–February 1996 issue of the magazine *Archaeology* ("The First Europeans," by Jean-Jacques Hublin, and "Treasure of the Sierra Atapuerca," by Paul G. Bahn) and the May–June 1997 issue ("Faces from the Past," by Juan Luis Arsuaga Ferreras).

Further Viewing

Reconstructions of the Terra Amata settlement as well as tools and other remains found during the excavations can be seen in the Musée de Paléontologie Humaine de Terra Amata in Nice.

CHAPTER

TWO

Lascaux

C. 15,000 B.C.

A painted cave

in the French Dordogne

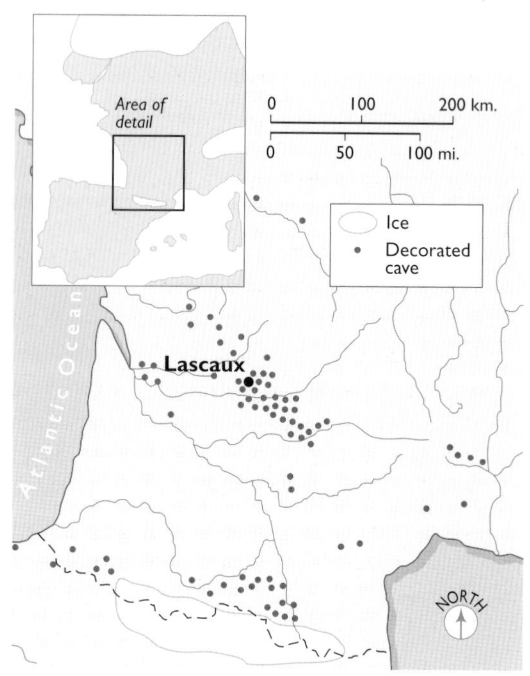

Imagine a prehistoric art gallery set deep below the earth, its rough rock walls emblazoned with polychrome paintings of amazing animals, troops of horses, mighty wild bulls, and long-antlered deer. Imagine the awe and wonder of encountering these mysterious images, lit only by the light of a stone tallow lamp—images that seem almost to spring into life and movement as the flame flickers and eddies. This is how Lascaux was made to be seen by the artists who painted and engraved the images on its cave walls some 17,000 years ago.

Lascaux is without doubt one of the most famous archaeological sites in the world, sharing with Altamira in Spain and the recently discovered Grotte Chauvet the accolade of being the most impressive of all the painted caves of western Europe. It was also one of the most visited prehistoric sites, receiving an incredible 50,000 visitors a year in the late 1960s. By this time, the pressure of visitors was having a seriously harmful effect on the cave's environment, raising the temperature and humidity and encouraging the growth of green algae, which began to invade some of the painted surfaces. The decision was made to close the cave for its own preservation, allowing access only to scholars. Mindful of the fame of Lascaux, however, the French authorities poured resources and expertise into creating a facsimile of

Lascaux, known as Lascaux II, nearby. Although built of concrete and sunk into an abandoned quarry, this is a painstaking replica of the most famous sections of Lascaux, and few visitors come away unmoved by the experience of viewing it.

The cave of Lascaux was painted around 17,000 years ago. We know this from the radiocarbon dating of charcoal recovered from sediments on the cave floor. They suggest that the cave was painted between 15,000 and 14,000 B.C. Of course, these early dates have the disadvantage that they date the occupation of the cave rather than the paintings on the cave walls. But we can be reasonably confident that this was a time when the cave artists were at work. The carbon used in the dating came from lamps and torches that had been brought into the cave to light its dark recesses and passages; no natural light reaches this deep.

Today, the Dordogne region where Lascaux is situated is a pleasant countryside of rolling hills, meadows, and woodlands. It is famous not only for its prehistory (center of one of the greatest known concentrations of Paleolithic caves) but also for its cuisine. Seventeen thousand years ago, the outlook was very different. Europe at the time was in the grip of the last Ice Age, and Lascaux lay in a cold, dry setting, some way from the glacier edge but still harsh and inhospitable. The great attraction of the region was its rivers, flowing westward into the Atlantic Ocean and home to salmon and other fish. Seasonal salmon migrations must have played a major part in the yearly rounds of the Lascaux people. There were also seasonal migrations of game animals. The deeper areas of the Lascaux cave where the art is found could never have been living places—people only went there infrequently and for special (perhaps ritual) reasons—but there were remains of hunted animals in the cave floor deposits, showing that the people relied heavily on reindeer. Almost 90 percent of the animal bones were of reindeer, which were twenty times more numerous than those of wild boar or roe deer, with red deer and horse still less abundant. Yet when we look at the art, we find that reindeer, wild boar, and roe deer are entirely unrepresented. This fact alone suggests that theories which see the art of Lascaux and other caves as a kind of hunting magic must be wrong—the animals that were good to eat were not the same as those that were good to paint.

If the people who painted and visited Lascaux cave didn't live there, then, where did they live? The answer is in the many caves and rock shelters that characterize this part of France. The limestone geology forms good natural caves and shelters, and many of them were occupied by groups of hunters and gatherers for tens of thousands of years. They improvised shelters under the rock overhangs, and built hearths and beds. Their lives were typified by continual movement—they didn't stay in the same place all year, but moved around the region, revisiting preferred camp sites, some of them in caves or rockshelters, others under skin tents in the open. They moved up and down the river valleys, following seasonal migrations of fish or game animals, some-

(*opposite*) Distribution of decorated caves in southwestern France, showing the location of Lascaux. The inset indicates the extent of glaciation in western Europe at the height of the last Ice Age (c. 20,000 years ago), when ice sheets covered much of the British Isles and smaller ice caps formed in the Alps and the Pyrenees. The fall in sea level caused by the locking up of water in the ice sheets altered the coastline, joining Britain to the Continent and Corsica to Sardinia.

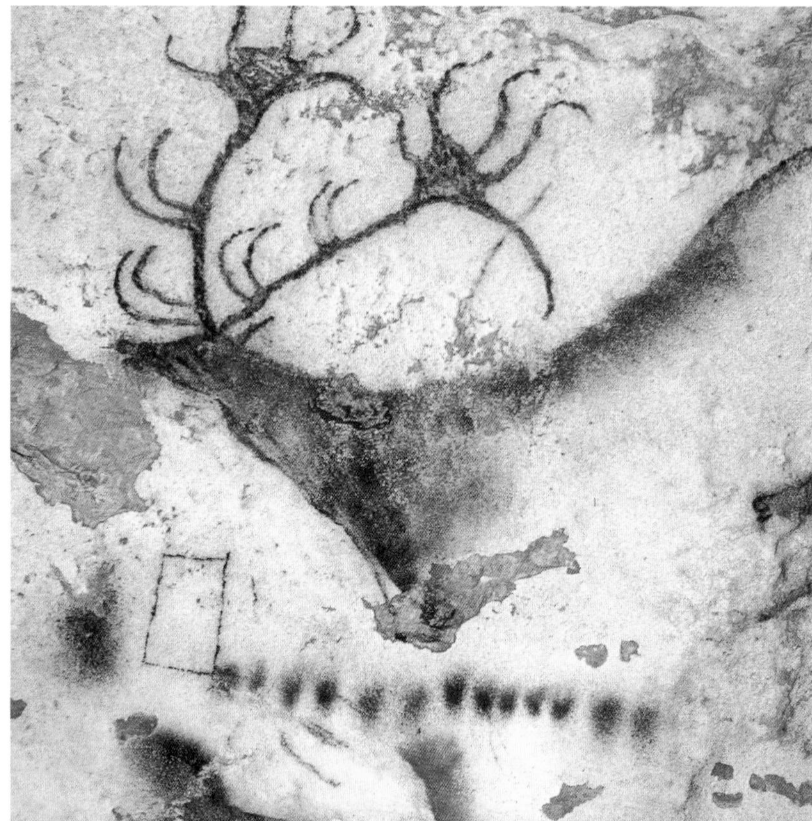

Male deer from the Diverticule Axial at Lascaux. The animal is shown in the act of "belling," the challenging call uttered by stags during the rutting season. The figure measures 5 feet (1.5 meters) across from the nose of the animal to the point where the rump fades into the cave wall. Below can be seen an enigmatic line of dots and an open rectangle. Such abstract marks are a common feature of western European cave art—more common, indeed, than the representations of animals—but their significance is far from clear.

times building traps and corrals to make the hunting easier. They also collected plant foods, among them nuts and berries from the trees and bushes that were able to thrive in this cold climate. And from time to time they engaged in rituals, descending deep into the limestone caves to visit or paint the art for which they are now so famous. Maybe it was only ritual specialists—shamans—who came here to commune with the spirits. Or it may only have been young people reaching adolescence who were allowed to do this; there are trails of young or adolescent footprints in the mud of some cave floors. Whatever the reason—and there are almost as many theories as there are painted caves—it has left us a striking and impressive record.

The Rediscovery of Lascaux

Southern France and northern Spain have some three hundred Paleolithic decorated caves. Many of these, however, have only a small number of marks or figures, and most of those are engraved—outline figures carved into the walls of the cave. Lascaux is altogether exceptional, with around 600 paintings and 1,500 engravings; only a few other caves can approach it for sheer quantity of art. Even at Lascaux, however, not all of the art is impressive, nor is it all representational. Alongside the spectacular polychrome bisons we have to reckon with hundreds of smaller marks—lines, grids, and dots that must have had meaning but don't seem to be pictures of anything from real life.

Given the profusion of decorated caves, it might be thought that they have been well known for many centuries. In fact, the real discovery of cave art began only in the mid-nineteenth century. There are hints of earlier visitors at some sites—for example, the Ruben de la Vialle who wrote his name in the famous Niaux cave in 1660—and there are papal strictures from the fifteenth century prohibiting worship in at least one decorated cave. Most of the art is in inaccessible regions of the caves, however, and even if some of it was visited, nobody recognized these paintings or engravings for what they really were.

The key discovery came in 1879, at Altamira in northern Spain, but even then it took fifteen years of angry debate for the paintings to be accepted as Paleolithic in date. Once that breakthrough was made, however, discoveries of new painted caves multiplied. They have continued up to the present day.

The story of Lascaux belongs fairly late in this history of rediscovery. It was four youngsters, led by Marcel Ravidat and Jacques Marsal, who were responsible. They knew from local tradition of a hole in the woods of Lascaux that opened into an underground chamber. One of their friends tells the story:

> On Thursday, 12 September 1940, on a pleasant autumn afternoon, the four youngsters Ravidat, Marsal, Agnel, and Coencas were walking through the wood, which was well-stocked in game, accompanied by their faithful dog Robot. Suddenly they saw the dog disappear down a hole full of brambles directly beneath a juniper tree. Time passed and the dog didn't reappear. Ravidat, whose faithful friend he was, decided to go into the narrow hole himself. . . . A stone which he cast rolled for quite a time, showing the depth beneath. Nonetheless, the young caver slid into this kind of shaft and ended up in a large chamber whose size he could at once make out even though the only light he had was a box of matches. Marsal and his two friends followed with difficulty, but since they had no other equipment for exploration, they climbed back up to the surface, swearing each other to secrecy on their discovery. The next day they began their investigations, armed with ropes and an automobile grease gun which had been converted into a lamp by the addition of a cotton wick. What surprise when they saw on the rock walls an immense cavalcade of fantastic animals!

This is the romantic version of Lascaux's discovery—the lost dog leading to the great surprise. The truth, as it can be pieced together from words of the discoverers themselves, gives Robot less of a role. Ravidat had already in fact discovered the hole five days earlier, but had covered it over again until he had time for a more thorough exploration. He was a garage apprentice in nearby Montignac, and when he returned with friends to Lascaux on 12 September he was already armed with the improvised lamp and some rope. After an hour or more spent enlarging the hole, Ravidat crawled inside, head first, and lit his lamp—but at that moment lost his grip and slid headlong to the bottom. The others joined him. They then began to explore, and holding the lamp above their heads were amazed to see animal paintings on the walls. This was the Salle des Taureaux. The boys returned for further explorations on each of the following days, and by the next Monday the find had become public knowledge. The president of the local Tourist Board was quick to spot the potential of the new discovery, and on 18 September erected a signboard to the cave at the exit from the village. The archaeologists, indeed, were rather late on the scene, the first of them—the distinguished Abbé Breuil—arriving only on 21 September.

The news of the discovery spread like wildfire, but proper scientific exploration had to wait until after the Second World War. The key figure was the Abbé Glory, who spent the best part of eleven years (1952–1963) studying and recording the cave of Lascaux. The potential of such a site is never exhausted, however, and analyses have continued in recent years, bearing on questions such as the date of the paintings and the nature of the coloring materials. There have also been numerous attempts to interpret and understand the art. Why was it made? The question has given rise to numerous theories and interpretations, but in many respects the art of Lascaux remains today as mysterious as it is impressive.

Entering Lascaux

The Lascaux cave is an underground gallery formed by natural processes in the limestone bedrock. Over hundreds of thousands of years, fault-lines in the limestone have been enlarged by the eroding action of water seeping through and along these cracks. The result is what we find today: a long, angled limestone cave with subsidiary arms branching to the right and left. There has only ever been one entrance to this complex, located approximately where Ravidat and his friends broke through in 1940. The prehistoric artists must have entered by the same route, making their way down a sloping ramp of limestone debris into the cave itself, some 65 feet (20 meters) below ground.

The main axis of the cave is formed by the Salle des Taureaux (Hall of the Bulls), the Passage, the Nef (Nave), the Galerie Mondmilch (literally "moon milk," a white claylike precipitate of calcium carbonate), and the Cabinet des Félins (Cats' Gallery). This sequence of chambers and passages measures just over 325 feet (100 meters) in length. Walls and ceiling expand and contract as we make our way further and further into the cave, and deeper and deeper as the floor slopes gently downward. Then comes the obstacle of the "chatière" or "cat-flap," a narrow opening that leads to an upsloping gallery giving access to the Cabinet des Félins and the farthest parts of the cave. For this last stretch the floor of the cave is very irregular and progress is difficult; at one point there is a 13-foot (4-meter) drop to be negotiated. It is not surprising that the art here is very different in nature and impact from that in the showpiece sections, such as the Salle des Taureaux.

In addition to this main axis of Lascaux, there are the two side passages we have not yet mentioned. One of them, more or less a straight continuation of the Salle des Taureaux, is the Diverticule Axial. Then, further into the cave on the right, is the "Abside" or apse, and the "Puits," or well. The cave floor here was covered with a thick clay deposit (now partly removed), which had accumulated before the art was made. A steep, uphill scramble (today assisted by steps) leads into the Abside. In the far wall a tall, irregular opening reveals the entrance to the last part of Lascaux, the Puits. This mysterious innermost recess was the most difficult to negotiate, since the opening from the Abside ends at a 16-foot (5-meter) vertical drop into the Puits itself. In the absence of strong lighting this appears like a real leap into the unknown.

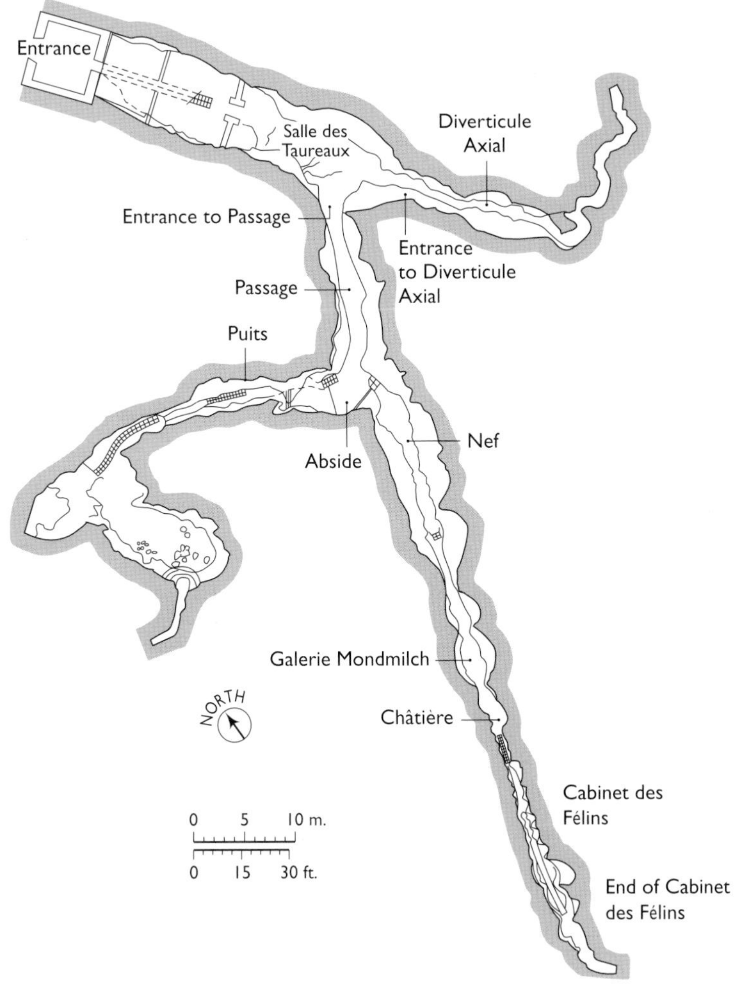

Plan of Lascaux, showing the modern entrance arrangements and the names given to the various parts of the cave.

Ravidat describes the dangers they faced in exploring this gulf, perched on the edge of the Puits:

> My friends were all afraid that they wouldn't be able to climb out again because they would have to hold on to a smooth rope. For myself, it wasn't that which made me hesitate since I had confidence in my arms; it was whether my friends' arms would be able to support my 70 kilos hanging loose without any hold. After making sure that the three of them would support me, with beating heart I began the descent and soon arrived at the bottom. Looking up, I realized that I had descended some 10 meters [in reality, only about half that]. I hastened to reassure my companions and began exploring again. I didn't go more than 20 or 30 meters since I was afraid of encountering a rock fall. So I turned round and examined the walls. Great was my surprise to see a human figure with a bird's head knocked down by a bison, the whole thing forming a scene 2 meters in length.

The human figure in the Puits is in fact the only one at Lascaux. Human figures are exceedingly rare in western European Paleolithic art, though animals abound. At Lascaux there are horse, aurochs, bison, deer, ibex, bear, large felines, and woolly rhinoceros. There is even a "monster" or mythical beast: the unicorn in the Salle des Taureaux. Yet other animals, common in other painted caves, are absent—no mammoth, no megaloceros (an extinct giant deer), not even any reindeer (save for one controversial engraving in the Abside), though reindeer is the most abundant species in the animal bones left by Paleolithic visitors to the cave. The artists were not simply painting the animals most familiar to them or most important to them in edible terms. Nor was it a random collection of creatures from everyday life. There was other meaning to the cave art, even if it remains hard to say exactly what that was.

Lascaux Today

Lascaux was discovered on 12 September 1940 and officially opened to the public in 1948. Fifteen years later, the pressure of visitors was such that the cave environment had been seriously disturbed, and patches of green algae, the *maladie verte*, were appearing on some of the painted surfaces. These were soon cured, but specialists noted with alarm a more pernicious problem, the *maladie blanche,* formed by calcite crystals on some of the cave walls. To prevent further damage, Lascaux was closed to the public on 20 April 1963. At the same time, work began on an ambitious new project to create a full-scale facsimile of the outermost sections of the cave, the Salle des Taureaux and the Diverticule Axial, which could be open to the public. The result, a faithful copy of these parts of the original (even down to using the same natural pigments), is what the visitor sees today: Lascaux II. It contains (in replica) much of Lascaux's most famous and spectacular art.

The ceiling of the Salle des Taureaux, one of the most spectacular areas of Lascaux. Images of aurochs (wild cattle), horse, and deer can be distinguished, together with an enigmatic creature at the far left known in French as the "licorne" or "unicorn" (though in fact it has two horns). The figures belong to several different periods and in most cases have been painted over each other.

The decoration of Lascaux begins some 80 feet (25 meters) from the entrance in the Salle des Taureaux, a vast underground cavern soaring to a height of 25 feet (7 meters) above the cave floor. The soft limestone here was unsuitable for engravings, but the Paleolithic artists turned this outermost part of the cave into a spectacular gallery of paintings. These are grouped in a frieze, 80 feet (25 meters) long, facing the entrance to the cave and framing the entrances to the Passage and the Diverticule Axial beyond. The eye is immediately caught by the great aurochs painted in bold outline, one (originally two) on the left, three on the right, facing inward toward the Diverticule Axial. Belonging to this same group at the far left is a fantastic animal portrayed in the same bold outline. Known as the "unicorn," it has in fact two straight horns pointing forward, not to mention circular marks on the flanks. Over these large figures have been painted a number of horses, two of them large and polychrome, the rest smaller and solid brown. All these are moving right, but there are also small, red-painted deer facing left, and three smaller red aurochs painted over the feet of the large aurochs.

This image is typical of the level of complexity to be found in the Salle des Taureaux. Clearly there is no single decorative scheme here, but rather a whole series of schemes. Curiously, prehistoric artists painted these schemes —at intervals that could be from years to millennia—one over the top of the other, leaving us the confusing palimpsest we see today.

Taking the left-hand opening (the only one available in Lascaux II) we enter the Diverticule Axial. This is sometimes called the "Sistine Chapel of Prehistory," because here the decoration on the side walls continues across the ceiling. This raises the question of scaffolding, since it would have been impossible to decorate the upper walls and ceiling without the aid of a raised platform. With this in mind, archaeologists have examined the walls of the Diverticule Axial with great care and identified a series of small holes and ledges which

Schematic diagram showing the layout of decoration in the Diverticule Axial. The ledges and holes in the cave walls are thought to have supported a wooden scaffold that the prehistoric artists would have needed to reach the upper walls and ceiling.

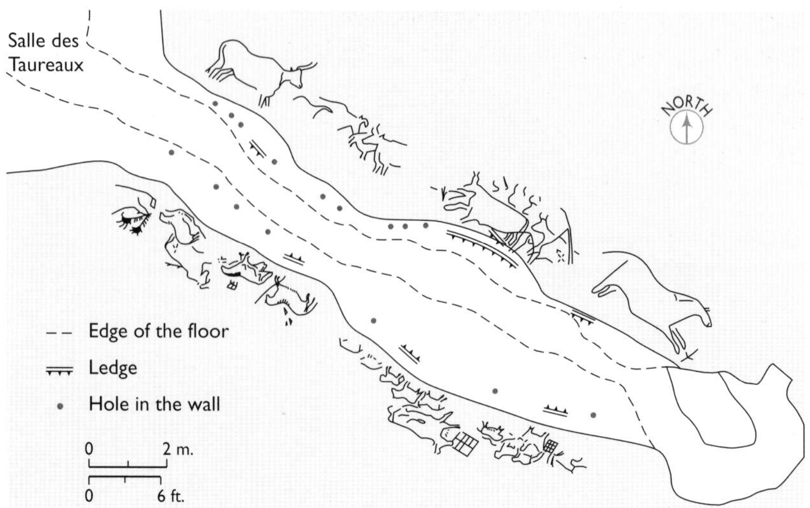

could have supported just such a platform. Similar scaffolds must have been constructed in the Salle des Taureaux and the Abside, but they have left little trace.

The phrase "Sistine Chapel of Prehistory" has other resonance beyond simply the ceiling paintings. The observant reader will have noted that two sections of Lascaux are named after parts of a church: the "Nef," or Nave, and the "Abside," or Apse. They are appropriate enough, insofar as Lascaux must have been a place of special significance, though of course they imply nothing specific about the use of the cave.

The decoration in the Diverticule Axial is in broad terms similar to that of the Salle des Taureaux. There are large animals in outline or polychrome; others in solid color. The left-hand wall has a series of bulls or cows, some superimposed, plus a couple of horses; on the opposite wall is a belling black deer, large cows, and smaller horses. Then comes a break in the art, a change of level in the cave, and a striking group on either side: on the left, a large black bull (with others painted beneath); on the right, a large black cow, which appears to be jumping, and a line of horses moving in the opposite direction beneath. Beyond, in the deepest part of the Diverticule, are more horses, including one (on the left) painted upside down.

The arrangement of the paintings clearly isn't arbitrary, but its meaning is far from obvious. In the 1960s, the French cave art specialists Annette Laming and André Leroi-Gourhan thought that the different animal species stood for female and male, though they failed to agree among themselves which species stood for male and which for female. But some species do tend to occur together in the art, both at Lascaux and at other caves. The best example is the frequent association of horse with either bison or aurochs. As we see, horse and aurochs are painted close together in the Diverticule Axial and the Salle des Taureaux, and indeed elsewhere in the cave. But why this is we don't know.

Quite a different theory comes from the rows of marks we see below the feet of the belling deer and the first horse in the Diverticule Axial. Might these be animal tracks or spoor? If so, they suggest that one purpose of the art was didactic—to teach youngsters to recognize the telltale traces of the animals they would have to hunt.

Killing the Images

Lascaux II ends at the Diverticule Axial, but in the cave itself we could retrace our steps toward the Salle des Taureaux and turn left into the "Passage." This was once richly decorated with paintings and engravings, but the friable nature of the calcite means that most of them can only have had a short life. Today, only a few engravings remain.

Passing the rocky projection on the left that forms the division between the Passage and the Nave, the sequence of painted art recommences with a pair of panels, one above the other. Here we are in a significant location, directly opposite the opening leading into the Abside and the Puits. The upper of the two panels, above a rocky ledge, portrays a group of eight ibex: seven males with long elegant curving horns, the eighth a hornless female facing the opposite way. More famous is the scene below the rocky ledge, the so-called Panel of the Imprint. It takes its name from a handprint found in the mud at its foot by the early explorers of the cave. The print is long since gone, but reminds us of the hand- and footprints found in the deeper galleries of other painted caves, such as the Réseau Clastres at Niaux or at Fontanet, where a child seems to have been chasing a dog. These traces bring the caves to life in a way no other evidence can, and it is regrettable that in most cases they have been unwittingly destroyed by visitors.

Bison from the "Panel of the Imprint," situated at the junction between the Passage and the Nave opposite the opening to the Puits. The image appears to have been "killed" by the scratching of oblique lines, which may represent spear or arrow wounds. It is evidence like this that has led to the view that the cave art is somehow connected with hunting magic.

The Panel of the Imprint itself is dominated by a large polychrome bison, head lowered to charge. This stands at the right-hand edge of a group of seven partly overlapping horses. These are splendid, vivid images, with shaggy manes and long flowing tails. Some clue to their purpose and meaning is given by the straight lines that have been scratched onto two of the horses and onto the bison. Seven oblique lines with hooked ends cut into the bison's flank from above; seven arrowlike lines are marked on the side of one of the horses, rising from beneath, and a single similar line is scratched on the haunch of its neighbor to the left. These appear to be "kill" marks representing spears or arrows embedded in the animals. They tie in with theories of cave art as hunting magic: that the hunters painted lifelike images to represent their prey, then ritually killed them in the hope that their real life analogues would more easily suffer the same fate.

Coloring the Picture

Continuing on from the passage we pass the entrance to the Abside on the right and then enter the Nave, a huge underground hall decorated with further paintings. High on the left-hand side, above a rocky ledge, is the Black Cow frieze. The prehistoric artists made use of the ledge as a kind of ground line for the animals above. The black cow itself is portrayed, like so many Lascaux figures, with huge body and tiny head. Around and beneath it are some twenty small horses, facing the opposite way, and divided into two distinct groups—those on the right characterized by their round, bloblike hooves. There is no way of knowing for sure that these horses were painted by different people at different times, but that is the likeliest explanation.

The ledge below the Black Cow frieze has another crucial interest: on it were stone lamps, coloring materials, and food remains left by the prehistoric artists. No fewer than 158 lumps of coloring material have been found at several places within the cave. The bulk of them were black (over one hundred pieces), followed by yellows, reds, and white. The cave artists used hematite or red ochre for the red, manganese dioxide for the black, kaolin for the white, and goethite (another form of iron oxide) for the yellow. Study of the local geology has shown that sources of all these minerals were available within 25 miles (40 kilometers) of Lascaux. Indeed the most common colors—blacks and reds—lay respectively only 3 miles (5 kilometers) and 0.3 miles (0.5 kilometers) from the cave.

How the colors were applied to the walls is a less easy question. It is obvious from the lumps of mineral pigment found at Lascaux and other sites that they were powdered and mixed with water to form a paste or liquid. The grinding was done by stone pestles and in mortars. Some of them were found at Lascaux and still contained pigment. Archaeologists have experimented in applying this kind of paint. They have achieved the best results by using animal hair brushes, but for some outlines the paint may simply have been

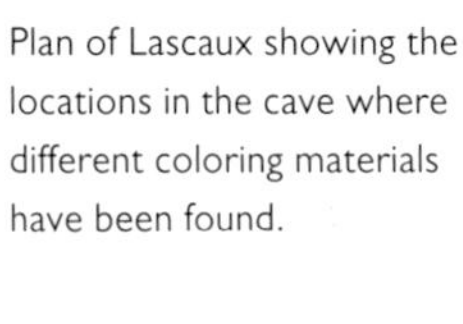

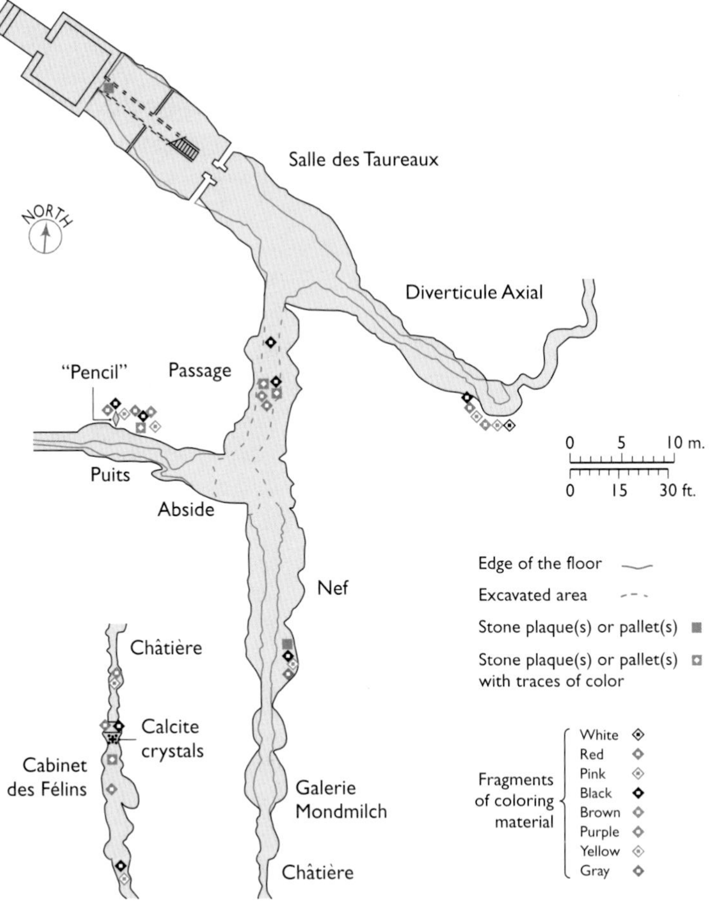

Plan of Lascaux showing the locations in the cave where different coloring materials have been found.

applied to the cave walls by finger. Pads may have been used for the infill coloring, or even for outlines where skins could have been cut to shape and placed against the rock surface to give the image a sharp edge.

Ancient Art and Modern Aesthetics

Modern audiences are familiar with the centuries-long tradition of Western art, and they cannot help but bring this knowledge with them when they view Lascaux. As a result, we all carry preconceived attitudes and approaches, which necessarily influence the way we look at the cave art. An example of this is the famous "Swimming Deer" frieze, on the wall of the Nave opposite the Black Cow. The heads of five deer with prominent antlers are portrayed in outline profile, above an irregularity in the rock wall. The row of heads emerging from the rock has suggested to many people the idea that they are swimming. Whether this was in the minds of the original artists, however, we shall never know. Like so many of the Lascaux paintings, photographs cannot do justice to the majesty of the "Swimming Deer." Each is around 3 feet high. The simplicity and elegance of the rendition is to modern eyes particularly pleasing—not so striking, perhaps, as the great polychrome figures, but in a certain sense more artful. In saying this we are imposing our own, twentieth-century aesthetic sense on paintings 17,000 years old, and purists may object. Yet it is hard to deny that the Lascaux paintings must have had some aesthetic quality for the artists who made them, even if they had symbolic meaning far beyond any mere "prettiness" or artistic impact.

The Swimming Deer provide an excellent illustration of another common feature of Paleolithic cave art: the way the artists used natural features of the rock walls to give depth and context to their art. This is seen even more strikingly at other caves, such as Niaux in the Pyrenees. Pondering this use of natural features by the prehistoric artists has led to new ways of thinking about the meaning of the art, even to the idea that the paintings and engravings were simply manifestations of images that were already there, hidden in the rock face. Did the painters of Lascaux imagine animals in the shapes and hollows of the cave walls? Were these the spirits with whom they came to commune?

Leaving the Nave and continuing deeper into the cave, we enter the long narrow gallery with walls coated in the spongy calcite known as "mondmilch." This presented no suitable surfaces to the Paleolithic artists and was left undecorated. It leads to the deepest region of art in Lascaux: the Cabinet des Félins, the Cats' Gallery. Here are several panels of engravings—of felines, horses, and ibex, and in one place a possible woolly rhinoceros, together with numerous "signs," abstract marks of one kind or another. The fact that carnivores are only found here, in the deepest part of the cave, must be significant, as must be the fact that the last marks of all are six painted dots, arranged in pairs at the far end of the Cabinet des Félins. It is difficult to know what these simple but enigmatic marks painted high up on the wall can mean.

This is the farthest limit of the Lascaux cave, as far as prehistoric art is concerned. It is true that there is a lower level, a vast underground chamber blocked by liquid mud and filled with asphyxiating gases. Nobody has yet been able to penetrate these obstacles, however, and it is unlikely that the lower level was accessible in Paleolithic times either.

Layers of Meaning

Having reached the limits of the cave we turn back to explore the final branching arm, which consists of the Abside and the Puits. The Abside is a tall, dome-ceilinged chamber opening directly off the main gallery at the junction of the Passage and Nave. It is one of the most richly decorated parts of Lascaux, with over a thousand paintings or engravings. They extend onto the ceiling, and scaffolding must have been installed to paint them. Some of the paintings are as large as those of the Salle des Taureaux. Here, as elsewhere in the cave, we are aware of the curious way in which the figures overlap, having been painted or engraved on top of each other. The images may individually be splendid, but the distraction of lines or colors from other animals placed above or beneath them detracts from the effect. The ideas of the Paleolithic artists were certainly different from our own. To call these figures art is to impose our own ideas and preconceptions. They are not equivalent to a Rubens or a Renoir, or even a Picasso. That is not intended as a comment on their value or quality, but on the reason for making them.

Accepting a difference in values, archaeologists have nonetheless endeavored to explain the phenomenon of overlapping and superpositioning, which is found in almost every major painted cave. It is not a question of limited space. Most caves have perfectly suitable wall spaces without any art, next to panels crowded with overlapping images. This suggests that location was of primary importance to the artists. They must have thought particular parts of the cave especially suitable for their images, and others unsuitable. Of course, the images were not all made in a short space of time: hundreds if not thousands of years may have passed between the first and last efforts at Lascaux. The cave may even have fallen out of use for long periods. That still does not explain why the latecomers chose to place their images above those of their ancestors. Perhaps the secret lies in the making: it may have been the creation of the image that was important, rather than the overall result. Painting or engraving a fine or spectacular image may have been the crucial act, endowed with all sorts of meaning and significance. Making such an image on the same rock wall where other images had already been carved may have been a recognition of the power or sacredness of those earlier images.

The Abside is notable not only for the sheer density of images but also for the abundance of red deer (seventy here, as compared with only a dozen in the rest of Lascaux). Horses are even more numerous (125), while aurochs and bison are relatively rare. Not knowing what the individual animals meant to the people who painted them, it is difficult to say more than that, once again, there is some specific intention in the portrayal of particular species. These are not randomly chosen images.

Beyond the Abside we descend into the Puits, where we find one of the most remarkable of the Lascaux paintings: a man "leaning" backward, neither truly upright nor lying down, in front of a bison. This is the only human image in the Lascaux cave, and one of the very few in western European cave art as a whole. Not surprisingly, it has given rise to an enormous body of speculation. Has the man really been knocked over by the bison, or is the juxtapositioning of the two images accidental? What is the meaning of the bird on a pole immediately below the human figure? Is it some symbol to indicate that he is no ordinary person but a shaman or ritual specialist? And why is the human shown ithyphallic, with erect penis? Is this the image of a shaman in a trance, conjuring up (perhaps) the bison that stands in front of him? Finally, we should note that the bison itself is not in the best of health, but has been disemboweled by a spear passing through its stomach.

The "Puits," or shaft, at Lascaux. Humans are rarely depicted in cave art, and that in itself makes this group of figures exceptional. It has been argued that the figures seen here form parts of a scene and that the human (with four fingers on each hand, an erect penis, and a bird-like head) is really a shaman or ritual specialist. The bison that faces him has apparently been disemboweled. Note also the bird or bird symbol on the stick nearby. Has the man (or shaman?) been felled by the bison he has killed? Or is the eviscerated bison merely a figment of his trance?

Lighting the Depths

Given the difficulty of access, the Puits might be expected to be a kind of inner sanctum, a place of particular significance. This idea gains support from the objects archaeologists found on the floor of the Puits: decorated harpoons, stone lamps, perforated shells, and coloring materials. They hint once again at rituals that must have been carried out in the cave. In contrast to these portable artifacts, the Puits has relatively little wall art. Apart from the man and bison already described, there is only a single horse, a single rhino, and a number of abstract signs or symbols.

One further discovery in the Puits deserves special mention. Today we are used to viewing the painted caves of western Europe under artificial light; either the lighting that has been set up in the caves to assist visitors or the lights used to illuminate the images for the glossy photographs reproduced in books and magazines. These lights allow us to see the art much more clearly than the original artists ever could. The people who painted and engraved these images deep in underground caves had only lamps or torches to guide them. The torches have left no trace, but archaeologists have successfully identified quite a number of lamps. Over a hundred have been claimed at Lascaux, but only one of these (plus a fragment of a second) is carefully shaped from red sandstone. The others are simply natural slabs of stone with cavities in one surface, sometimes with traces of burning. Only thirty-six of them can be accepted as genuine Paleolithic lamps. The fuel was probably animal fat, with a wick of lichen, bark, or wood. The carved lamp from Lascaux had remains of juniper wood as its wick. Significantly, this elegantly shaped object was found in the clay of the Puits, at the foot of the painting of bison and man, one of the most remarkable in the entire cave.

Lamps such as these would have been essential, but not particularly bright. We must imagine a restricted halo of flickering light surrounded by profound darkness. We must envisage the artists of Lascaux working on scaffolds barely able to see the cave floor only a couple of yards below them. And we must imagine them returning to view their handiwork, a procession of faint lamps and torches lighting their way and revealing turn by turn the images that appeared almost to jump at them out of the cave walls.

(facing page, bottom) Decorated stone lamp from the Puits at Lascaux, with engraved signs on the handle. When found, there were remains of burned material in the circular bowl. Analysis showed these to consist of juniper charcoal and ash from a resinous conifer, suggesting that this may have been an early perfume burner as much as a light source. Length of lamp: 9 inches (22 centimeters).

The Meaning of Lascaux

The descent into the Puits marks the end of this description of Lascaux. Along the way, various theories have been noted that have been put forward to explain

ICE AGE ART

It is ironic that the earliest evidence for what we might call "art" comes from a period of hostile climate, when ice sheets advanced over northern Europe and much of the rest was reduced to cold tundra. Lascaux is probably the most famous example of Ice Age art, but the evidence is not confined to cave walls. It also takes the form of carved objects of bone, stone, and ivory. Among the most famous examples of this portable art are the "Venus" figurines—female figures of plump or exaggerated proportions with breasts and pubic triangle emphasized. The best known of these is the "Venus of Willendorf" from a site in Austria; another, closer to Lascaux, is the "Venus of Lespugue." Willendorf and Lespugue are extreme examples; other Venus figurines are more normally shaped. Nonetheless, it is clear that Venus figurines are stylized representations of female bodies rather than female individuals.

Venus figurines are only a minor element of the Ice Age portable art. Much more common are carvings of animals, such as horse, deer, or ibex. Sometimes these carvings are decoration on functional objects. A good example is the antler spear–thrower from Le Mas d'Azil in the French Pyrenees. The working end is carved in the form of an ibex, from whose rear emerges a column supporting two birds; one of these is the hook in which the spear-butt would be engaged for throwing. Such pieces illustrate the imagination of the Ice Age artists. They also show their skill in working with materials such as antler, which are hard to carve, especially when we recall that they only had flint tools. And we must remember that these images weren't only shaped, but painted too; the Venus of Willendorf still has traces of red ochre, a common coloring material also used on the walls of Lascaux.

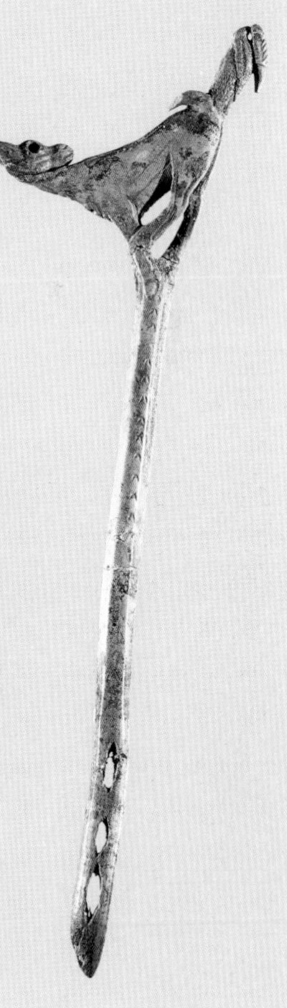

Antler spear-thrower from the cave of Le Mas d'Azil in the Pyrenees. This is roughly contemporary with some images at Lascaux and illustrates how the Ice Age artists worked in the round as well as on cave walls. The end of the piece is carved in the form of a young ibex, apparently looking on with surprise as two birds perch on an emerging turd. The tail of the second bird forms the hook with which the end of the spear would have engaged. An example of Paleolithic humor?

these vivid and impressive images. None of them, however, is entirely satisfactory. Nor can we say how the cave was used by the prehistoric communities who produced the art, despite the stone lamps and food remains that have been found there. Yet there is an essential quality of observation in these images that we still find familiar today.

Lascaux is far from being the oldest of the western European painted caves. The oldest of all, the recently discovered Grotte Chauvet, is in fact twice as old, with art dated to around 30,000 B.C. as compared with Lascaux's 15,000 B.C. Both of them belong to what has been called "the human revolution," the development of fully modern humans with languages and other skills just like our own. They fall at the end of the long period of human evolution that began with the earliest hominids in Africa four or five million years before. The painted caves, along with similar evidence from Africa, Asia, and Australia, are evidence of the dramatic change in human abilities and perceptions that marks our arrival at the fully modern stage. Hence, the significance of Lascaux goes far beyond the splendor of its images: it tells us something about the very essence of being human.

Further Reading

Most of the vast literature on Lascaux is naturally in French. A good place to start is the account by André Leroi-Gourhan in *L'Art des Cavernes. Atlas des grottes ornées paléolithiques de la France* (Paris: Ministère de la Culture, 1984, entry on "Lascaux" pp. 184–200). More detailed studies are collected together in *Lascaux Inconnu*, edited by Arlette Leroi-Gourhan and Jacques Allain (Paris: CNRS, 1979). Lascaux figures prominently in every general account of Paleolithic art. The following are especially recommended: Paul Bahn and Jean Vertut, *Journey Through the Ice Age* (Berkeley: University of California Press, 1997); Ann Sieveking, *The Cave Artists* (London: Thames and Hudson, 1979); and André Leroi-Gourhan, *The Dawn of European Art* (New York: Cambridge University Press, 1982). For stunning photographs of the Lascaux art, see Mario Ruspoli, *The Cave of Lascaux: The Final Photographic Record* (New York: Abrams, 1987).

Further Viewing

Material from Lascaux is held in the Musée des Antiquités Nationales at Saint-Germain-en-Laye, west of Paris. Copies of some finds are displayed in the entrance to Lascaux II. A few miles from Lascaux is the Musée National de Préhistoire at Les Eyzies-de-Tayac, which has rich collections of Paleolithic material from this region of France.

CHAPTER

THREE

The Côa Valley

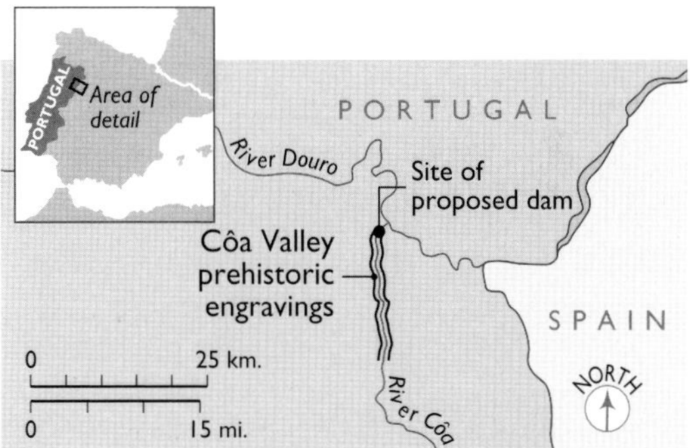

c. 18,000 B.C.

Paleolithic carvings

in northeastern Portugal

The Côa valley is a relatively recent addition to the list of Europe's prehistoric highlights. Hidden away in a remote area of northeastern Portugal, the amazing array of carvings and engravings was only discovered in 1992, and first became public in 1994. Yet such is their importance that the Côa valley is already famous—not only for the figures themselves, some of which may date back 20,000 years or more, but also for the controversy surrounding their date and for the struggle to ensure their preservation. The saga had a happy outcome, but for several months the future of the Côa petroglyphs hung in the balance. Deeply enmeshed in the arguments about preservation were the efforts of archaeologists to demonstrate that these carvings, scattered on exposed rock surfaces along a 10-mile (17-kilometer) stretch of the Côa valley, were indeed as old as was claimed.

Open-Air Art

The Côa river is a minor tributary of the Douro, in the heart of Portugal's port-producing country. This is a peaceful, rural landscape of sheltered valleys and forested hills, far from any major towns. To reach it today, you travel northeast from Lisbon to the valley of the River Douro, then strike inland, heading

The principal groups of prehistoric rock art in the Côa valley. The site of the proposed dam lies immediately to the north of Canada do Amendoal (site no. 3).

for the small town of Vila Nova de Foz Côa, a little way upstream from the Côa's junction with the Douro. Here, only 10 miles (17 kilometers) from the Spanish frontier, lies a priceless piece of prehistoric heritage: the greatest concentration of open-air Ice Age art so far discovered in Europe.

In itself, Ice Age art is by no means new to European archaeologists. Far from it. The painted caves of Lascaux and Altamira, and now the recently discovered Grotte Chauvet, are among the most famous prehistoric sites anywhere in the world. The cave of Altamira has been studied and visited by archaeologists since the nineteenth century. Other more recently discovered decorated caves have been splashed over the pages of newspapers and color supplements. They form the subject of weighty tomes and their popular interest has given birth to numerous coffee table books.

What makes Côa so exceptional is that its art is not hidden away in a cave but scattered on exposed rock surfaces in the open air. Archaeologists have long pondered whether there might not once have been open-air art in Paleolithic Europe. Those of a gloomier disposition thought that no traces would have survived, and therefore no one would ever be sure. On the whole, they assumed that even if there had been any such art, it would long since have disappeared. It would have been destroyed, they thought, by the ravages of time and the enormous changes in climate that separate the last Ice Age from the present day. All that was left, it seemed, were the spectacular paintings and engravings preserved in the sheltered environment of the caves. The Côa valley has changed all that; it has literally brought Paleolithic rock art into the light of day.

Several hundred figures have so far been discovered, and more are coming to light all the time as Portuguese archaeologists broaden and intensify their exploration. The area in which they fall stretches up the Côa valley from its confluence with the River Douro for approximately 10 miles (17 kilometers). The total extent has yet to be established. Most of the engravings are in the lower part of the valley, on naturally smoothed rock faces a little above the river. Some of them, in fact, lie slightly below water level, which has risen since the Pocinho Dam was built twelve years ago. This makes them difficult to see and will ultimately destroy them as the water erodes the rock faces. Many more of the engravings would have been lost, however, if the project to build a new dam at Côa itself had been carried through to completion. Only a decision by the Portuguese government saved them from this fate.

The Côa Engravings

The Côa art consists of pecked and engraved images, showing in outline form the animals that populated this part of Europe at the height of the last Ice Age some 20,000 years ago. There may originally have been paintings, too, but if so, the paint has not survived. Another possibility is that the pecked and engraved outlines were themselves colored, but again, no traces can be seen.

The absence of coloring distinguishes Côa from the famous painted caves, but we should bear in mind that most Paleolithic cave art consists of engravings; the stunning painted animals of Lascaux or Altamira are very much the exception.

Côa nonetheless resembles the art of the decorated caves in some important respects. In the first place, there are the subjects depicted: Ice Age mammals. Second, there is the style of depiction—the twist of the horns, the swollen abdomens. Then there is the fact that the animal outlines are often superimposed, just as in cave art. Archaeologists have used these features to argue that the Côa engravings must be contemporary with the decorated caves. But the closest parallels seem to be with the portable art (engraved stone slabs) of Parpalló near Valencia, in Spain, which is dated to around 18,000 B.C.

Not all of the Côa art was made at the same time, however, and this date should be regarded as only a general guide, a central point within a range that must have spanned several thousand years. Archaeologists who have looked closely at the Côa engravings claim they can trace an evolution in the style of the figures. They place the earliest of them in the Gravettian period, around 25,000 years ago, and the most recent in the late Magdalenian, some 10,000 years ago. This argument is supported by the way some of the carvings cut across others, which shows they must be different in date. There are also marked differences in the weathering or patina of the figures. This means that when new carvings were made, earlier ones had already been exposed for many hundreds or thousands of years.

We can be fairly sure, then, that the Côa engravings were made over a long period of time, down perhaps to the late Magdalenian period at the very end

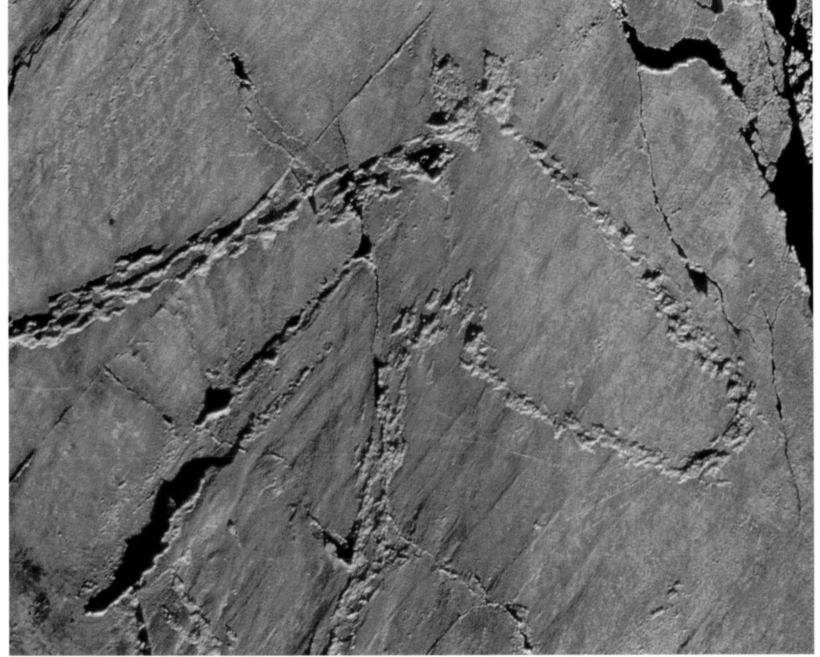

Horse engraving from the Canada do Inferno in the Côa valley. Note the pecked technique used to produce the outline. Length of head: approx. 6 inches (15 centimeters).

Aerial view across the Côa valley at Ribeira de Piscos, with a vineyard on the right.

of the Upper Paleolithic, or even beyond. But not all archaeologists have been convinced by these arguments. Some, as we shall see below, have proposed much younger ages for the Côa valley art.

Techniques and Subjects

The Côa figures are engraved or pecked in the surface of the schist bedrock or on large schist blocks, sometimes so lightly that they are almost invisible today. Portuguese archaeologists who have studied the carvings distinguish four different techniques. First, there are figures formed of finely incised lines made with a sharp, pointed instrument. Next come figures with a pecked outline, created by hammering a line across the rock face with a stone implement. The third technique is abrasion, where an initial narrow groove is worn into a wider channel, to make the figure stand out more clearly. Finally, there is the technique of scraping, where the whole of the area within the outline is scraped or roughened, to create a contrast between the figure and the surrounding rock.

That is how the figures were made. But what did they depict? The Paleolithic artists of the Côa valley in fact chose a relatively restricted range of subjects. All the carvings, save one, are of animals. In overall numbers, large herbivores predominate, with aurochs (wild cattle) in first place, followed by horses, and then ibex and red deer. The large size of the images makes them particularly striking: many of them are over 2 feet long, and some of them as much as 5 feet (1.5 meters). But there are also smaller species, in smaller scale.

Among these are fish, low down near the original water's edge. Many of the fish engravings have already been lost below water as a result of the Pocinho Dam, but occasionally the level drops and they come back into view.

Before leaving the subjects of the art, we mustn't omit to mention the one nonanimal figure from Côa. This is a human figure, finely engraved, at Ribeira de Piscos. Human figures are rare in Paleolithic art, and some have claimed that this one must be more recent than the other Côa engravings. In style, however, it is quite similar to human portraits engraved on stone slabs from La Marche in western France. The La Marche engravings belong to the Magdalenian period, over 10,000 years old. There is really no reason to think the Ribeira de Piscos carving is not Paleolithic, a rare image of an actual individual—one of those, perhaps, who actually created the art.

The animals shown in the Côa engravings give us a glimpse of the wildlife that inhabited the valley at the height of the last Ice Age. The valley itself, or the broader Douro valley to the north, may have been a regular route for the seasonal migrations of deer and horse. Ibex would have lived on the sloping (and sometimes precipitous) valley flanks, aurochs on the lowland valley floor. The deeply incised valleys offered a sheltered habitat, shielded from the extremes of cold. That may be one of the reasons why we don't find depictions of cold-adapted species such as mammoth, woolly rhino, bison, or reindeer. In fact, no skeletal remains of any of these cold-adapted animals have been found in southern or western Iberia from deposits of the last Ice Age. Those animals simply weren't present there. By contrast, archaeologists working in Portugal and Spain do find the bones of ibex, aurochs, red deer, and horses—the very species that are portrayed at Côa.

Where did the Côa artists live? This is a question it is really too early to answer, since archaeologists have only begun to explore the valley in detail. One open-air camp site has already been found, however, at Cardina, toward the southern end of the rock art zone. Initial excavations by Portuguese archaeologists show that some parts of the Cardina site were occupied at the end of the Ice Age, in the so-called Final Magdalenian period (10,000–8000 B.C.), but other soundings went back to the Late Gravettian (c. 20,000 B.C.), broadly contemporary with the date proposed for the engravings. The people who lived at Cardina—a small band of hunters and gatherers—would have exploited the richer vegetation of the valley floor for plant foods, and hunted both on the valley floors and the higher lands around. They made tools of flint and rock crystal, hafting them in wooden or bone handles to make efficient spears and knives.

Archaeologists have recently begun work at a second Paleolithic settlement in the Côa valley. This is only a few hundred yards from the major rock art site of Quinta da Barca, and dates from the Magdalenian period (15,000–8000 B.C.).

As more work is done, we can expect to gain a much clearer picture of Paleolithic life in the Côa valley, but already we can discern some of the key

ART BEYOND THE CAVES

The discovery of open-air Paleolithic art at Côa must mean there were once similar sites throughout southern Europe. This is a remarkable but unmistakable conclusion. It overturns a long-standing belief that the earliest European rock art was restricted to caves. Archaeologists used to think that open-air art (such as the famous Valcamonica carvings) began only after the end of the Ice Age. We now know that the early modern humans who occupied Europe at the height of the Ice Age, some 20,000 years ago, made carvings not only in caves but in the open.

The number of open-air art sites now stands at six. All of them, for the moment, are in southwestern Europe, in Spain, Portugal, and southern France. Why should this be? One possibility is that the inhabitants of other regions simply didn't create open-air art. After all, there is little enough cave art outside Spain and southern France. But another, more convincing explanation is that southwest Europe, with the moderating influence of the Atlantic Ocean, suffered from a less extreme climate than the rest of Europe. There was probably less frost damage to the exposed rock surfaces, and so the art has survived.

Locations of open-air rock art sites in Iberia and southern France that may be of Paleolithic age (over 10,000 years old).

Côa, in fact, is the most recent of the six sites to be discovered. Not far away are two earlier discoveries, both of them, like Côa, in the upper Douro region near the Spanish–Portuguese frontier. The first to be found was on the Portuguese side in 1981, when archaeology student Nelson Rebanda reported a panel carved with three animal figures at Mazouco. It had long been known to locals but was a major surprise to archaeologists, who realized

elements in the art, in the local topography, and in these first settlement excavations.

Côa Art: The Principal Sites

The Paleolithic art for which Côa is now so famous was first recognized at Canada do Inferno in the northern end of the valley in 1992. Then in the winter of 1994–1995, systematic exploration led to the discovery of a whole series of sites, stretching 10 miles (17 kilometers) upstream. Most of the known carvings are concentrated at five major localities.

Canada do Inferno remains one of the most important of the rock art sites. It has a dramatic location, at a point where the steep-sided Côa valley is joined by a smaller side valley. The carvings are on the west side of the Côa river, on schist outcrops overlooking the floodplain. They include figures of

that here for the first time was Paleolithic art in the open air. At Siega Verde, on the Spanish side of the frontier, there is a much richer site than Mazouco, with well over five hundred engravings, mainly of horses.

Engraved horse, one of three ancient figures at Mazouco in northeast Portugal. The horse measures over 2 feet (62 centimeters) in length, but its appearance has been altered by chalking and painting since its discovery.

At around the same time as Mazouco, Spanish archaeologists found Upper Paleolithic rock art further east at Domingo Garcia, on the edge of the Meseta plateau. A few years later, yet another group of engravings came to light at Piedras Blancas in Almeria. The list of discoveries is completed by Fornols-Haut in the French Pyrenees, where a huge schist block is covered with fine engravings. To date, this is the only one of these sites north of the Pyrenees.

Compared with the three hundred or more decorated caves, these six open-air sites may not seem very exciting. Yet in truth they are, for they open a whole new window on Ice Age art. They show us that the early inhabitants of western Europe didn't just decorate caves, but carved images in all sorts of outdoor locations. We can scarcely even begin to imagine what it all meant—rock faces engraved with animals, scattered over the landscape. But it shows that the landscape itself was rich with significance. We can sense there were deep beliefs behind the images, though we may never know precisely what those beliefs were.

aurochs, horses, and ibex, but two rocks also have engravings of fish. Since 1995, Canada do Inferno has been the subject of a systematic recording program, the first to be undertaken in the valley. It will be followed by similar work elsewhere.

The second important site is upstream at Ribeira de Piscos, where the Côa valley begins to open out. There are fewer figures here, but a number of horse engravings in fine line technique are especially impressive. Here, too, is the sole human figure in this collection of Paleolithic art. It has been carved over the earlier engraving of an aurochs with a striated body (where the outline of the animal is filled with multiple fine incisions).

Still further upstream, where the valley floor broadens, is the important art site of Penascosa. Some of the blocks here are naturally split, and it is interesting to see how the Paleolithic artists have made use of the flat surfaces presented by the cleavage of the schist. Horse and ibex, together with aurochs and a few fish, are present. One particularly notable carving shows a stallion mounting a mare—a rare example in this art of animals interacting. The Penascosa art has another interesting feature. Several of the animals are shown with two or three heads, carved on top of each other in slightly different positions. The artists may have done this to convey a sense of movement. The same treatment occurs at Canada do Inferno and Quinta da Barca.

Quinta da Barca, opposite Penascosa, is the fourth of the Côa sites. Carvings are scattered about a wide area, both on the valley floor and on the higher slopes behind. Finally, 4 miles (6 kilometers) upstream from Penascosa, is the more inaccessible site of Faia. Here the Côa river runs once again within a narrow, steep-sided valley, flanked by granite cliffs 650 feet (200 meters) high. The Faia rock art occurs in small rock shelters and includes paintings of men and animals. These are probably only four thousand or five thousand years old, but alongside them is a series of older engravings, some of aurochs, which probably belong with the Paleolithic art.

Disputes and Dates

European archaeologists generally believe that most of the Côa engravings (as distinct from the later prehistoric paintings) were made during the Upper Paleolithic period. Experts have compared the style of some of the figures to

Upper part of Rock I at Canada do Inferno, showing superimposed engravings of horses, aurochs, and ibex.

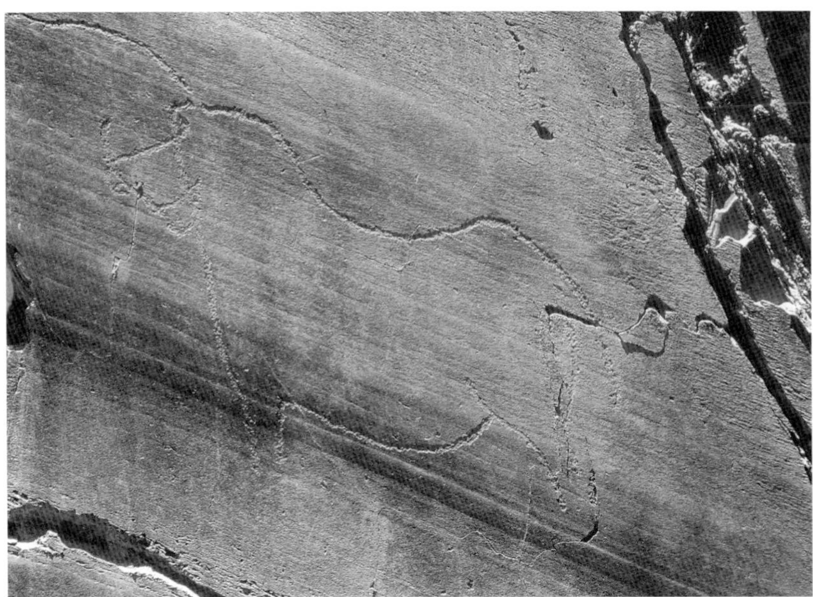

Engraving from Ribeira de Piscos. What at first sight looks like an animal with horns is in fact two horses with overlapping heads. The complete horse figure shown here measures 24 inches (60 centimeters) across.

those on the portable art from Parpalló, and on that basis have given them a general age of around 20,000 years. Future studies may well show that there are several distinct phases within the art. But all the evidence of style and representation points to them being Upper Paleolithic.

This opinion is reinforced by the heavy weathering patina which covers the Côa engravings. Clearest of all are those few cases where more recent carvings overlie the Paleolithic engravings. At the site of Vermelhosa, for example, where the Côa joins the Douro, there is an Iron Age carving of a mounted warrior, fresh and new in comparison with the finely engraved Paleolithic deer over which it has been carved.

The argument gains further strength from the fact that horse and ibex, which figure so prominently in the Côa art, became extinct in the Côa region at the end of the last Ice Age around 10,000 years ago. The position regarding the extinction of the horse is a little less sure. Some archaeologists believe it survived in limited numbers after the Ice Age, but overall it is much more likely that, like the ibex, it disappeared from the region around 10,000 years ago and was absent for the next 5,000 years. Horses were reintroduced to Spain and Portugal as a domestic animal by humans during the third millennium B.C. All in all, it is hard to avoid the conclusion that the carvings of horse and ibex must be more than 10,000 years old, and perhaps considerably older. This means they are Upper Paleolithic.

Against this consensus of opinion, however, are the voices of certain specialists who think the Côa engravings are much more recent than this. The dispute arose when attempts were made to date the carvings directly. This was done in order to decide whether they were indeed Upper Paleolithic, as archaeologists were claiming them to be, and hence worth preserving.

Dating rock art is never easy. What, after all, is there to date, apart from the style of the engraving itself? The answer is given by new techniques that have been developed specifically to give a direct date for rock engravings in the open air.

These new techniques rely on one of two things. The first is the presence of tiny carbon flecks trapped in the silica skin, which wind-blown dust deposits on the surface of the rock (known in arid regions as "desert varnish"). Even tiny amounts of carbon like these can now be dated by radiocarbon dating. The second approach is to measure the erosion or exposure of the engravings themselves.

Both have been tried at Côa but without much real success. The first set of carbon dates showed the engravings might well be Paleolithic, and were certainly over two thousand years old, while the second set suggested they were under two thousand years old! Studies of erosion gave an age of up to 6,500 years, and measures of chlorine-36 (produced by the action of cosmic rays on exposed rock) showed that the rock surfaces had been exposed for over 100,000 years. In sum, the whole exercise was a failure, and none of the methods provided a clear and reliable date. But there is certainly nothing about them to make us abandon the generally held view that many Côa engravings are Upper Paleolithic. We come back to the simple fact that the animals most prominent at Côa—horse and ibex—have been extinct in Portugal for over 10,000 years. And the style of the engravings is Upper Paleolithic.

The Battle for Côa

Dating is not the only battle that has been fought over the Côa engravings. The real struggle was to save them from being drowned beneath the waters of a hydroelectric scheme.

The drama began in 1989 when plans were made to build a hydroelectric dam at the end of the Côa valley, near the town of Vila Nova de Foz Côa and about 1 mile (1.5 kilometers) upstream from the junction with the River Douro. Following usual practice, the state-owned company building the dam, Electricidade de Portugal (EDP), commissioned an environmental impact study. This included a look at the archaeology, but the company came away with the conclusion that there was nothing of great archaeological significance to worry about.

In fact, the Paleolithic engravings were first noticed three years later, in 1992. But even then they weren't officially reported until November 1994. By that time, work on the $150 million dam had already begun. Had it been completed, the 700-foot (200-meter) high structure would have drowned out thousands of acres of land, including not only the Paleolithic engravings but Quinta Erva Moira, one of Portugal's top port vineyards. Not surprisingly, there was opposition to the scheme at both the local and national levels, and many people—even those well-placed to know—argued that it wasn't really needed.

The two-year delay in reporting the discovery of the art led many opponents of the dam to suspect a cover up. An international campaign was quickly mounted to try to halt the building work and persuade the Portuguese government to preserve the carvings. In February 1995, a team of specialists from the United Nations Educational, Scientific and Cultural Organization (UNESCO) visited the area and pronounced the Côa rock art of world-class importance. They urged the government to call a halt, at least temporarily, to the hydroelectric scheme. The campaign had enormous support at the local level, too: children from the high school in Vila Nova de Foz Côa collected hundreds of thousands of signatures on their petition to save the art.

Faced with such unexpected opposition, the government and the electricity company began to reconsider their options. One possibility was to physically cut away the carved rocks and carry them to safety elsewhere, allowing work on the dam to proceed. That, after all, is what had been done in Egypt in the

Dam construction in progress in the Côa valley in 1994. Work on the dam (which would have resulted in the flooding of most of the Côa valley engravings) was only halted in November 1995.

1960s when the Aswan Dam was built, and the rock-cut temples of Abu Simbel were moved. But in the Côa case this would have risked serious damage to the art, and it would have been expensive.

Before reaching a decision, the electricity company decided to undertake proper tests to establish whether the Côa art really was as ancient as archaeologists claimed. Enter the dating experts discussed above. In an ideal world this should have resolved at least one part of the controversy, but as we have seen, the results of the dating attempts were contradictory and unconvincing. It led some people—including advocates of the dam—to claim that the Côa art was not Paleolithic at all, but much more recent. Overall, however, few people were completely persuaded by these dating experiments.

In the end, it was the politicians who saved the day. On 1 October 1995, the Portuguese voters went to the polls to elect a new government. In place of the center-right Social Democratic Party, who had supported the Côa Dam project, the election brought to power the opposition Socialist Party, led by Antonio Guterres. On 7 November, Prime Minister Guterres announced what the archaeological world had been waiting anxiously to hear: work on the dam would be halted.

The Côa valley has now been turned into an archaeological park, where visitors from around the world can explore this unrivaled collection of open-air Paleolithic art. It will shortly become one of Europe's leading archaeological attractions. Reception centers in the villages of Castelo Melhor and Muxagata, and a museum in the town of Vila Nova de Foz Côa, organize guided tours by off-road vehicles down to Penascosa, Ribeira de Piscos, and Canada do Inferno respectively. The valley has changed much since ibex and aurochs roamed its flanks and forests, and prehistoric hunter-gatherers camped on the valley floor. Without the art, it would be just another European valley, with a scatter of archaeological sites. But the art makes us think of the valley as a Paleolithic landscape in which our distant ancestors moved about to gather and hunt, and left some echo of their beliefs and concerns in the vivid images carved on the rocks.

Further Reading

Little has yet been published in English on the Côa engravings, though that will change as research gathers pace and the new visitor arrangements take shape. Most useful is the booklet *Côa Valley Rock Art and Prehistory,* written by António Faustino de Carvalho, João Zilhão, and Thierry Aubry, and published by the new Parque Arqeológico of the Vale do Côa in 1996. The story of the discovery and the efforts to save the art, up to June 1995, are described by Paul Bahn in "Cave Art Without the Caves," (*Antiquity* 69, 1995, pp. 231–237). The controversy over the dates is taken up by Robert Bednarik and João Zilhão in the December issue of the same journal (*Antiquity* 69, 1995, pp. 877–901). The essential specialist publication (mainly in Portuguese) is the 590-page *Dossier Côa,* edited by Vitor Oliveira Jorge (Porto: Sociedade Portuguesa de Antropologia e Etnologia, 1995). For a general background to Paleolithic art (though written before the Côa engravings were discovered), *Journey Through the Ice Age* by Paul Bahn and Jean Vertut is indispensable (Berkeley: University of California Press, 1997).

Further Viewing

Reception centers for visitors wishing to view the Côa Valley rock art have been established at Muxagat, Castelo Melhor, and at Vila Nova de Foz Côa, where there are also plans for a museum.

CHAPTER

FOUR

Carnac

C. 4500–2500 B.C.

Long mounds and standing stones in southern Brittany

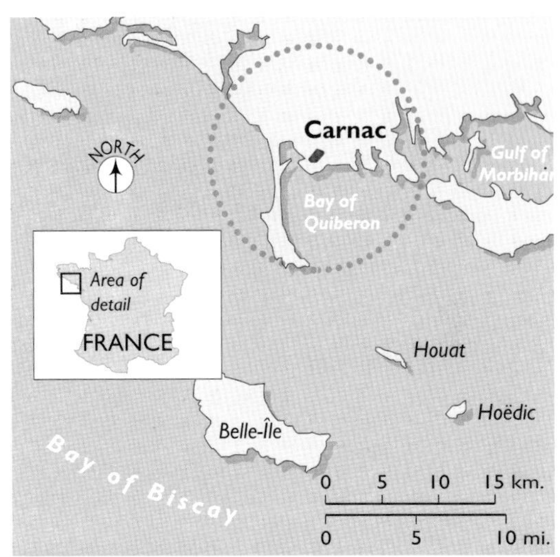

Few areas of Europe have such a diversity of Neolithic monuments of such a size and importance as those of the Carnac region of southern Brittany. Here we find not only burial mounds and stone arcs or semicircles, but enormous alignments formed of serried ranks of standing stones stretching nearly a mile across the landscape. There are also remains of the largest single standing stone ever erected in prehistoric Europe, and a profusion of megalithic art in the passage graves. Above all, perhaps, it is the longevity of the tradition that is astonishing: the first of the monuments date to around 4500 B.C., while the last of them were probably built just around 2500 B.C. Like Avebury in Britain or the Boyne Valley in Ireland, this is a megalithic wonderland.

The modern town of Carnac lies near the coast in the French département of the Morbihan. It is a landscape of drowned valleys; long, thin promontories; and small offshore islands, framed in the west by the projecting Quiberon peninsula and in the east by the Gulf of Morbihan, an almost landlocked bay. The prehistoric builders chose carefully when siting their monuments. Some locations were selected especially to be visible from the sea. This is obviously the case for present-day island sites such as the passage grave of Gavrinis or the stone semicircles (more accurately horseshoes, circles with breaks) of

View across the Le Menec alignments at Carnac in Brittany.

Er Lannic. It is also true of the Grand Menhir Brisé, the massive though now fallen menhir at Locmariaquer, and of the conspicuous burial mounds of Petit Mont and Tumiac on the Arzon peninsula. Tradition holds that the Tumiac mound is the viewpoint from which Julius Caesar watched the Roman defeat of the local Veneti in the sea battle in the Gulf of Morbihan in 56 B.C. Tradition may be right, but Tumiac itself is much older than the Romans, and dates probably from the fourth millennium B.C.

MEGALITHIC TOMBS IN BRITTANY

La Table des Marchand and Gavrinis are only two of the several thousand burial mounds with stone chambers that were built in northern and western Europe in the Neolithic period. Great efforts have been made to establish where the idea of building these tombs may have originated, and how it spread. No consensus of opinion has been reached, but the tombs of Brittany do seem to be among the very earliest. They were built by small-scale fishing and farming communities, groups of families who may have regarded the tombs as the resting places of their ancestors.

In Brittany, the first megalithic tombs were constructed around 4500 B.C., while the latest of them date to around 3000 B.C. (Gavrinis and La Table des Marchand belong around 3500 B.C.) During this enormous time period, longer even than that which separates us from the Romans, an incredible profusion and variety of tomb-types were created. The prevailing fashion seems to have been communal burial, where bodies were placed together in the tomb without any attempt to keep the bones separate. Whether at certain periods everyone was buried in this way, or whether only special individuals merited this treatment, is unclear. The rules must anyway have varied from place to place. What is clear is that very few objects were placed with the dead. Treasure hunters who over the centuries have been lured by the size of the burial mounds have inevitably been disappointed by the poverty of their pickings. These were in any case Neolithic monuments, built by societies who had no knowledge of metal, and whose cutting tools were of flint or polished stone. The nature of technology makes the construction and decoration of these tombs an even more impressive achievement.

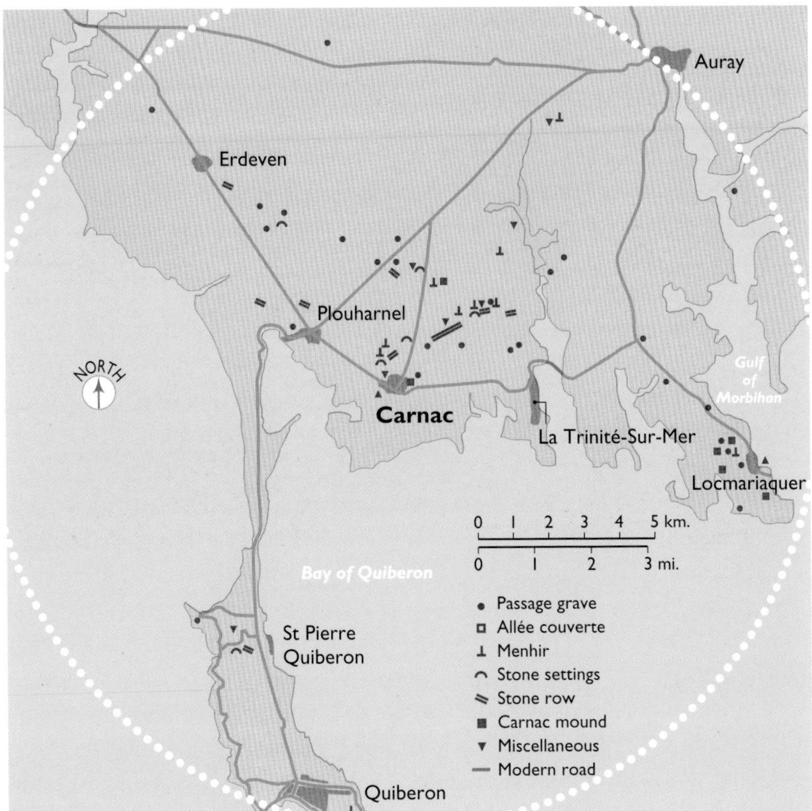

Positions of the major Neolithic monuments of this area. Note: passage graves and allées couvertes are categories of megalithic tomb; stone settings are arcs or horseshoes of standing stones (to be distinguished from the famous stone rows, which, however, they sometimes adjoin).

Landscape with Monuments

Mention of Er Lannic and the sea leads to one important question that must be resolved before reading too much prehistory into the present day landscape, for the standing stones of Er Lannic today are partly below sea level. Indeed, one of the semicircles is entirely submerged. There could be no more graphic evidence of sea-level change in the period since it was built. The visitor who takes a boat at Larmor-Baden to the small offshore islands of Gavrinis or Er Lannic is making a journey that would have been impossible 5,500 years ago. At that time, when sea level was lower, the shallow strait between these islands and the mainland was marshland, and the islands themselves were part of a low promontory at the junction of two broad estuaries: the River of Auray to the west and the River of Vannes to the east. The vegetation, as well, was very different, and in place of the present heathland and scrub we must try to imagine forests of deciduous trees such as oak and elm, interspersed in more fertile areas with the clearings of the early farmers.

There is such a concentration of monuments in the Carnac area—and such a variety—that it is hard to know where to begin. The task isn't made any easier by the fact that chronology—when the individual monuments were built or extended—is far from settled. Perhaps the best way to start is to enumerate the different kinds of monuments found in the Carnac region. At the broadest level they can be divided into two categories: mounds and stones.

The mounds themselves can be further subdivided into long mounds and round mounds, the latter usually much smaller in size and covering a stone-built passage grave. Alongside these there are mounds of less regular shape, such as Petit Mont at Arzon, most of which are also associated with passage graves.

The stones divide naturally into four groups. First, there are single standing stones; next there are modest alignments of standing stones; then there are the enormous alignments that contain hundreds of standing stones arranged in parallel lines; and, last but not least, there are stone arcs or semicircles, such as the submerged examples of Er Lannic.

Two further comments are needed by way of preamble, before we turn to the monuments themselves. First, stones and mounds are clearly associated. The tradition and technology seen most conspicuously in the stone rows are also represented in the stone-built passage graves under some of the mounds. Furthermore, stone rows in one case run over the top of one of the long mounds. There can be no clearer demonstration of the close association between them.

The second comment concerns the spans of time and the numerous modifications that have been made to many of these monuments. It wasn't simply a case of raising a standing stone row or building a mound and then moving on to something else. Subsequent generations came back to the same monuments, enlarging, rebuilding, or sometimes destroying the work of their predecessors. This was in every sense a living tradition in a continually revisited and constantly changing form.

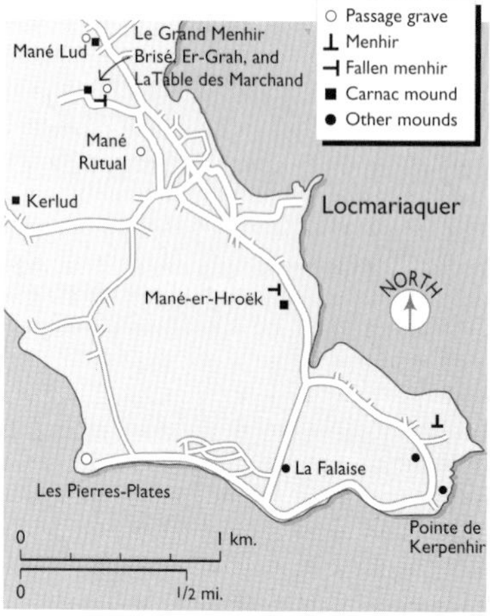

The Neolithic monuments of the Locmariaquer peninsula.

Revelations at Locmariaquer

The visitor to the Carnac region will find many of the sites clearly marked and easily identified. Several of them lie within or around the small town of Carnac itself. But it may be most logical to begin some 6 miles (10 kilometers) to the east, at Locmariaquer.

Here there is a group of three monuments, closely clustered together. It is hard to say which is the most prominent: the massive fallen fragments of the Grand Menhir Brisé, the huge long mound of Er-Grah, or the neater ovoid tumulus of the Table des Marchand chambered tomb. All three have long been known, but it is only within the last ten years that archaeologists have made a thorough investigation of the complex, excavating both within and between them. The results have been surprising in a number of ways, above all in what they have told us about the history of these monuments.

One of the main objectives of the recent excavations was to untangle the relationship of the Grand Menhir Brisé to the long mound of Er-Grah. The

The Grand Menhir Brisé, now broken into four fragments, must originally have stood 65 feet (20 meters) tall. At 350 tons, it was the largest standing stone ever erected in prehistoric Europe. It was quarried from an outcrop of orthogneiss at Roguedas, a few miles to the northwest, and then laboriously dragged to the site and erected in a specially shaped stone-hole. On the upper face of one of the fallen fragments is the low-relief carving of an object called an "axe-plow"—perhaps simply a prehistoric plow. This and the rest of the stone may well have been painted, making it still more striking and impressive.

long mound is one of several in the region. In its center is a small tomb chamber, constructed of megalithic slabs, but this is almost certainly a later insertion. In its earliest form Er-Grah was a long, chamberless mound built in three sections: the center part of rubble and the two ends of earth faced in stone. Altogether it measured almost 650 feet (200 meters) long, though today it is so badly damaged and dilapidated (the northern end has been quarried away to make room for a parking lot) that it is hard to imagine how impressive it must originally have been. But its size places it among the special category of Carnac mounds that we shall meet once again in the tumulus Saint-Michel.

Archaeologists have dated Er-Grah to around 4000 B.C.; they have also shown that it once extended almost to the foot of the Grand Menhir Brisé. This menhir is now broken into four huge fragments, and people had argued for decades about whether it ever stood upright. Some claimed that there was a fault in the stone, which caused it to break when the prehistoric builders were trying to erect it. Others held to traditions that said it had fallen in the seventh century A.D., or alternatively, as recently as the eighteenth century. What now emerges as a result of the new excavations is that the Grand Menhir was most likely quarried, pummeled into shape, and raised upright in the Neolithic period. The hole carefully cut for it has been found by the archaeologists. But it didn't stand alone, for stretching away to its northeast the excavators traced a line of eighteen smaller holes, each of which had once held a standing stone. It was even possible to say (from fragments of stone found in the holes) that those nearest the Grand Menhir were made of orthogneiss (like the Grand Menhir itself), the next few were migmatite, and those furthest away of granite.

This line of menhirs was probably the first monument to be built at Locmariaquer, perhaps around 4500 B.C., though we can't date it precisely. It was on a different alignment to the Er-Grah long mound, and that in itself

Reconstruction of the Grand Menhir Brisé (a), showing the so-called "axe-plow" carved in low relief on the second of the fallen fragments; a reconstructed menhir (b) formed by fitting together the decorated menhir fragments reused in the passage graves of La Table des Marchand and Gavrinis, shown here together with a third undecorated fragment from the chamber in the Er Grah long mound. The original menhir may have stood in the Locmariaquer complex; the map shows the findspots of the three fragments.

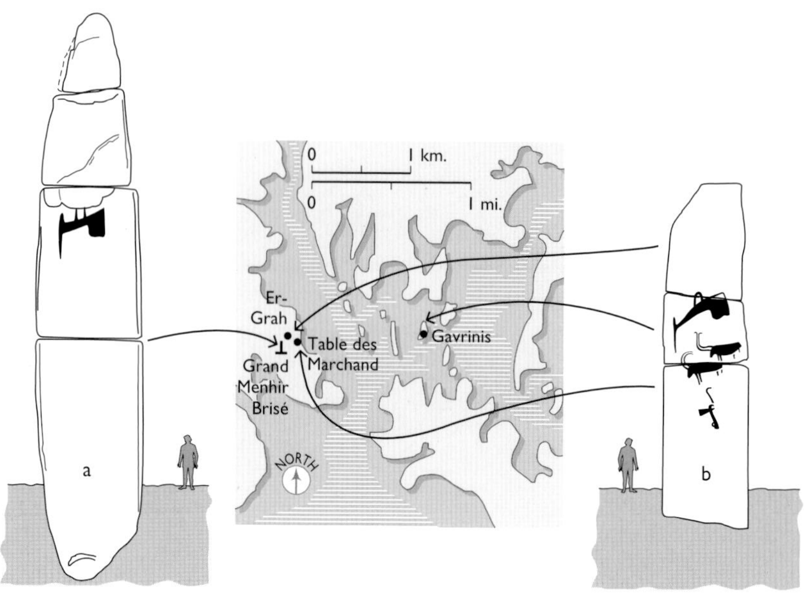

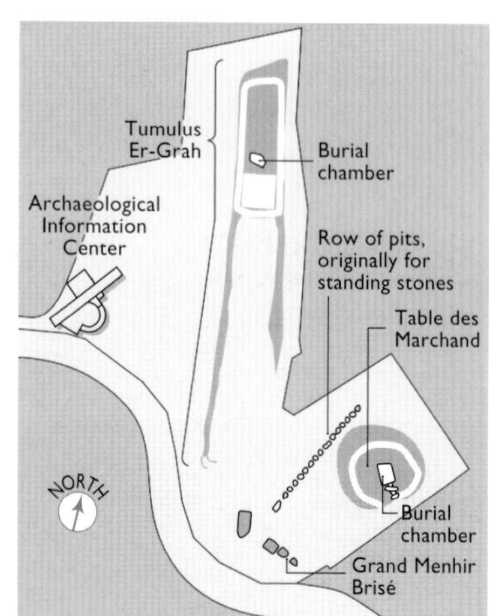

The archaeological complex at Locmariaquer: the Grand Menhir Brisé, once the tallest standing stone in Europe; the massive but much damaged and eroded tumulus of Er-Grah, one of the enormous Carnac mounds; and the famous passage grave of the Table des Marchand, incorporating reused menhirs in its construction.

suggests it wasn't part of the same plan. The Grand Menhir Brisé was carved and possibly painted; so too may have been the others, making an impressive line of colored pillars, culminating in the massive Grand Menhir, several times larger and taller than the others. But apart from the fallen Grand Menhir and a few fragments in the stone-holes, none of these standing stones survives. How can they have disappeared so completely?

The explanation is to be found in the third of the Locmariaquer monuments: the Table des Marchand. This is later in date than either the Grand Menhir or Er-Grah, built only around 3500 B.C., but it incorporated parts of two earlier monuments. The first is the curiously shaped pointed stone that forms the back wall of the burial chamber. This carries row upon row of curved lines, thought to represent "crooks" (symbols of power) or even axe hafts. Whatever their true significance, they were clearly symbols of importance, since they are found on many other Breton Neolithic monuments. What is surprising is that the back face of this stone is also decorated (though less ornately). Might it once have stood alone, in the open, and only later have had the tomb chamber built around it? The theory is given greater weight by the capstone of La Table des Marchand. This too carries a carving, of a polished stone axe in its haft.

Refitting the Fragments

To follow the rest of the story the reader has to travel east, across the waters of the Gulf of Morbihan to the small island of Gavrinis. Here again there is a megalithic chambered tomb, of about the same date as La Table des Marchand. And here again the capstone of the chamber is a massive block, but in this case the carvings are on the upper surface. Hence, once this enormous stone was set in position only its lower surface would have been visible; the top was covered by the rubble mound heaped over it. It was only when archaeologists removed the mound in the early 1980s that they were able to inspect the upper surface of the stone, hidden from view since the Neolithic.

Three separate carvings could be made out. The first, toward one edge of the capstone, was a large shape known as an "axe-plow." According to some this represents a polished stone axe set in a wooden haft or handle with a back-loop; others see it as a primitive kind of plow. There was no ambiguity about the other shapes on the stone. One was a near-complete carving of a bull or cow with long, curving horns. The third shape was a pair of curving horns from a similar animal, not disembodied but broken away at the edge of the slab. Part of the axe-plow, too, was missing, cut short by the break at the capstone edge.

These broken engravings showed that the Gavrinis capstone had originally been part of a larger stone that had been broken up or trimmed to size. Then archaeologists realized that the curved horns fit exactly onto the carved body of a quadruped on the capstone of La Table des Marchand. Careful study of the breaks along the edges of the two slabs showed that they had once been part of the same stone. What, then, about the truncated axe-plow at the other edge of the Gavrinis capstone? No precise match has been found, though in

CARNAC MOUNDS

The Carnac area is famous not only for the sheer quantity of Neolithic monuments but also because some of the types found there are rare outside this region. Among these are the huge burial mounds known as "Carnac mounds," which typically measure over 300 feet (100 meters) in length and, where well-preserved, can be 30 feet (10 meters) high. Most of them are elongated in plan, but the ovoid example at Tumiac (160 feet [50 meters] across and 50 feet [15 meters] high) is no less impressive. They seem to have been designed to cover a closed burial chamber, and are therefore different from the passage graves, such as Gavrinis or La Table des Marchand, where the megalithic passage allowed regular and repeated access to the burial chamber at the heart of the mound. The burials in the Carnac mounds were much more richly furnished than those in passage graves. The enclosed chamber of Mané Er-Hroëk at Locmariaquer is the richest known of them, with no fewer than 106 axes of jadeite, fibrolite, and other special rocks, not to mention 49 variscite beads.

Where did this idea of large, long mounds come from? The likeliest source is the much smaller long mounds that are also found in the Carnac area. The best known is Le Manio, which now lies partly beneath the Kermario stone rows at Carnac. This is a small, trapezoidal structure, 115 feet (35 meters) long and 50 feet (16 meters) wide at its broader end. It was excavated in 1922 and found to contain numerous small stone chambers, without human bones. But the most prominent feature was a large standing stone, which was bedded into the rock below the mound and had five undulating lines carved on it. At its foot lay a closed burial chamber with a carving of a hafted axe on its capstone. This is just the kind of carving found on the early menhirs at Locmariaquer. It allows us to sketch an outline of developments: beginning in a first phase around 4500 B.C. with modest long mounds of the Le Manio type and decorated menhirs, including the Grand Menhir Brisé; followed by a second phase of enormous Carnac mounds, probably around 4000 B.C.; and finishing with a third phase of passage graves around 3500 B.C., which also involved the breaking up of the earlier menhirs and their reuse as capstones.

terms of dimensions it would make a good fit with the capstone of the burial chamber in the Er-Grah long mound.

Putting the three capstones together gives us one large stone, 45 feet (14 meters) long, decorated on one face with an axe-plow, two long-horned cattle, and an axe, not to mention parts of three curved shapes known as "crooks," which may in fact be axe hafts or animal horns. The carvings themselves are enormous: the axe-plow is 9 feet (2.8 meters) long, the cattle each about 6 feet (2 meters) from horns to hindlegs. The pounding of the surface of the monolith, which has left them standing in raised relief, must have taken many weeks to complete. Picked out in paint (which they probably were, though all traces have vanished), they would have made an impressive monument.

This decorated stone was not made to be broken up and hidden within the body of the local burial mounds. It was meant to be a large upright standing stone, probably sited at Locmariaquer near the Grand Menhir Brisé. It may indeed have stood for decades, or even centuries, but eventually was felled by human hand and broken up. Two fragments were reused as capstones in megalithic tombs at La Table des Marchand and (probably) Er-Grah; the third, itself weighing around 19 tons (17 metric tons), was carried by water across the estuary of the Auray River to Gavrinis, where it too became part of a newly built tomb.

The other menhirs in the Locmariaquer alignment may have suffered a similar fate. It is clear above all that the Grand Menhir Brisé did not fall through storm or earth tremor, nor did it break as it was being raised into position. Not at all. The 65-foot (20-meter) menhir was intentionally felled and broken up by the people who were building megalithic tombs nearby. The only difference is that they simply left the debris where it fell; they didn't redeploy the fragments as capstones. So it is that they lie today as the mutest of testimony to important and dramatic events: to the raising and decoration of

The tumulus Saint-Michel at Carnac. The central chamber within this mound contained 136 beads of jasper and variscite and 39 polished stone axes, including some made of jadeite that may have come from the Alps. Largest and most impressive of the so-called Carnac mounds, the top of this huge monument was later leveled to create a platform for a Christian chapel dedicated to Saint Michael.

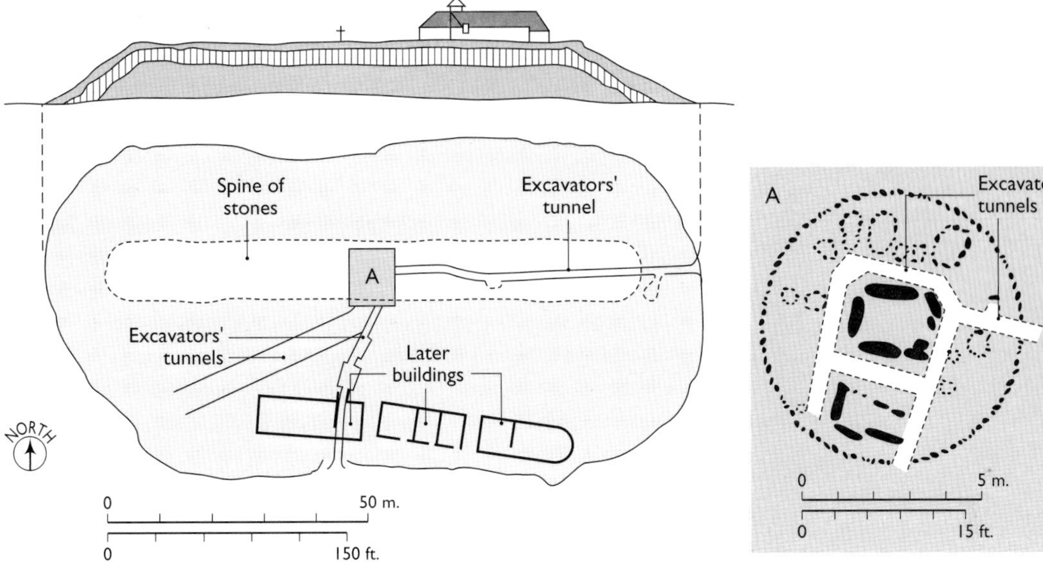

Plan and section of the tumulus Saint-Michel at Carnac, showing the initial spine of stones enclosed within the larger mound. In outline are the tunnels dug by the early excavators. The inset shows the megalithic burial structure at the heart of the monument, which contained axes, beads, and pendants of jadeite and other special stones. The chapel on the summit of the mound and the line of buildings along the southern fringe of the mound—including the apsidal structure—are of post-prehistoric date.

enormous standing stones, and to their destruction a few generations later when new beliefs or priorities carried the day.

Memorials of Power?

We have now encountered almost all of the main Carnac monument types: standing stones, passage graves, and long mounds. But the long mound of Er-Grah, despite its length, is not an impressive example of its type. To appreciate that, we need to retrace our steps northwest to Carnac itself. There, on the northeastern edge of the town, is the long mound to cap all long mounds: the tumulus Saint-Michel. This enormous mound is so big that an entire chapel was built on its summit but still left plenty of space free. The ground dimensions are 410 by 200 feet (125 by 60 meters) wide, and the tumulus Saint-Michel is around 30 feet (10 meters) high.

The tumulus was excavated in the 1860s and then again just after the turn of the century. These explorations took the form of tunnels, minelike galleries driven toward the heart of the tumulus, coupled with more conventional open-air excavations around its edges. Despite their unorthodox nature and the less rigorous standards of the time, the archaeologists were able to show something of the internal features buried deep within the body of the mound. They found that the Neolithic builders had begun with a lower and narrower mound of stones, laid out along the long axis. At the center of this was a small megalithic chamber, 8 feet (2.5 meters) by just under 7 feet (2 meters) across and less than 3 feet (1 meter) high, covered by a massive capstone. Despite its unpretentious dimensions, this chamber yielded an extraordinary array of Neolithic artifacts—136 beads of jasper and variscite (remains of a necklace),

Aerial view across the Le Menec alignments north of Carnac, showing the parallel but irregular lines of stones.

9 pendants, and 39 polished stone axes, 11 of them of jadeite (these can be seen today in the museum at Vannes). Two of the axes had been intentionally broken, as if ritually to "kill" them before they were placed in the grave. The jadeite must have come from the Alps, 500 miles (800 kilometers) distant. The individual buried in the tumulus Saint-Michel was evidently a figure of some importance. This is backed up by the group of fifteen smaller "tombs," all stone-built, that surround the main grave. When archaeologists opened these they found only cattle bones, perhaps ritual food offerings to support the deceased on the journey to the next life.

From the central chamber in the tumulus Saint-Michel at Carnac came these ninety-seven beads and nine pendants of variscite, an attractive greenish-blue stone. They probably formed parts of a necklace such as the one reconstructed here.

Unlike the passage graves, the central chamber in the tumulus Saint-Michel was not made to be accessible to the outside world, and sometime after the burial the mound was dramatically enlarged, covering in the initial stone structure and sealing the central chamber. A thick layer of clay was laid over it all, then a further covering of earth and stones, which form the present surface. At some point, perhaps during this enlargement, a small passage grave was inserted into the east end of the mound. Until recently, visitors could enter the tumulus by a tunnel cut into its south side, heading straight for the center where the early chamber and the smaller surrounding structures can be seen. Then the tunnel turns sharply to the right and leads along the long axis of the tumulus to the eastern end, where it passes by the later passage grave just before emerging again into the outside world. No visit to the tumulus Saint-Michel, however, is complete without the view from the summit, via the narrow, stepped path up to the chapel. It is hard to believe that what we are standing on here is not a natural hill but a prehistoric burial mound, erected by human hands around six thousand years ago.

The tumulus Saint-Michel is the classic example of the "Carnac mound," a monumental, not to say overgrown, long barrow. The fact that there are several of these in the Carnac area (hence the name), and that they are larger than the long mounds found in other regions of Brittany, suggests that this was a special focus of power in the Neolithic period. It may have been equivalent to the Avebury area in southern Britain and the Boyne valley in Ireland, all of them focal points—in ritual and perhaps secular terms—for the whole of their surrounding regions. We may imagine ruling families—powerful lineages of chiefs and their retainers—but we still don't know exactly how these societies were organized or who was in charge.

The "Army of Stones"

We have yet to come to the most famous and impressive of all the Carnac monuments: the stone rows. These multiple lines of standing stones stretching remorselessly in straight lines across the landscape have long caught the popular imagination. In the eighteenth century, one French savant speculated that they might be grave monuments to Celtic warriors who had fallen in single combat on this field of battle. Others attributed them to the Romans.

Artist's reconstruction of the Kerlescan alignments, fanning out and rising in height as they approach an open rectangle (with a "hedge" of stones on three sides and a long mound on the fourth). In the distance beyond the Kerlescan rectangle can be seen the approaching files of the Kermario alignments, with a long mound in their midst.

By the nineteenth century, the Druids had become firm favorites as builders of the stones. Others pointed to possible astronomical alignments, a theory that has been resurrected (still unconvincingly) in recent decades.

The Carnac alignments are now known to have been erected in the Neolithic period, though without further excavations their date can't be fixed exactly. In any case, what we see today is probably the result of centuries of addition and modification, beginning perhaps in the fourth millennium B.C., and ending perhaps around 2500 B.C. There are in fact half a dozen separate alignments, each on a different axis. The four best known are Kermario and Le Menec, each with over one thousand stones, and the smaller Petit Menec and Kerlescan with only a few hundred apiece. In each case what survives today is only a remnant. There are gaps in the rows, and many stones have fallen or been intentionally felled and broken up.

The most famous of the stone rows are those of Le Menec. Here 1,050 standing stones are arranged in ten rows stretching almost a mile. The rows are not strictly parallel, but converge steadily toward the east. Nor are the rows rigorously laid out in terms of the spacing of the stones—there are many minor deviations and irregularities. At the western end the alignment begins as eleven rows spaced roughly evenly over a breadth of 325 feet (100 meters); half way along the width has reduced to 280 feet (85 meters) and there are only ten rows. At the eastern end the ten lines (some claim eleven—it isn't easy to be sure) span little more than 200 feet (60 meters).

The irregularity of the arrangement makes it highly unlikely that these stone rows had any precise astronomical alignment. What, then, were they for? The question is hard to answer, but it may be useful to consider what the alignments run from and to. At the western end of the Le Menec alignments, there is a ring of standing stones, in plan a flattened-oval though incomplete on the north. At the other end there are scanty traces of a similar stone ring. The stones of the alignments become taller as they approach these terminals. This in itself suggests that the stone rows were perhaps built as complex processional ways leading to ritual enclosures. At the ends of the Le Menec rows, the ritual areas are marked merely by oval stone settings, but the shorter Kerlescan alignment has a more impressive arrangement. This alignment begins on the east with eight rows of small standing stones. As we move west the stones increase steadily in size and extra rows are added. By the time we reach the western end of the alignment there are thirteen rows of large stones, up to 10 feet (3 meters) high. The alignment ends at a roughly rectangular enclosure, 260 by 300 feet (80 by 90 meters) across, marked out by standing stones placed close together save on the north, where the ritual area runs up against the side of the Kerlescan long mound. Here mortuary monuments and ceremonial avenues come together at last, complementary parts of a single ritual landscape.

The Broader Setting

Stone rows aren't unique to Carnac, but nowhere else in Brittany are they so extensive or so numerous. They show once again how Carnac is special. But this special character isn't confined to Carnac itself. It stretches beyond the whole of the southern Morbihan. We have already considered the monuments of Locmariaquer, southeast of Carnac town. But in addition to Er-Grah and

La Table des Marchand, the Locmariaquer peninsula has three more enormous "Carnac" long mounds and several more passage graves. Further east still there are the monuments of the Arzon peninsula and the islands in the Gulf of Morbihan, including the richly decorated tomb of Gavrinis and the partly submerged stone settings of Er Lannic. It all adds up to an impressive array of monuments, many of them megalithic, spanning over two thousand years of time.

The Carnac area today is a popular tourist destination, as much for its beaches and bays as for its prehistory. Pressure of visitors has forced the authorities to close off parts of the Le Menec alignments, just as the center of Stonehenge is now closed. Yet many of the smaller sites are still little visited, and there are few pleasanter ways to spend a few days—good weather permitting—than to search out the sites by car or bicycle, or take ship across the waters of the Gulf of Morbihan, imagining, if we can, how it must have looked when the first farmers raised their menhirs here.

Further Reading

The English-speaking visitor to Brittany is fortunate in having available an excellent guide to the megalithic monuments of the region: *Megalithic Brittany* by Aubrey Burl (London: Thames and Hudson, 1985). For a more discursive account, see Mark Patton, *Statements in Stone: Monuments and Society in Neolithic Brittany* (London: Routledge, 1993). Most of the other literature is in French. A good place to start is *Carnac. Les premières architectures de pierre* by Gérard Bailloud, Christine Boujot, Serge Cassen, and Charles-Tanguy Le Roux (Paris: CNRS, 1995). Also of interest are Le Roux's brief guide to *Gavrinis* (Paris: Imprimerie nationale, 1985) and Anne-Elisabeth Riskine's *Carnac. L'armée des pierres* (Paris: Imprimerie nationale, 1992).

Further Viewing

The principal museums covering the prehistoric monuments of the Carnac area are the Musée de Préhistoire Miln-Le Rouzic in Carnac itself and the Musée de Préhistoire at Vannes. There are also visitor centers at Locmariaquer and (less satisfactory) the so-called Archéoscope near the Le Ménec alignments, a short distance north of Carnac.

CHAPTER

FIVE

Tarxien

C. 3500–2500 B.C.

Megalithic temples on the Maltese Islands

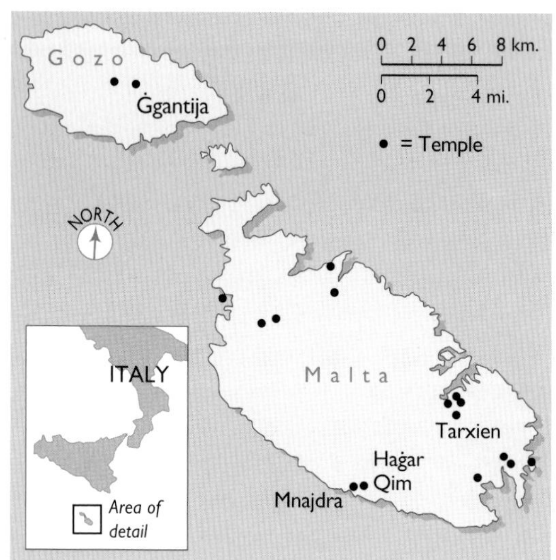

In the suburban outskirts of Valletta, the capital of Malta, lie two of the most impressive prehistoric monuments in Europe; not so famous, perhaps, as Stonehenge or Newgrange, but just as remarkable. They are Tarxien (Tar·sheen), a set of three (perhaps four) megalithic temples, and Hal Saflieni, a rock-cut hypogeum, or underground burial place. These two sites form part of a prehistoric temple-building phenomenon spread throughout the Maltese Islands. Archaeologists have long speculated why they were built, and what was so special about Malta in prehistory. The Maltese temples are all the more remarkable in being without parallel in Europe and the Mediterranean, at least for the period when they were constructed. Radiocarbon dates show that they are around five thousand years old, older by several centuries than the pyramids of Egypt. They are some of the first monumental temples to have been built anywhere in the world.

Malta is one of the smallest Mediterranean islands, part of a group along with neighboring Gozo and tiny Comino. Their combined land area is only 120 square miles (314 square kilometers). Nor are they particularly fertile islands. Today they are largely bare of tree cover, and soil erosion has exposed expanses of the underlying rock in many places. In fact, some 60 percent of the islands' surfaces are classified as arable land, though many of the soils are thin and rainfall is low and unpredictable. The prehistoric landscape was probably not very different —there is no evidence of large timbers being available—and if there was perhaps more soil cover than today, it can't have added more than 10 percent to the total.

Yet the Maltese Islands were certainly workable by early farmers, who settled and grew crops there from around 5000 B.C. These early farmers were the first people to colonize Malta. They had come from Sicily, the nearest landfall, lying some 50 miles (80 kilometers) north of Gozo. The pottery made by the earliest settlers is similar in shape and decoration to the so-called Stentinello pottery in use in Sicily at that time. They kept up their contacts with Sicily and southern Italy in the centuries that followed. Archaeologists know this from discoveries of imported materials at Maltese prehistoric sites. The imports include obsidian (a volcanic glass used for cutting tools) from the Lipari islands, red ochre (a coloring substance) from Sicily, and greenstone (for polished stone axes) from the Calabria region of southern Italy. But the imported materials are not numerous, and they fluctuate in quantity from period to period: most common around 4000 B.C., less so after 3500 B.C., and relatively rare in the greatest period of temple construction, between 3000 and 2500 B.C. Indeed, it looks as though the Maltese Islands became increasingly isolated as the centuries passed, and it seems that this isolation stimulated the development of the Maltese temple-building tradition. But we are still unsure whether this isolation was physical—simply an absence of overseas contact—or cultural, a conscious attempt to remain separate and apart.

One problem would have been boats. Since Malta was short of trees and timber, the prehistoric occupants would have had to rely on skin boats, with animal hides stretched over a wooden frame. It is possible to construct quite a seaworthy vessel in this technique, but the method places a limit on size, and the Mediterranean can prove perilous at times. The voyage to Sicily appears straightforward to a person standing on the heights of Gozo and looking across the straits. From this vantage point, Sicily is clearly visible on the horizon (at least in good weather), but it disappears from view at sea-level, and blind navigation is needed for the first part of the journey. It can't have been an easy undertaking for prehistoric navigators. It is also difficult to see what produce the Maltese might have offered that the Sicilians could not have found more easily nearer to home.

Isolation, then, is a key feature of Maltese prehistory. The islands have excellent natural harbors, not least the Grand Harbor of historic Valletta, but these would have been of limited use to the temple-builders if there was not much contact with the outside world during that period. The early communities of Malta seem to have become inward-looking, trapped within the limited horizons and resources of their island home. Left largely to themselves, they developed along idiosyncratic lines, choosing to invest their energies in megalithic temples and rock-cut burial places. They weren't alone in this. Other island societies have produced remarkable monuments as if in response to their very isolation. The most famous of all is probably Rapa Nui (Easter Island) in the depths of the Pacific, where competing clans raised huge monolithic statues to assert their importance and win favor with the ancestors. Island societies seem often to have created strange monuments out of all proportion to their land area and population. Prehistoric Malta was no exception.

One further reflection is necessary to complete the scene-setting before moving on to Tarxien itself. That is the role of geology. We have already referred to soils and rainfall, but it is the underlying rock that provided the material from which the temples were made. This is limestone, a common building material. Maltese limestone, however, is of two very different kinds. On the surface, and deep down, is the hard coralline limestone, difficult to work though very durable. In between is a much more easily worked material, the golden-colored globigerina limestone, which the temple-builders preferred for their finer work. Globigerina also supports the best arable soils. Over much of eastern Malta and central Gozo, erosion has removed the upper layer of coralline limestone and exposed the globigerina below, and it is here, very logically, that most of the temples are found: near the best soils.

Discovering Tarxien

The prehistoric Tarxien temples stand on the limestone plateau about 1 mile (2 kilometers) to the south of the Grand Harbor at Valletta. Two reasons lead archaeologists to believe that the harbor was important even in prehistoric times. The first is that the Tarxien temples are not the only ones in this area. Overlooking the harbor itself are the three Kordin temples, similar to those at Tarxien but less elaborate and less well preserved. Then even nearer to Tarxien there is the hypogeum at Ħal Saflieni. Thus, there is a remarkable concentration of monuments, all belonging to the temple period 3500–2500 B.C.

The second indication that the Valletta area was especially important is the elaborate nature of the Tarxien temples themselves. There are eighteen classic temple sites on the Maltese Islands, but only at Tarxien do we find as many as four temples together, and only there is there a temple with six apses. Furthermore, no other Maltese temples can rival Tarxien in the richness of decoration. Even if overseas contact was relatively rare, the deep sheltered inlet of the Grand Harbor obviously conferred a special status on the communities who controlled it.

Today, the Tarxien temples have been swallowed up within the suburban growth of Valletta. When they were first found, however, this area was open fields. It was a local farmer who brought them to light, complaining to Dr. Themistocles Zammit about the stones he kept hitting whenever he tried to dig deeper than usual. Zammit was a remarkable man with no fewer than three successful careers—archaeology, medicine, and education. When the Tarxien farmer came to him in 1913, he was director of the National Museum in Valletta and was just completing excavations at the Hal Saflieni hypogeum. Zammit visited the field in question and saw the blocks of stone and prehistoric pottery that were being turned up. Convinced of their importance, he began serious excavations at Tarxien in 1915, which he continued every summer until 1919. What he revealed went far beyond his expectations. The Tarxien temples were not as well preserved as some of the others—those of Ġgantija (Je·gant·ia) on Gozo, for example, or Mnajdra and Haġar Qim on Malta itself. But in their ground plan and decoration they surpassed even these.

They had one other claim to fame. Here, for the first time, was an opportunity for archaeologists to excavate a Maltese temple complex that had lain undisturbed and unknown since its abandonment some forty-five centuries ago. Zammit kept meticulous records of his work, and the findings he made at Tarxien make them the best documented of all the Maltese temples. Perhaps we should emphasize here why we think they were temples—there is no domestic debris, for example, to suggest that anybody lived in these impressive complexes; nor are there any burials—they certainly weren't built as tombs. But the precise nature of the rituals and beliefs, as at so many prehistoric sites, still eludes us. We shall consider the various clues as we come upon them.

Tarxien Today

The general plan of Tarxien is of three temples (southern, central, and eastern) crowded cheek-by-jowl in the western sector of the site, with a court and a possible further temple in the less well-preserved eastern sector. The most striking feature of the plan is the "lobed" arrangement. These lobes or apses are usually paired on either side of a passage, sometimes with an additional lobe at the apex. All the Maltese temples have this kind of plan, though they differ in detail and complexity. The simplest have a trefoil plan; others have four or five apses. The central temple at Tarxien, exceptionally, has six.

A further point to bear in mind is that not all the Tarxien temples are contemporary. This is perhaps most obvious in the case of the central temple, squeezed awkwardly into the space between the southern and eastern temples. It may have been added to create a specially sacred "holy of holies," in a secluded position reached only through the western temple. The offset plan means that the casual passerby would not have been able to see into the central temple when looking from outside into the southern temple.

The southern and eastern temples at Tarxien share the same alignment and are probably contemporary. They were constructed earlier than the central temple. Pottery found beneath the floors suggests, however, that they belong to the so-called Tarxien phase of Maltese prehistory (3000–2500 B.C.). They were not the first buildings on the site. That distinction must go to the poorly preserved "early temple" at the eastern edge of the site, which is thought to date from the preceding Ġgantija phase (3600–3000 B.C.).

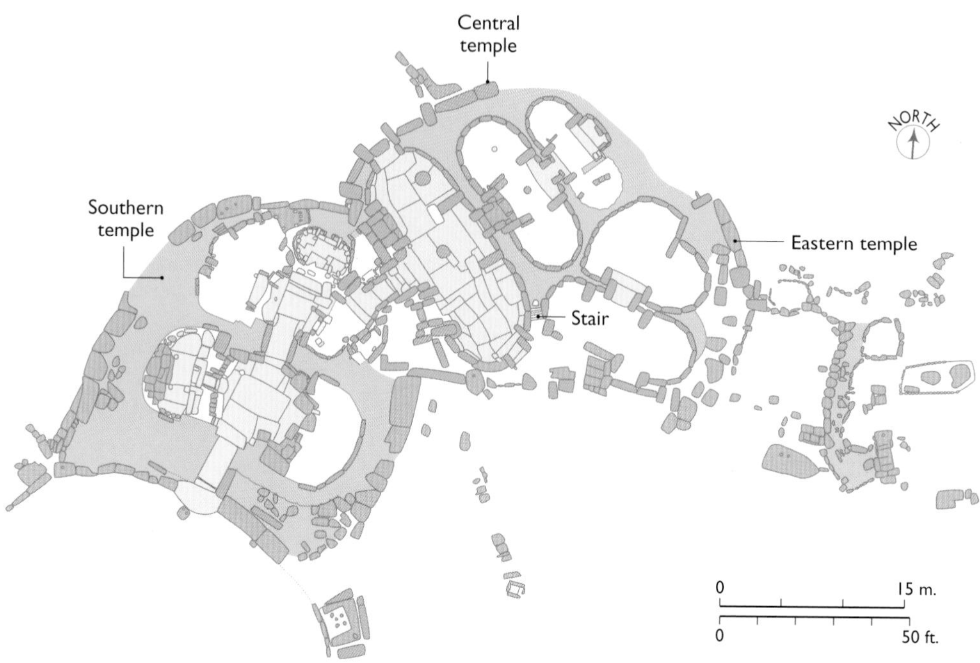

(*above*) Plan of the Tarxien temples.
(*facing page, top*) Double seated figurine from recent excavations at the Brochtorff Circle on the Maltese island of Gozo. This depicts a pair of obese, probably female figures seated on a wickerwork couch. Carved in the local globigerina limestone, traces of the original polychrome coloring (notably a striking red) have survived. Conventional thinking interprets figures such as these as mother-goddesses, though other identifications are possible. Width of figurine: approx. 5 inches (14 centimeters).

A note on materials: Tarxien, along with the other Maltese temples, is "megalithic," incorporating large stone blocks up to 24 tons (20 metric tons) in weight. These are usually of the harder coralline limestone, which is difficult to work to a smooth or decorated surface but is hard-wearing and can be quarried and split to give reasonably regular blocks. Slabs of coralline limestone were used for the outer walls of the temples. We know these slabs were maneuvered into position on stone balls, since groups of balls were found during Zammit's excavations, buried beneath the temple floor. Some have been left on display in front of the southern temple and one can still be seen in situ beneath the floor slab of the central temple's eastern outer apse. Inner walls are sometimes of dry-stone construction (originally covered in painted plaster), but in the later temples such as Tarxien, carefully worked slabs of the softer globigerina limestone are also used, sometimes with designs carved in relief. Between the inner and outer walls, the temple-builders piled earth and rubble for greater solidity. Floors were of stone slabs, a limestone cement known as torba, or occasionally simply cut into the bedrock. Today the temples are open to the sky, but that can't have been the case originally. One striking clue to their appearance is provided by small temple models (several from Tarxien itself), which show flat-topped structures. This kind of roof simply isn't tall enough to have been vaulted in stone, and despite the shortage of trees on Malta there must have been a ceiling of wooden beams. Whether the whole of the floor area was roofed is another question; roofing may have covered the apses only, leaving the central courts as passageways open to the dry Maltese climate.

The Southern Temple

The Tarxien temples have been a regular tourist attraction ever since they were discovered, and it is therefore not surprising to find they have been tidied up and restored for presentation to the public. The most obvious sign of this is the concrete capping that has been applied to some of the stones. Luckily this is easily made out and there is little risk of confusing original work with modern additions. The most obvious restoration of all is the entrance to the southern temple. To understand what the entrance facade originally looked like we need to turn to one of the better-preserved temples such as Hağar Qim: a concave line of massive coralline limestone slabs set edge to edge, with a low bench at their foot. In the center of the facade stands the temple entrance, a trilithon structure with two supports and a capstone, each of them monolithic. At Hağar Qim, two courses of limestone blocks laid lengthwise complete the temple frontage.

Access to Tarxien is by a wooden walkway, raised above the original floor. It leads through the southern temple into the outer bay of the central temple and then passes in front of the entrance to the eastern temple. Visitors who cross the threshold of the southern Tarxien temple find themselves in the outer bay of a four-lobed structure. Turning first to the right, an irregular line of low limestone blocks divides the central space from the eastern apse. These

(*below*) Facade of the temple at Hağar Qim, on raised ground overlooking the southern coast of Malta. Although partly reconstructed, this facade gives a good impression of the original appearance of the Maltese temples.

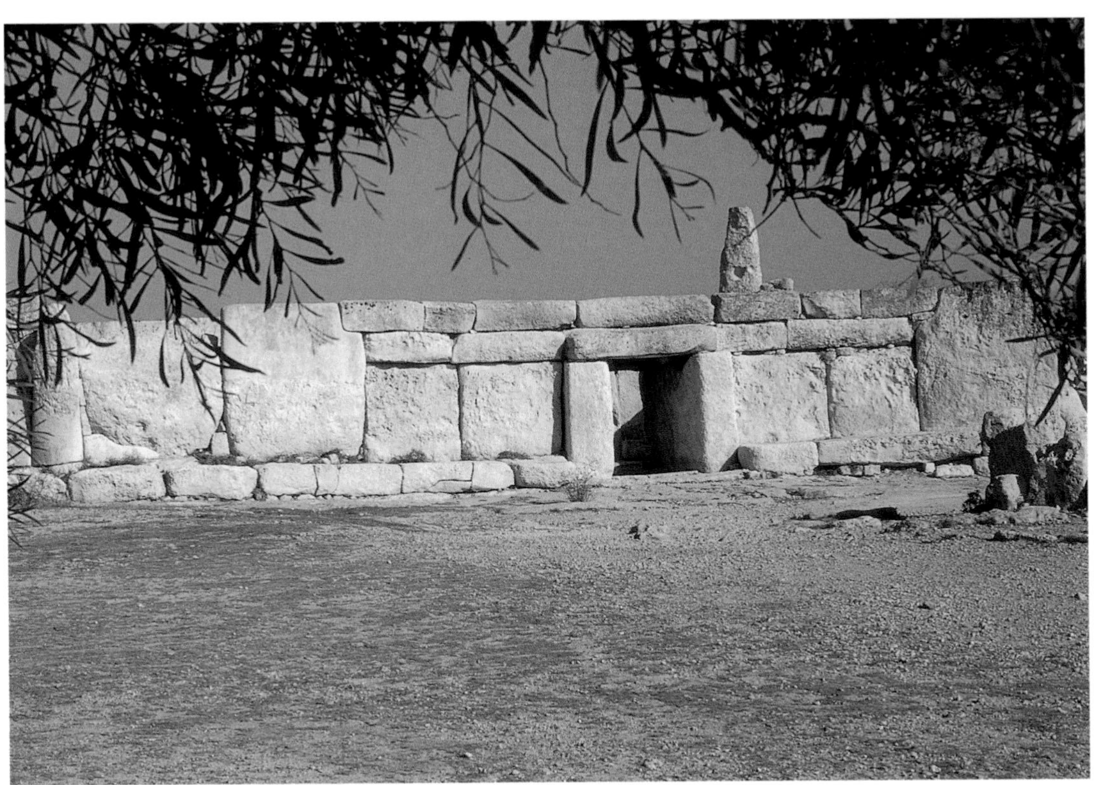

are easily stepped over, and there is no trace that they once supported a screen, as elsewhere in these temples. The blocks are decorated with abstract designs of scrolls and running spirals in raised relief. Like most of the decorated blocks at Tarxien, these are stone copies. The originals were moved for safekeeping to the National Museum of Archaeology in Valletta, where they are on display. The most remarkable feature of this apse is not the decorated blocks, however, but the lower part of a massive seated statue. All that survives today is a fringed skirt and a pair of enormous swollen legs supported by relatively dainty feet. This, too, is a copy of the original, which can be seen in the National Museum. The original is in fact much less complete than the copy suggests and lacks a good part of its left side (marked by a rough diagonal break). The back of the statue is also rough and incomplete. The plinth on which it stands is a separate decorated slab, carefully shaped to receive the base of the colossal figure. Most people identify it as female and think in terms of a mother goddess or earth goddess, though there is no certain indication of sex. They see this colossal statue as the image of the divinity worshipped in the temple, but this, again, is speculation. It was certainly a dramatic image, tucked away just inside the entrance to the temple. Fragments of several similar smaller statues were found at Tarxien, but for a better idea of what it must have looked like when complete we should turn to the recently discovered sculpture from the Brochtorff Circle on Gozo, showing twin figures seated side by side. The Brochtorff example bore traces of polychrome paint, and we must imagine the colossal Tarxien statue in its original state, standing 7 feet (2 meters) high and painted in bright polychrome colors. It would have been an eye-catching image.

Turning our back on the eastern apse, the western apse presents a similar appearance, with a line of carefully cut decorated blocks at ground level. Here, however, there is a break in the middle of the line and a passage flanked by upright slabs giving access to the apse itself. At the back was a kind of altar, but only a part of the base survives, decorated with a procession of animals—a ram, a pig, and four goats of the moufflon variety. Just in front of this a pair of connecting holes are cut in the stone slab floor, through which a rope could be tied. There are quite a number of these at Tarxien (including one outside the main entrance to the southern temple). The best guess is that they were for tethering animals that had been brought to the temples for sacrifice.

Another altar stands just to the right of the passage leading into the inner bay of the southern temple. This is a different type of altar: the so-called spiral altar, a large block decorated with running spirals in raised relief. The particular curiosity of this piece is what lay within it and what stood above and behind it. Within was a deep cavity, its opening in the face of the altar block plugged by a tightly fitting stone carved with a continuation of the relief frieze, so that it was "camouflaged," though not very effectively. The cavity contained charred animal bones (mainly goat) and potsherds, probably the remains of sacrifices that may have been offered on the altar above. Here an arrangement of slabs formed a kind of false portal. A corresponding altar, though less elaborate, stood on the other side of the passage.

How did these apses work? Archaeologists have recently pointed out that the carvings in the left-hand apse are of male animals while the right-hand apse has the colossal statue, often interpreted as female. Does this indicate a sexual division of the temple into left/right–male/female? And how could worshippers outside the temple participate in sacrifices carried out in the apses, which they could not see? The implication must be that only a privileged elite were allowed to take part directly in the rituals; most people simply had to wait at a distance, watching where they could.

The passage leads from the outer bay to the inner bay. To the right and left once again are semicircular apses, but the most striking element is the terminal niche, flanked by curved stone benches, and the enormous threshold slab just in front of it, carved with running spirals. The purpose of the threshold slab was to separate this space both physically and symbolically from the rest of the temple. We don't know what went on in the niche, but its ritual importance can be judged from the fact that fragments of two temple models and two carved stone phalli were found inside it.

Colossal figurine from the southern temple at Tarxien. Note the fringed skirt and enormous swollen legs supported by relatively dainty feet. Usually identified as female (though there is no sure indication of sex), this statue has been regarded by some as a priestess and by others as a representation of the deity who was worshipped in this temple. Neither identification is secure.

The Central Temple

One of the most curious features of Tarxien is the way that you enter the central temple through the apse of the southern temple. In fact, the apse of the southern temple was partially dismantled in order to create this passage when the central temple was built. This arrangement makes the central temple even more secluded than the southern temple, and the seclusion increases as we look toward the terminal niche. Again, there are various traces to show how the temple must have worked.

The most striking feature of the outer bay is the circular stone basin in the middle, set into a huge megalithic floorstone. When Zammit first found this it contained burned limestone, and it was probably a fireplace. We may imagine the smoke rising and filling the enclosed space, making the rooms beyond seem even more mysterious, especially if there were no windows. Perhaps aromatic herbs were burned here to complete the sensation of otherworldliness. The message was made the more striking by the dramatically decorated sillstone which stood in the narrow passageway between outer and central bays. Carved with two enormous spirals, this would have looked still more impressive when it had its original paint. The present threshold block is a modern stone copy of the original, which resides in the National Museum in Valletta. The visitor will be reassured to note that the original in the museum is in a much better condition than the copy on site, which has been heavily eroded since it was placed in position only a few decades ago. The soft globigerina limestone used for most of the decorated blocks erodes much more quickly than the harder coralline limestone used for the temple walls. Many people have fancifully imagined the spirals as a pair of eyes, staring at the worshipper who has had the temerity to penetrate so far into the temple, warning them against going any farther.

The outer bay has one further feature to attract our attention: small chambers are worked in the thickness of the back walls, entered through trilithon openings. What were these little rooms for? The one in the right-hand apse has carved slabs showing bulls and a sow suckling her piglets. Again, the conjunction of male and female animals may have been of significance, though we can only speculate whether the temples were used for fertility rituals. Still odder is another slab with a small square opening cut through it at ground level. Was this to carry sacrificial blood? This is a common if speculative explanation. The small space beyond, in the thickness of the temple wall, was roofed by a corbelled vault and contained a heap of animal bones, once again perhaps the remains of sacrifices.

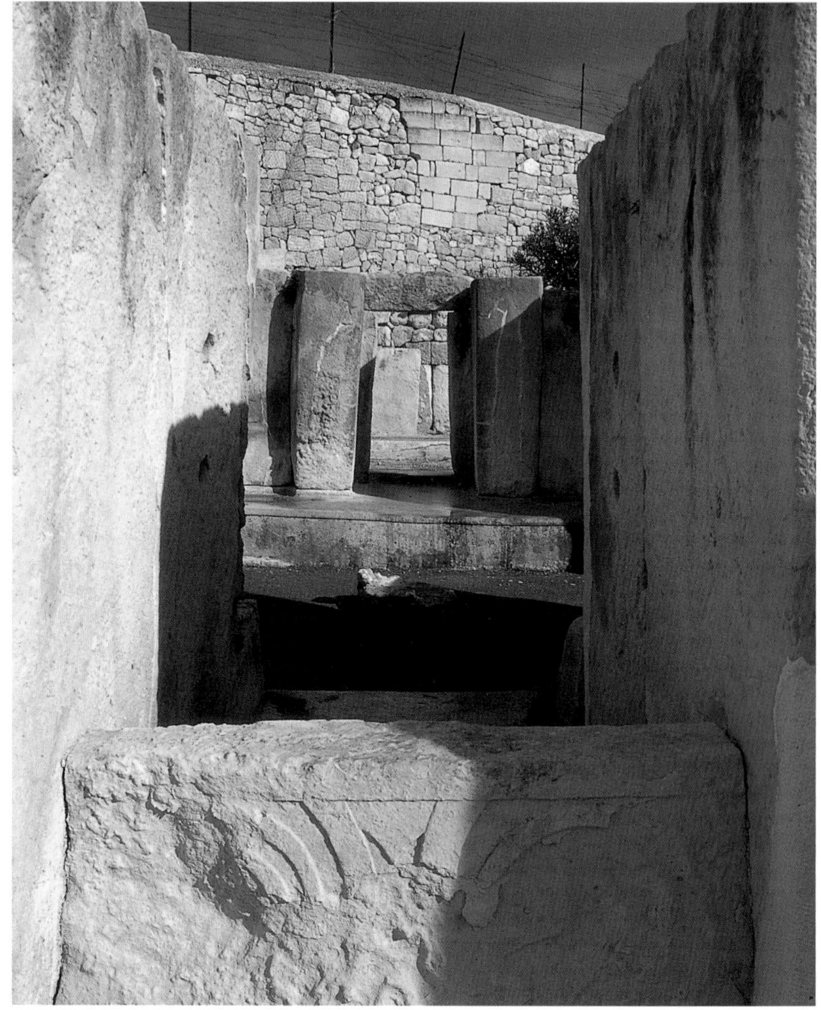

The double-spiral sillstone in the central temple at Tarxien, decorated with a bold double-spiral motif. The carving is now heavily eroded, but fortunately this is only a copy, since the original was removed to safety in the National Museum in Valletta. The sillstone marks the division between the outer part of the temple and the two inner bays, and its height and visual impact may be intended to indicate that only privileged individuals were allowed beyond this point.

To get to the inner reaches of the temple we would have to cross the double-spiraled sillstone. The visitor today is prevented from doing so by the modern railing, but beyond can be seen a corridor with apses to either side, both of them separated from the central space by an elaborately decorated screen slab. The expertly carved blocks are displayed in the hallway of the National Museum of Valletta. Once more we have the impression that each apse had its own individual function in the overall scheme. If we were to turn to the left into the left-hand apse, then left again, we would find a small, double-shelved niche tucked into the corner. It held animal bones and horn cores, as did other niches in the Tarxien temples. The special interest of this particular niche is what Zammit found in front of it, on the floor of the apse: fragments of three baked clay figurines. They depict individuals, probably male, with elaborate hairstyles and wearing pleated skirts. Many people have suggested they are portraits of the priests who controlled the Tarxien temples.

Baked clay "priest" statuette found by Zammit in his excavations in the central temple at Tarxien. It was one of three small statuettes on the floor of the left-hand inner apse, in front of a wall niche containing animal bones and horn cores. The suggestion that this may be a priest raises the question of what the temple figures (including the colossal statue and the small Brochtorff figurine, pp. 77 and 74) actually represent: are they ordinary humans, mythological beings, or divinities?

Another threshold slab leads into the innermost bay of the central temple, though this, too, is currently inaccessible to visitors. It is in any case badly damaged by Roman buildings whose footings are still visible in the right-hand apse. It was, however, the most secluded part of the Tarxien temples and may have been the "holy of holies," the place of greatest sanctity.

The Other Temples

In comparison to the southern and central temples, the other temples at Tarxien are much less well preserved. The eastern temple reverts to the four-lobed plan, with a terminal niche like the southern temple. Especially notable is the fine tooling and fitting of the megalithic slabs that form the left-hand outer apse. Another interesting feature is the "oracle hole" cut through at the join between two of the slabs of the inner right-hand apse. This small square opening communicates with a small room within the thickness of the wall, which can only be reached from outside (from where the visitor can see it today). Zammit thought that the oracle hole itself may originally have been camouflaged with a cover of wood or leather, and that a priest concealed within the small room gave messages and pronouncements to a worshipper in the apse. There is even a narrow sinuous channel by which an amulet or other sacred object could be slipped, to appear mysteriously at the worshipper's feet. This is of course pure speculation, but it draws our attention once again to the workings of these temples.

The eastern temple is the third and last of the principal structures at Tarxien, but before leaving the site there are two further structures to the east that deserve brief mention. The first is a rectangular court, lined by stone blocks. It may originally have been a covered room. Beyond lie the remains of another temple, of which only one side survives. It probably had five apses. It is the oldest structure at Tarxien, dating back to the Ġgantija period (3600–3000 B.C.). Beyond this again, outside the excavated area, there were traces of further build-

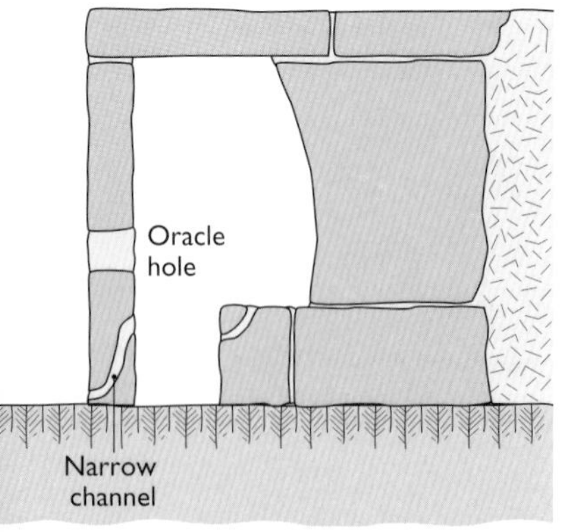

Cross-section through the "oracle room" in the eastern temple at Tarxien. Zammit thought that this "secret" chamber hidden within the thickness of the temple wall and accessible only from outside might have been devised for some "magical" practice. A priest concealed within the chamber may have spoken through the oracle hole and slipped objects down the sinuous channel to appear mysteriously at the worshipper's feet.

ings. Establishing the whole extent of the Tarxien religious complex is a task still awaiting future archaeologists.

Rituals, Beliefs, and the Dead

The purpose of this account of the Tarxien temples has been not only to describe what they are, but to seek an explanation of why they were built. We cannot now hope to know exactly what beliefs were held by the Maltese people at this distant period, since there are no written records, but that does not mean there are no questions we can ask.

A first question is who was allowed inside the temples. As we have seen, monolithic threshold slabs divide the temples into bays and suggest that if ordinary worshippers were allowed inside at all, they were only permitted to enter the outer apses. Most may have been restricted to standing in front of the temple. The impressive concave facade for example, which is preserved at Haġar Qim, may have been designed to face a crowd of worshippers in the open air, waiting while the rituals were performed in relative seclusion within the temples. Some ceremonies may have involved rituals on the temple roofs, where they could have been seen by people outside; a narrow stone stair leading upward is squeezed in between the central and eastern temples at Tarxien.

Another clue to the rituals is provided by the special contrivances built into the structure. These include the altars—for animal sacrifice?—the cupboards and niches in which the animal bones and horn cores were stacked, and the "oracle" hole in the eastern temple. It is difficult to say precisely how they functioned, but they give an impression of dramatic ritual ceremonies in a setting carefully designed with an eye to effect. The effect would have been all the greater when the temples had their original paintwork, when they were roofed and dark, when fires or aromatic herbs (perhaps even hallucinogens) were burned in hearths or braziers, and when the drama of the ceremonies was intensified by music or chanting.

Exactly what the rituals were designed to achieve we can hardly guess. The truncated colossal statue from the western temple may be a female fertility deity. Smaller versions are known from Tarxien, and as we have noted, a small statuette of twin-seated female deities was recently found in excavations at the Brochtorff Circle near the town of Xaghra on Gozo. The carvings of male and female animals might also suggest a fertility theme, especially the sow with her suckling piglets. But there are few unambiguous representations of female deities, and it may be that power and prestige were the real driving forces behind the Maltese temples. The restricted access suggests that exclusivity was important; only the privileged few were allowed into the temples. The human bones from the Brochtorff Circle show relatively few of the medical disorders normally associated with agriculturalists. Could this mean that what we have here are the remains not of ordinary people but only of this privileged elite? Only further analysis can confirm this hypothesis. But the Brochtorff Circle introduces another theme, for this was not a temple but a subterranean burial complex. Were the rituals carried out in the Tarxien temples connected with death and the ancestors? Support for this idea comes from the remarkable Hal Saflieni nearby.

The Hypogeum

Hal Saflieni is a hypogeum, an underground complex of burial chambers. It was cut from the soft globigerina limestone, beginning probably during the Zebbuġ phase (4100–3600 B.C.; the sequence runs Zebbuġ-Ġgantija-Tarxien), and continuing into the Tarxien phase. The hypogeum was discovered by accident in 1902 when workmen were cutting a cistern in the rock. They tried to conceal their discovery, but it came to the attention of the authorities who entrusted investigation of the monument to a Jesuit priest, Fr. Magri. When he left for the Far East in 1905, responsibility for the excavation passed into the more competent hands of Themistocles Zammit, whom we have already encountered at Tarxien. Unfortunately, however, much of the monument was cleared in a rather casual manner. Zammit records that under Magri's direction the human bones were piled into a heap and discarded, and only the best of the finds were kept.

The hypogeum is arranged on three main levels. It shows remarkable parallels to the Tarxien temples in the spiral decoration (here painted rather than carved) on walls and ceilings, and in the trilithon structures either carved into the rock or made of separate stones. The original entrance had been badly

Rock-cut facade in the hypogeum at Hal Saflieni, less than half a mile northwest of Tarxien. The pillars and beams must mimic features of above-ground architecture in timber or stone (probably the latter, as trees are very scarce on Malta). Traces of painted decoration survive in some parts of this underground burial complex.

VISITING THE MALTESE TEMPLES

In addition to the temples of Tarxien, near Valletta, a number of other Maltese temples are well worth a visit. Tarxien is distinguished by the richness of its decoration. It is also one of only two temple sites to have been excavated this century; the others were simply "cleared," beginning with Ġgantija in the 1820s. But Tarxien is far from the best preserved of the temples in terms of its overall structure; that accolade must go to Haġar Qim, with its impressive (though partly rebuilt) entrance facade, closely followed by Mnajdra and Ġgantija. Nine other temples or groups of temples are known, less well-preserved but many of them still showing features of interest. This probably represents only part of the original total; there are at least five other "temples" of irregular plan, not to mention scatters of megalithic slabs that may represent the final ruin of further examples.

The Hal Saflieni hypogem has been closed to visitors for conservation and refurbishment. It is scheduled to reopen in late 1998, though access will be limited to small groups of people at any one time.

Aerial view of Haġar Qim, the most complete of the Maltese temples.

damaged by house-building, but a few large stone blocks remained that suggested it had had a megalithic entrance. Just inside the entrance was a trilithon, and then a series of roughly hewn chambers that were the earliest part of the complex. The middle and lower levels of the hypogeum were reached by descending a vertical fall in the rock floor and by a flight of rock-cut steps respectively. The most elaborate were the inner chambers of the middle level, farthest from the original entrance. Rooms 18 and 20 had ceilings covered with running spirals in red paint. Rooms 24 and 26 had wonderfully carved trilithon facades cut into the rock. These may have been shrines (though rather inaccessible ones), but it is clear that one of the main purposes of Hal Saflieni was for burial. Zammit estimated that it had originally contained the bones of seven thousand individuals. These were not in articulation, but had been moved around after the bodies themselves had decayed.

The findings at Hal Saflieni have been confirmed by the recent excavations at the Brochtorff Circle, a similar site on Gozo. Burials, probably numbered in the thousands, have been recovered from a complex of modified natural caves. The Brochtorff Circle is only a little distance from the Ġgantija temples, the main temple complex on Gozo; Hal Saflieni is less than half a mile from Tarxien. In each case, we have a major temple complex and a major burial place in a paired arrangement. There may well be other hypogea still to be discovered close to other major temples on Malta. Temples and tombs shared common features of architecture and belonged to a common system of ritual and belief.

British archaeologist Colin Renfrew has taken the geographical location of the Maltese temples and shown that they can be divided into clusters. There are five of these clusters on Malta, and one on Gozo. Renfrew suggests that these are centers of prehistoric territories, each controlled by a chieftain who may also have been a priest. It was competition between these territories that led to the construction of ever more elaborate temples, as each elite struggled to outdo the others, and of huge mortuary hypogea, in which remains of the ancestors were housed.

The end of the process might easily have been foreseen. It is exactly what happened on Easter Island only five hundred years ago. The Easter Islanders exhausted their resources in a frenzied round of competitive building and fell into violent discord and decline. Archaeologists speculate that the Maltese temple-builders may have suffered a similar fate. A key interest in studying the skeletal remains is to see whether there is anything to suggest a decline in the population's health as the temple period neared its end.

Further Reading

Despite recent work, the standard account of the Maltese temples remains *The Prehistoric Antiquities of the Maltese Islands* by J. D. Evans (London: Athlone Press, 1971). This is an exhaustive and lavishly illustrated catalogue of sites and finds, prefaced by a discussion of Maltese prehistory. A short guide book to the main sites is also available: David Trump's *Malta: An Archaeological Guide* (London: Faber and Faber, 1972). For early excavation at Tarxien, see *Prehistoric Malta* by Themistocles Zammit (London: Oxford University Press, 1930). The significance of the temples is the subject of chapter 8 in Colin Renfrew's *Before Civilization* (New York: Cambridge University Press, 1979). For the most recent fieldwork at the Brochtorff Circle, see Simon Stoddart et al., "Cult in an Island Society: Prehistoric Malta in the Tarxien Period" (*Cambridge Archaeological Journal* 3, 1993, pp. 3–19).

Further Viewing

Sculptures and other finds from Tarxien are displayed in the National Museum of Archaeology, Auberge de Provence, Valletta.

CHAPTER

SIX

Avebury

c. 3600–2200 B.C.

Neolithic rituals

in southern Britain

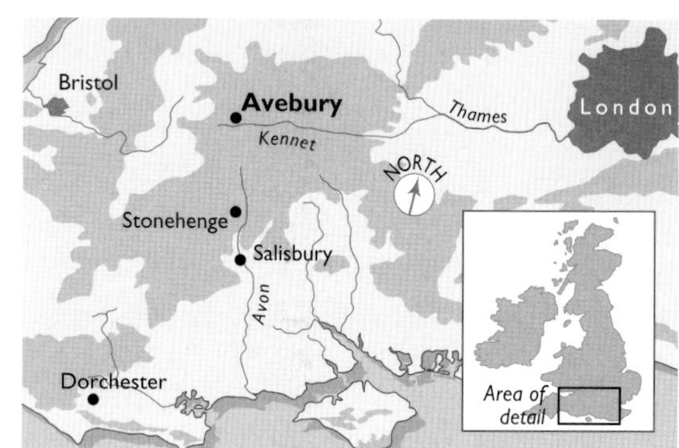

Neolithic Britain survives today most conspicuously through its ritual monuments. There are long burial mounds, causewayed camps, henge monuments, and stone circles, all evidence of the effort made by prehistoric people to modify the landscape and to imbue it with new meaning and ritual significance. Nowhere can we gain a better impression of this preoccupation than at Avebury, in the heart of historical Wessex. The Wessex region takes its name from the West Saxons, the dynasty of rulers who seized control of central southern Britain in the Anglo-Saxon period (fifth–eleventh centuries A.D.). But Wessex is also famous for the relics of a much earlier age, and has within its confines some of the most famous prehistoric sites in Europe. Best known of all are Stonehenge and Avebury, impressive stone circles testifying to beliefs and rituals on which antiquarians and archaeologists have spent centuries of exploration and speculation in an effort to understand them.

Today, a village straddles the great ditched henge enclosure built at Avebury in the third millennium B.C. But the Avebury henge is only the central feature of a larger ritual complex including prehistoric monuments spanning a period of over two thousand years, from the early Neolithic, around 3600 B.C., to the end of the Early Bronze Age, circa 1500 B.C. They show that Avebury remained an important center throughout this period, with new features being added as old ones fell into disuse. It makes Avebury an ideal center for anyone interested in prehistory. Here, within a relatively small area, the visitor can see the Neolithic long barrow of West Kennet, the Windmill Hill causewayed enclosure, the Avebury henge and Silbury Hill, a selection of Bronze Age round barrows, and the finds displayed in the Alexander Keiller Museum, adjacent to the Avebury henge in the middle of the whole complex.

Landscape and Clearance

The Avebury landscape is an area of rolling chalk hills dissected by the valley of the River Kennet. In visiting the various sites we can take advantage of the varied panoramas that open before us: from the West Kennet long barrow, looking north and west over Silbury Hill and Avebury toward Windmill Hill in the distance; from the Windmill Hill causewayed enclosure, looking south; or from the Avebury henge itself, looking upward and outward between the stones, across the remains of the massive enclosure bank, to the hillsides that

THE AVEBURY SEQUENCE

Chronology is one of the major headaches in archaeology. How can we determine when sites were built and used? Radiocarbon dating of organic remains such as bone or charcoal is the principal means of establishing when and in what order the different monuments or parts of monuments were built at Avebury. It shows us that the West Kennet long barrow and Windmill Hill enclosure came first, around 3600 B.C. It also tells us that the Avebury henge was built between 2900 and 2600 B.C. But it is too imprecise to answer all of our questions. We would like to know, for example, whether the stone circles were put up at the same time as the bank and ditch. Some archaeologists have speculated that the two inner circles came before the rest of the monument, and that the large outer circle may have been added only after the bank and ditch were completed. We need more information and better dates before we can answer these questions.

Another question arises from the plan of Avebury. The West Kennet avenue, which adjoins the henge, isn't straight, but as it approaches the southern entrance to the henge it goes through a particularly awkward change of course. In fact, strictly speaking, there may even be a break between the stones in the henge entrance and those of the avenue proper. Does this mean that the avenue was built first, and only later adjusted to link up with the henge? These are details, perhaps, but if we are ever truly to gain a better understanding of the Avebury monuments we need to know which of them were built separately and which as part of a single coordinated scheme.

ring the horizon. These complementary viewpoints, looking from monument to monument, emphasize the intervisibility and interconnectedness of all that we might call the Avebury complex.

Six thousand years ago, the view would have been radically different. At that time the landscape was wooded, with mature oak forests covering the rolling chalk uplands. Farmers were just beginning to fell woodland to make clearings for their crops. By clearing the trees, they set in motion the changes

The principal prehistoric monuments of the Avebury area.

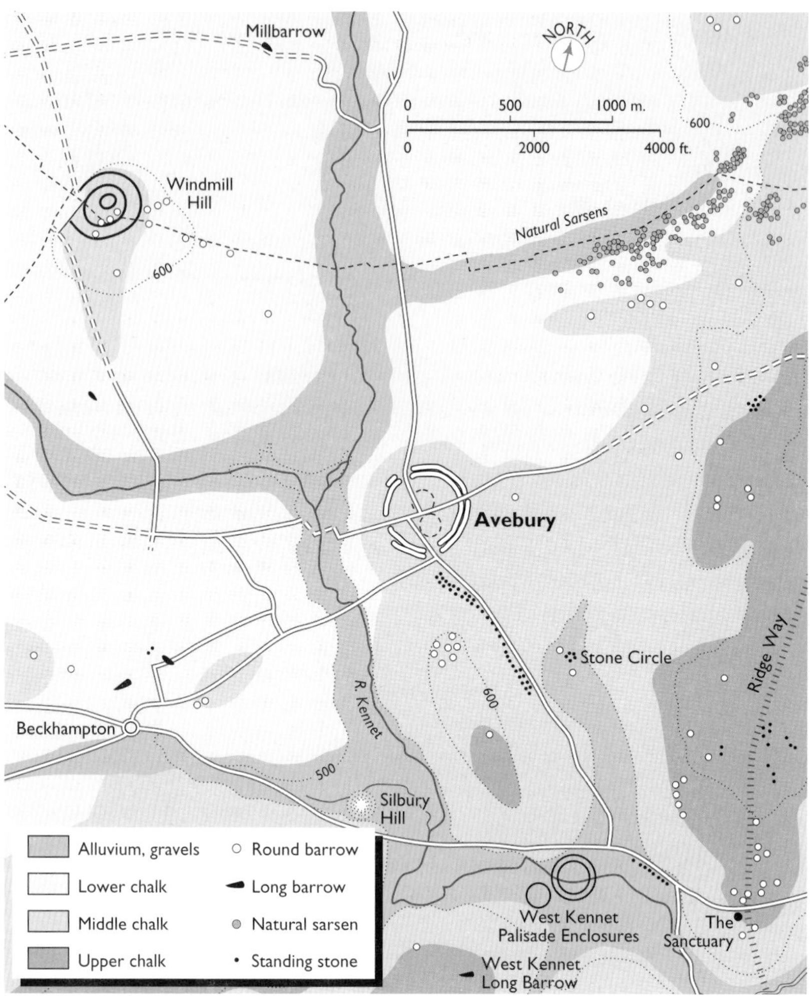

that have made the landscape what it is today. Exposed soil proved vulnerable to erosion, especially when it was plowed and tilled, and much of it ultimately washed away into the river valley. The uplands became grassland for pasturing cattle and sheep.

For the early farmers, however, clearings were hard work to create and restricted in size. Each of them may have centered on a small settlement, perhaps little more than a farmstead. Many of them were probably impermanent—occupied for a few years, then abandoned when the community moved to new land elsewhere. They grew crops, but they also had herds of cattle. Indeed they may have lived mobile lives like cattle pastoralists of more recent times, rather than as peasant farmers with fixed fields and villages. But in time, as these communities grew in size, their members began to make a lasting mark on the physical landscape. This took the form of long mounds for burial and causewayed enclosures for feasting and ceremonies.

The First Monuments: West Kennet and Windmill Hill

The long barrows of the Avebury region are of two kinds. On the one hand are the so-called unchambered long mounds. These are only "unchambered" in the sense that their burial chambers were of timber and have long since disappeared. The other kind are the chambered long mounds, with passages leading to stone-built (often megalithic) chambers under one end of the mound.

The most famous chambered mound in the Avebury area is without question West Kennet, and it is here that our tour of the Avebury monuments can properly begin. The West Kennet long barrow stands on a hilltop south of the village and appears from below as a long, low eminence spread out along the ridge. Those visitors who make the climb to the top find themselves confronted by a gently curved facade of massive stones, almost concealing the entrance into the passage behind. There are in fact five separate cells or chambers in the tomb, two on either side of the passage and one at the end. When archaeologists excavated them (in 1869, then again in 1955–1956), they proved to contain remains of at least forty-six individuals, but not whole skeletons, only fragments. Those who have studied the bones conclude that the bodies must have been exposed before they were placed inside West Kennet, a practice we know of from other tombs of this kind.

Nor were the bodies spread randomly between the different cells. The one at the end had only males; the inner pair of side cells held males and females, but only adults; while the outer cells had young individuals as well. It may be that only privileged individuals had the right to be buried in the inner reaches of the tomb. Add to this the likelihood that bones were added or extracted after the skeletons had been deposited and we begin to appreciate the complexity of rituals and beliefs that were in play in these tombs.

Beyond the burial chamber stretches the long mound of West Kennet, some 330 feet (100 meters) in length. Why the Neolithic builders made it so long is unknown, since the burial chambers are clustered at one end. Perhaps burial was only one of the activities carried on here. The mound itself may have been built as a platform for special ceremonies or as a landmark. It would certainly have presented a striking appearance when first built—a gleaming monument of freshly quarried chalk.

West Kennet is one of eight long mounds around the edges of the Avebury "area." They belong to an early stage of the Neolithic period, around 3600 B.C. Each may have been the ritual focus for a cluster of communities, like the parish churches of more recent times, though the communities themselves were probably quite small. There must also have been a kaleidoscopic quality to the landscape as some settlements withered and others grew. The Avebury area was not yet a densely inhabitated region. But neither could these communities have functioned as isolated social units. They must have been in continuous contact and interchange, both among themselves and with

Plan (*right*) and isometric cutaway view (*below, right*) of the burial chambers at the east end of the West Kennet long barrow. On the cutaway view, the original concave facade can just be made out behind the massive (later blocking) stones (the space between them is filled with rubble). In the center of the original facade an entrance gave access to a passage, roofed with slabs and leading past two sets of side chambers (northeast and southeast, northwest and southwest) to a terminal chamber at the end of the passage (west chamber).

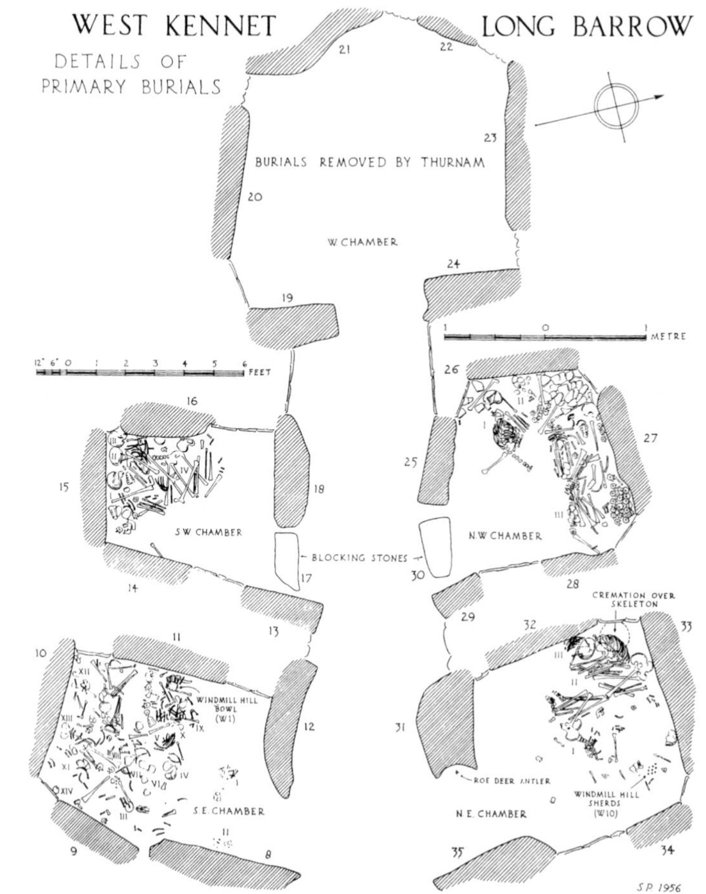

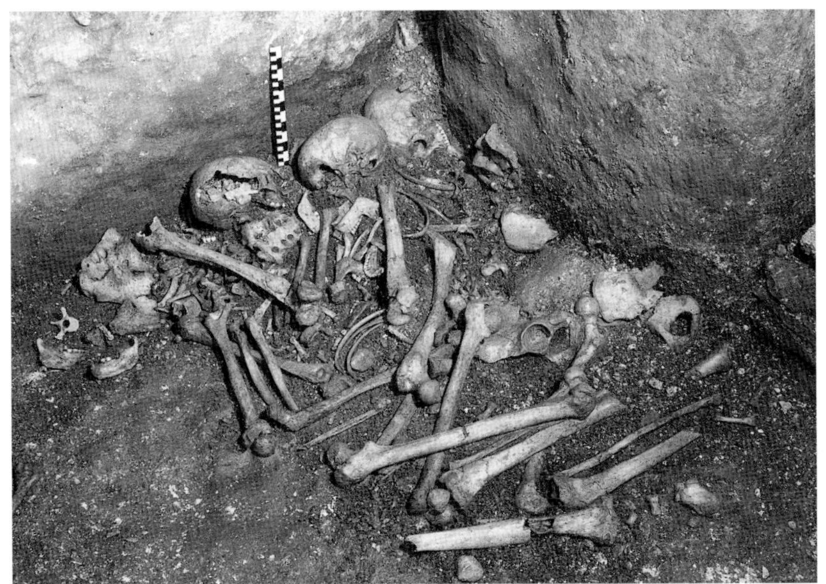

Human skeletal remains in the southwest chamber at West Kennet. The chambers were used for collective burials, so remains of several individuals became mixed together. The practice may have been intended to promote the idea that at death, individual identities were merged in the collective identity of the ancestors.

communities from other neighboring regions. And it must only have been by banding together that they were able to construct the causewayed enclosure on Windmill Hill.

Windmill Hill is at the northwestern corner of the Avebury area; to reach it we have to descend once again to the Kennet valley and travel west and then north, passing Avebury itself on the right-hand side. Causewayed enclosures are so called because of the number of breaks in their ditches. These were cut into the chalk, and the excavated material piled up to form a low bank. Neither banks nor ditches, however, were continuous, and causewayed enclosures were certainly not made for defense, as was formerly argued. Rather they were places for ceremonial and ritual activities—perhaps, among other things, for communal feasting at certain key moments in the year. The Windmill Hill causewayed enclosure consists of three circuits of ditch and bank, one within the other. They aren't truly concentric, but slightly off-center. Nor is the site placed on the top of the hill, but to one side of the summit. The innermost circuit can only be seen from the north. The two outer ones, on the other hand, look as if they were made to be visible from the south, from the direction of Avebury and West Kennet. Perhaps they were built by different communities.

The West Kennet long barrow and Windmill Hill causewayed enclosure are roughly contemporary, built around 3600 B.C. They may have continued in use for several centuries, but around eight hundred years passed before the next monuments were built in the Avebury area. These were on an altogether different scale: the Avebury henge and Silbury Hill. They show that during this crucial period, Avebury had progressed from being a rather ordinary part of the Wessex landscape to a major regional center.

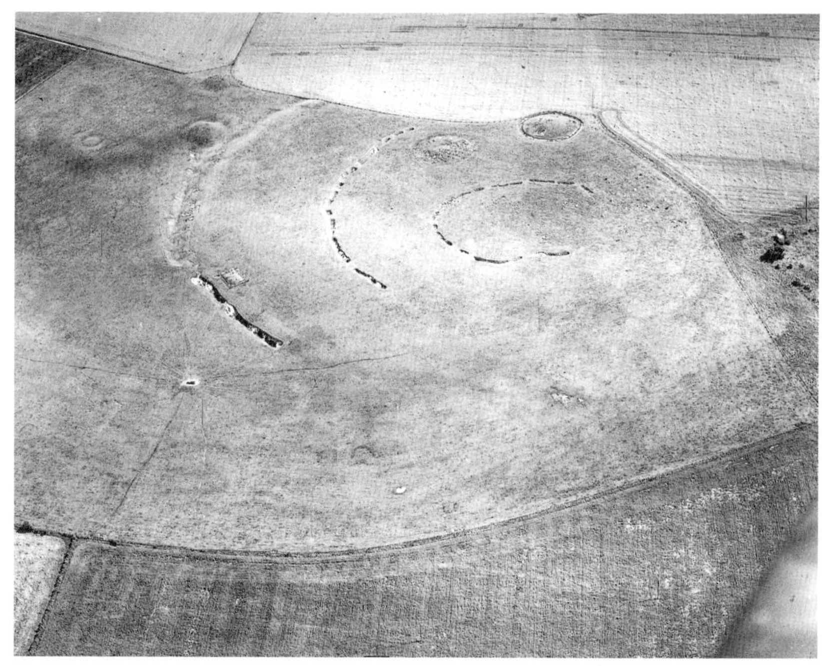

Aerial photograph of the Windmill Hill causewayed enclosure showing the three circuits of Neolithic ditches and the later (Bronze Age) round barrows.

The Avebury Henge

To the nonspecialist, the word "henge" raises images of Stonehenge. That, indeed, is where the term originates. But as perversity will have it, Stonehenge is an unusual example of its type. Archaeologists today use the word "henge" to describe not a stone circle, but a ritual enclosure defined by a bank and ditch. The bank is outside the ditch, an arrangement that shows that these are not defensive enclosures. Henges vary greatly in size and are often very regular in plan. They may have one or two entrances, marked by gaps in the bank and breaks in the ditch. Where there are two entrances, they are usually diametrically opposite each other. No stone is involved, though some henges had timber uprights.

Alongside these henges is another class of monument, the stone circle. These are clustered in the north and west of Britain, where stone is abundant. They consist simply of a ring of standing stones and range from small circles (some under 50 feet [15 meters] across) with modest-sized stones to massive rings with stones of megalithic proportions.

Avebury has both standing stones and a ditch and bank. How then does it fit into this scheme? First of all, at over 1100 feet (350 meters) in diameter, it is much larger than the general run of henges. Second, it is less regular in shape than most of the smaller henges—nowhere near a true circle, though some believe it consists of a number of regularly curving arcs. It belongs in fact to a special class, the "major henge," known only from half a dozen examples in the Wessex region.

Given its size, it is hard now to appreciate that the Avebury henge was discovered by accident. It was antiquarian John Aubrey who came upon it in January 1649 while out foxhunting. He was amazed at the scale of the monument, "wonderfully surprized at the sight of those vast stones" and maintained that it "does as much exceed in greatness the so renowned Stonehenge as a Cathedral does a parish Church." That is a view echoed by many modern visitors to the two sites: Stonehenge is the more famous of the two, but Avebury is the more truly impressive.

The Avebury henge is the largest stone circle in Europe. There are in fact three stone circles rather than just one. The main circle, running around the inner edge of the ditch, consisted of ninety-eight standing stones. Within it were two smaller circles, but when we say smaller, it is salutary to remember that both are substantially larger in plan than the central circle at Stonehenge. The northern inner circle was double, centered on an enigmatic structure

Aerial view of the Avebury henge from the west, illustrating the massive dimensions of the enclosure, with a circuit of standing stones around its inner lip. Fragmentary remains of the two inner stone circles can be seen to the right and left just beyond the central crossroads.

known as the "Cove," formed of three enormous sarsen (hard sandstone) blocks, among the very largest used at Avebury. The southern circle was smaller and simpler, though again with a central feature—in this case a former monolith known as the "Obelisk." These weren't the only internal features —geophysical survey and aerial photographs have revealed other stone holes in the chalk and at least one ring ditch.

The greatest glory of Avebury is not the internal features but the outer stone circle and the massive ditch and bank. The site is best appreciated by taking time to walk along the crest of the bank. The enormous size of the ditch is immediately obvious, even in its partially silted state. Excavations from 1908 to 1922, and by Alexander Keiller, the marmalade magnate, in the

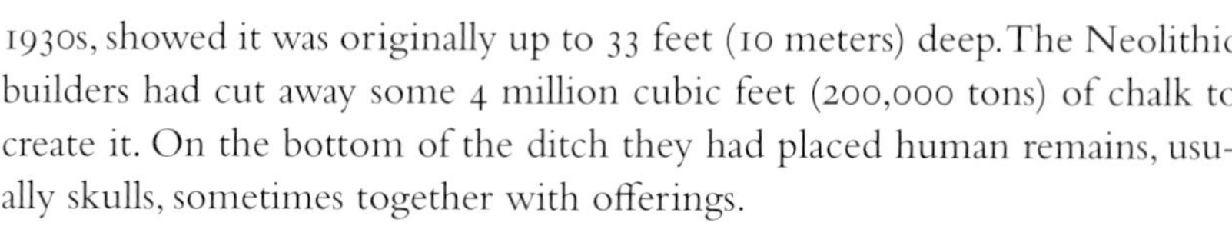

1930s, showed it was originally up to 33 feet (10 meters) deep. The Neolithic builders had cut away some 4 million cubic feet (200,000 tons) of chalk to create it. On the bottom of the ditch they had placed human remains, usually skulls, sometimes together with offerings.

The Avebury henge had four entrances, arranged like the points of a compass though on an axis somewhat to the west of true north. Next to one of the entrances the builders had departed from their usual practice and buried in the ditch not just a skull but an entire human body, an adult female. It isn't easy to say what this might have meant. The entrances themselves were made more impressive by scraping away the surface chalk to enhance the height of the banks to either side. The Neolithic builders certainly weren't averse to a little stage-management.

The ditch of the Avebury henge under excavation in 1922. This is one of the deepest sections of the ditch, and the old photograph illustrates the scale of the work effort involved in its construction.

Beyond the Henge

At the southern entrance to the henge it is possible (with care) to cross the modern road and visit another of Avebury's wonders: the West Kennet avenue. "Avenues" are processional ways marked out by parallel lines of upright stones, running in this case 50 feet (15 meters) apart. The western (Beckhampton) avenue is the subject of serious doubt. It was drawn by William Stukeley in the eighteenth century, but only as part of a fanciful view that showed Avebury and its avenues in the form of a huge serpent. When archaeologists looked in 1989 they found no trace of the stone holes, and there is no clear evidence for it apart from Stukeley's claims. The southern or West Kennet avenue, by contrast, can still be followed for part of its course.

Many of the stones have been removed or destroyed, but even so it is clear that the West Kennet avenue was never straight. Instead, it follows a sinuous course, ending one and a half miles from Avebury on top of Overton Hill, at an enigmatic monument that John Aubrey labeled the "Sanctuary."

Little remains of the Sanctuary today, though the hilltop on which it stands provides breathtaking views across the Avebury landscape. When Stukeley visited it around 1720, he saw two concentric circles of standing stones, one within the other, but by 1724 both had been destroyed. The site was rediscovered only in 1930, when excavations showed not only the stone settings but also a complex series of six timber rings, represented by the post-holes in which they had stood. (Stone-holes and post-holes are now indicated by concrete markers.) Until recently, archaeologists believed that the Sanctuary had begun life in around 3000 B.C., before the Avebury henge, as a circular timber building with a thatched conical roof. According to this view, the building was enlarged several times and the stones came only at the very end of the sequence. We now think this is mistaken, and that all of the stone and timber settings were built at the same time, within a century or so of 2500 B.C. This makes it contemporary with the Avebury henge and the West Kennet avenue, built perhaps as part of a single coordinated scheme.

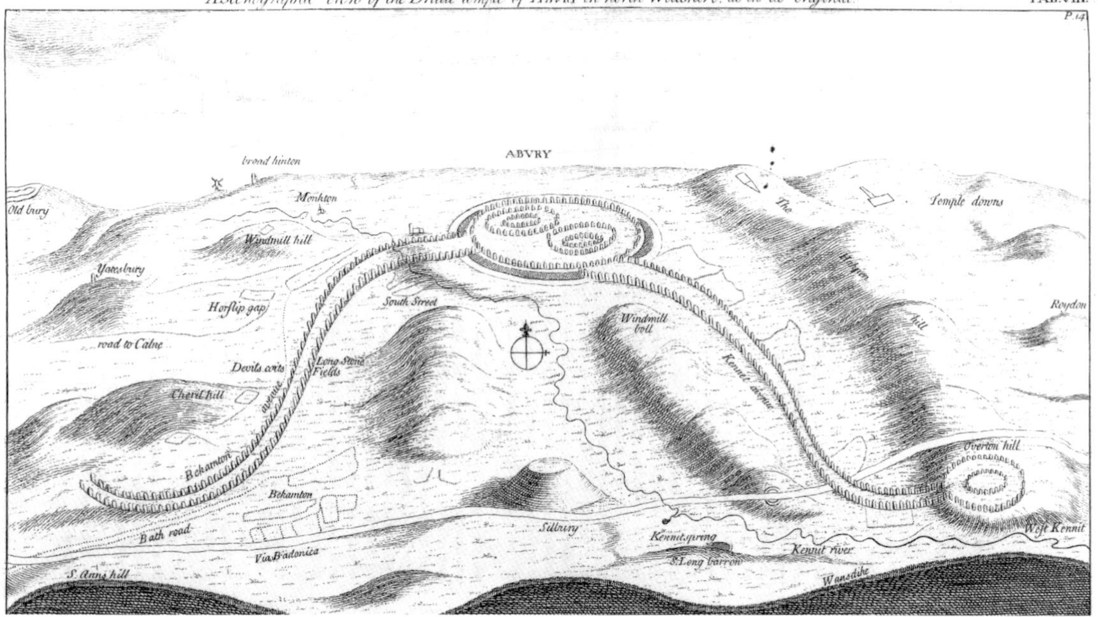

Building the Henge

William Stukeley's imaginative eighteenth-century reconstruction of the Avebury complex. It shows the great henge (labeled "Abury") top center, with twin avenues leading from it. The right-hand or West Kennet avenue still survives, terminating in the so-called Sanctuary on Overton Hill, but no sure trace has been found of the left-hand or Beckhampton avenue. In the center foreground rises the conical Silbury Hill, with the West Kennet long barrow below it to the right. Note the title of the drawing, "A Scenographic View of the Druid Temple of Avebury." Stukeley was the leading proponent of the erroneous view that prehistoric monuments such as Stonehenge and Avebury were associated with the Druids referred to by Caesar and Tacitus.

The Avebury henge represents an enormous concentration of building effort. The bank and ditch alone must have taken at least one and a half million working hours to construct. The achievement is all the more astonishing when we remember the builders used picks of red deer antler and shovels made from cattle shoulder-blades. They left some of them in the ditch, as if to remind us of the simplicity of their tools.

But it wasn't only an earthwork: there were also the two hundred or so stones of the circles to be dragged from the Downs a mile or more to the east of Avebury. The largest stones weighed over 55 tons (50 metric tons), and the combined strength of two hundred people would have been required to maneuver them. Each stone would have had to be pulled to the site strapped to a timber sledge, placed near the hole specially dug into the chalk to receive it, and laboriously levered into an upright position. And then there are the stones of the avenues, an additional several hundred massive megaliths.

We don't know how many years the scheme took to complete—perhaps a couple of centuries. Nor do we know how many people were involved, how they were organized, or where they lived. The work may have been seasonal, bringing people together from far afield for a few weeks each year. Who was in charge? There are no traces of individual leaders or chiefs, no lavish graves that might be their resting places. The project may have been very much a communal effort, but however egalitarian the society of the period, there must have been somebody to design, organize, and direct the building of Avebury.

How it was built is one puzzle. What it was intended for is still more difficult to answer. In the eighteenth century, Stukeley argued that the inner circles were dedicated to the sun and moon respectively. He "restored" Avebury to the Druids, the native priesthood of Britain described by Julius Caesar and other Roman writers. We know now, of course, that Avebury had been built and abandoned more than two thousand years before Caesar. But archaeologists today continue to believe it is connected with worship and ritual. How else could we explain these elaborate constructions? There is little trace of astronomical alignments, however, and nothing to document the kind of sun-symbolism seen at Stonehenge or Newgrange. Nonetheless, Avebury is the work of a prehistoric society that believed strongly enough to create a massive ritual monument, perhaps the focus for people over a wide area of southern Britain, who may have gathered there at certain times or seasons not only to build it but also—perhaps—to worship at it.

Schematic cross-section through Silbury Hill, showing the four principal components of the mound: (1) the initial turf stack, edged by a ring of stakes; (2) the primary capping of alternating layers of soil and chalk, edged by a bank of clay and chalk; (3) a secondary mound of chalk, again edged by a bank of clay and chalk; and (4) the final covering of chalk to give the enlarged mound we see today. Richard Atkinson, who excavated Silbury Hill in 1968-1970, saw this as evidence of three phases of construction following one another in quick succession: the turf stack and primary capping (Silbury I), followed by the secondary mound (Silbury II), and the final mound (Silbury III). The dating evidence is ambiguous, however, and the construction process may have been both more complex and more prolonged.

Did the enclosure contain or exclude? Was the idea of the bank to keep people out, to symbolize the division between those who were allowed inside, a privileged elite or ruling lineage? Or was it simply a sacred space, marking off the ritual world that participants entered as they crossed into the circle? We may never know for sure, but these are ideas to ponder as we wander among the stones or marvel at the length and depth of the enormous ditch.

Silbury Hill

Impressive though it is, in terms of sheer effort the Avebury henge is dwarfed by Silbury. This flat-topped conical mound rises from the valley of the River Kennet, about a mile to the south. Today, the main trunk road (A4) skirts by the edge of Silbury Hill, and though the mound itself is fenced off and out of bounds, it can easily be inspected from the modern viewing platform. The Roman road—predecessor to the A4—made a slight southward detour in order

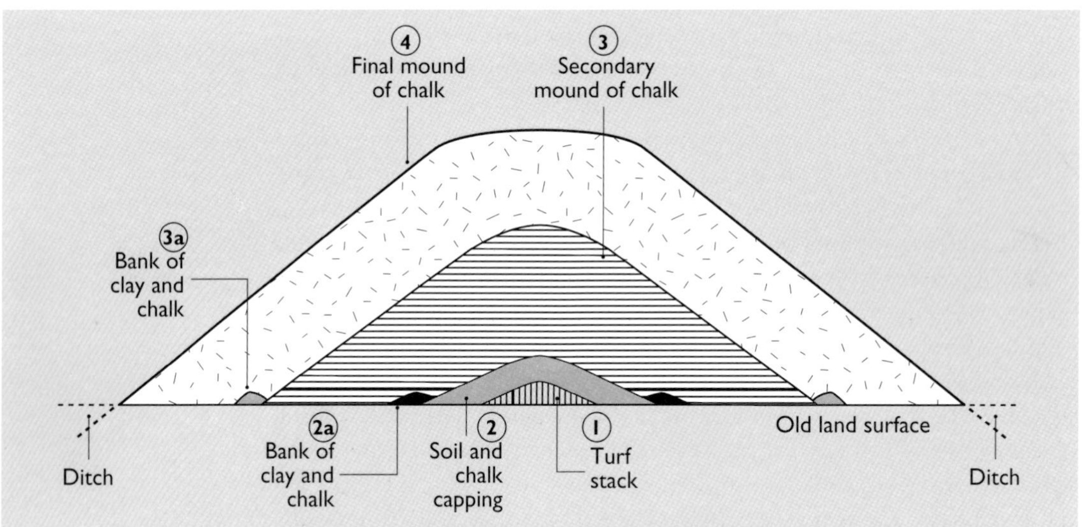

to avoid Silbury Hill. This was one of the observations used by William Stukeley to argue that Silbury Hill was a pre-Roman, prehistoric monument.

It is in fact the largest humanly made prehistoric mound in Europe, 120 feet (37 meters) high and 520 feet (160 meters) across at its base, containing some 12.5 million cubic feet (more than 300,000 cubic meters) of material. Yet no one has been able to establish why it was built. First thoughts were that it must be an oversized burial mound. Circular burial mounds are common in the area in the Early Bronze Age. They cover or contain the graves of community leaders, who were often furnished with elaborate grave goods such as metal tools or weapons, and sometimes amber necklaces or even gold. John Aubrey brought King Charles II to Silbury in 1663. He records in *Monumenta Britannica* that "no history gives any account of this hill. The tradition only is that King Sel or Zel, as the country folk pronounce, was buried here on horseback, and that the hill was raised while a posset of milk was seething." Stukeley in 1723 reached a similar conclusion: "Silbury is indeed the most astonishing collection of earth, artificially raised, worthy of the king who was the royal founder of Avebury as we may plausibly affirm . . . 'tis the most magnificent mausoleum in the world, without excepting the Egyptian Pyramids."

Naturally enough, this notion led several people to dig into Silbury Hill in the search for possible buried treasure. The Duke of Northumberland brought Cornish tin miners here in 1776 to dig a tunnel down from the summit. They found nothing. In 1849, a second attempt was made, this time tunneling in from the side. The tunnelers reached the center of the mound and found the old ground surface, where they expected to discover a splendid tomb, but came away disappointed on both occasions. Other excavations followed in 1886, then again in 1922, but all to no avail. The final attempt was made in 1968–1969, under the bright lights of the television cameras. Mining students and archaeologists from Cardiff University reopened the 1849 tunnel from the edge of the mound. The media watched with bated breath as the center was reached, but there were no surprises, no traces of a burial, and no rich finds.

The 1960s excavation was a useful exercise nonetheless, since the archaeologists were at last able to understand the structure of Silbury Hill. They followed up the tunnel with a series of trenches on top of the mound. Their findings showed that Silbury Hill had been built in several phases, beginning with a circular stack of turves, capped by chalk and earth and measuring 120 feet (35 meters) across and 18 feet (5.5 meters) high. This primary mound became the core of a large structure, the first Silbury Hill, built of chalk rubble and measuring 240 feet (73 meters) across and about 55 feet (17 meters) high. But this was not even finished when the builders decided to enlarge it. The third and final structure, built over the previous ones, was surrounded by an irregular quarry up to 70 feet (20 meters) wide and over 20 feet (6 meters) deep. This final mound, too, had a chalk core, though the builders covered it

Plan of the Late Neolithic palisade enclosures on the valley floor at West Kennet.

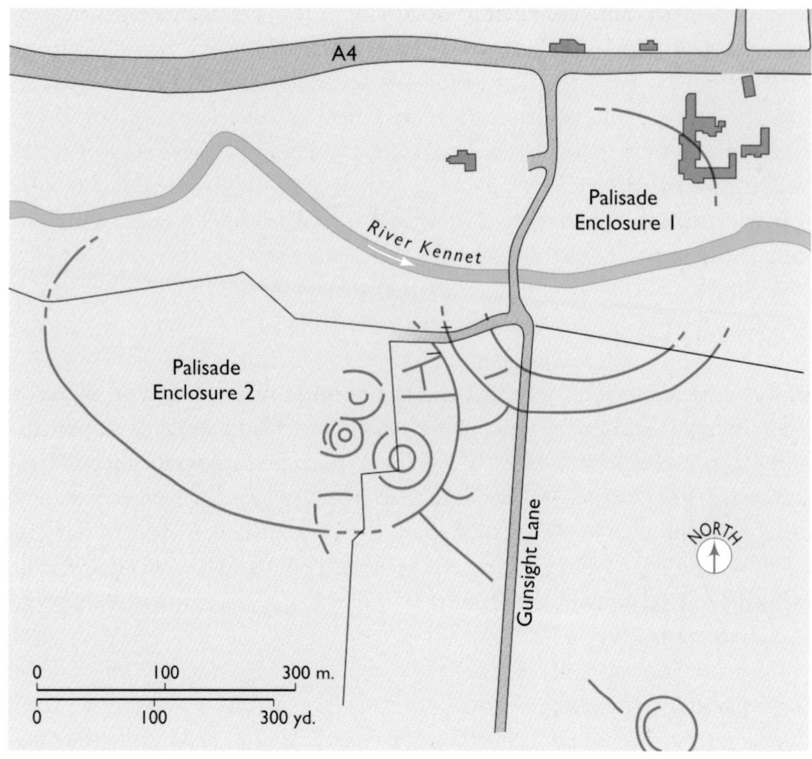

with a layer of earth to give Silbury Hill the smooth-sided, truncated-conical shape it has today. The only irregularity to be seen is a ledge or terrace, running right around the mound about 16 feet (5 meters) below the summit. Some archaeologists think this is an original feature, but it could also be a much later Saxon modification.

These discoveries still don't tell us why Silbury Hill was built. Nor do we know exactly when it was built. Radiocarbon dates from samples collected in 1968–1969 weren't very precise. Turf from the primary mound gave a date of around 2600 B.C., which could mean that Silbury Hill was getting under way just as the Avebury henge was being brought to completion. It is possible, however, that construction at Silbury ran on (or indeed began) rather later than this, since antler picks from the base of the quarry gave radiocarbon dates of 2400–2100 B.C. As so often in archaeology, a precise chronology eludes us.

The fact that Silbury is built on relatively low ground hints that there was more to the significance of the massive mound than height alone. The precise location must itself have been important, perhaps in relation to other Avebury monuments or to the surrounding topography. Two of the most obvious roles are as a landmark—something to look at—and a viewing platform—something to look from. Silbury Hill is in fact just high enough to be seen from a whole series of positions in the surrounding landscape. It can also be seen from a few points within the Avebury henge, its top just breaking the skyline. Perhaps more convincing is the idea that it was a viewing platform. For a start, it has a flat top 100 feet (30 meters) in diameter. Then there is the terrace (possibly old, possibly Saxon) just below the summit. One suggestion (assuming the earlier date) is that summer sunrises were observed from here, one part of the rituals that may have been carried out at the Avebury complex. We know that the builders of Stonehenge, working at about the same time, took careful account of midsummer sunrise when they planned and raised the great sarsen trilithons.

The Twilight Years

Silbury Hill, the Avebury henge, and the avenues were all created within a relatively short space of time, between about 2900 and 2400 B.C., or perhaps a little later in the case of Silbury Hill. They remained in use for several centuries, but the main focus of new building seems to have switched southward away from the henge and east of Silbury Hill in West Kennet. Here on the valley floor two large palisaded enclosures were constructed, probably one after the other, around 2300–2200 B.C. They were built of massive timbers, set in ditches up to 6 feet (2 meters) deep. If the depth is any indication of the height of the palisades, the posts may have been as much as 25 or 30 feet (8 or 10 meters) long. One of the enclosures was double; the other, Enclosure 2, had several smaller double-rings within it, and was connected by a fence line with an outlying double ring upslope to the southeast—an arrangement reminiscent of Avebury, the West Kennet avenue, and the Sanctuary on Overton Hill.

Nothing of these enclosures can be seen today, though the track leading up from the road to the West Kennet long barrow passes just to the east of Enclosure 2. They were evidently much less labor-intensive to build than Avebury or Silbury Hill, but enclosures on this scale were still a considerable undertaking and if their timbers really stood 20 or 25 feet (6 or 8 meters) high they must have been an impressive sight. So here we have yet a further stage in the ritual landscape of Avebury, though how exactly the two enclosures functioned—whether for example people lived within them—we can't say for sure.

We know that Avebury and the avenues continued to be venerated to the end of the third millennium because new burials were placed at the foot of the stones. By 2000 B.C., however, the focus had shifted away from the major Avebury monuments. The area was still occupied; that much is shown by the round barrows. These circular burial mounds were built in small groups on the uplands around Avebury well into the Bronze Age. Some of them can be seen on Windmill Hill, within the ditches of the by-now long-abandoned causewayed enclosure.

There were also field systems—layouts of small rectangular fields still visible in places on the Marlborough Downs and at Bishop's Canning. So while the great Neolithic monuments mouldered slowly to ruin, weathering and merging more and more into the landscape, people still lived and farmed the

Avebury landscape. In the first millennium B.C. there were Iron Age hillforts. During the Roman period, a major road was built passing by the foot of Silbury Hill, though by this time the Avebury area was something of a backwater. The Romans haven't left many other significant remains.

Then, in the Anglo-Saxon period, the present village of Avebury was founded. The new settlers didn't leave the prehistoric monuments untouched for long. During the eleventh century A.D., a wave of Christian reform swept through southern Britain. Reformers saw the Avebury stones as symbols of devil-worship and began to fell and destroy them. Worse was to follow in the seventeenth century, for as Avebury village expanded, more and more stones were toppled and broken up for building stone. Numerous stones were lost in this way, but we are fortunate that so many have survived the onslaught of both religion and economics. They present us today with one of the most impressive archaeological sites in Europe, mysterious yet powerfully evocative of prehistoric times.

Further Reading

The best accounts of Avebury are those by Aubrey Burl, *Prehistoric Avebury* (New Haven: Yale University Press, 1979), and Caroline Malone, *Avebury* (London: Batsford, 1989). Neither of these was able to take account of the important new fieldwork at several of the Avebury monuments undertaken by Alasdair Whittle. Whittle has also reassessed the development and meaning of the Avebury complex and written up the 1960s excavations at Silbury Hill. For all this, see *Sacred Mound, Holy Rings: Silbury Hill and the West Kennet Palisade Enclosures* by Alasdair Whittle (Oxford: Oxbow Books, 1997). Earlier excavations at Avebury monuments are detailed in *Windmill Hill and Avebury* by Isobel Smith (Oxford: Clarendon Press, 1965), and Stuart Piggott, *The West Kennet Long Barrow* (London: HMSO, 1962). For a general account setting these monuments in a broader context, Tim Darvill's *Prehistoric Britain* (New Haven, CT: Yale University Press, 1987) is especially recommended.

Further Viewing

A display of finds from and photographs of Avebury, including pictures of the excavations in the early 1900s, is in the Alexander Keiller Museum in Avebury village.

CHAPTER

SEVEN

Skara Brae

C. 3100–2500 B.C.

A Neolithic village in the Orkney Islands

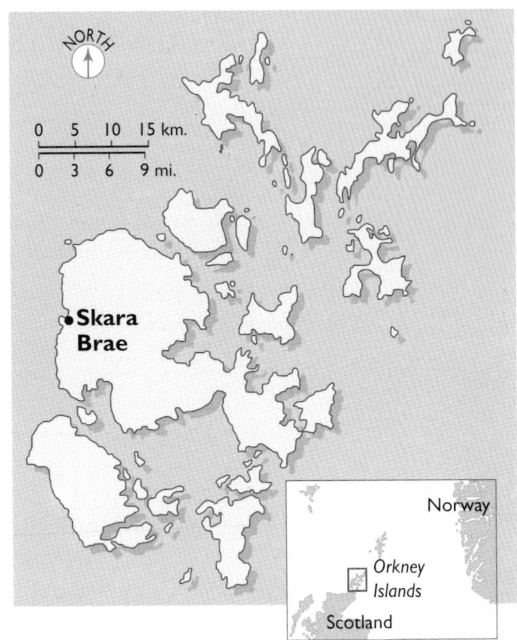

It is a strange feature of prehistory that the more out-of-the-way places often yield the most spectacular remains. This is especially true of small islands, and no account of European prehistoric sites could possibly be complete without mention of the Orkney Islands off the north coast of Scotland. In the first place, the Orkneys have one of the greatest known concentrations of Neolithic chambered tombs. But Orkney has another claim to fame, for in this treeless, open landscape timber was rare, and the early farmers built their houses as well as their chambered tombs of stone. Most of the houses have been destroyed by the ravages of time and tempest, but tempest, too, has led to remarkable rediscoveries, not least when in 1850 at Skara Brae a storm laid bare the best preserved prehistoric village in northern Europe.

Walking around Skara Brae today we can get a vivid impression of what life was like in an Orkney village some five thousand years ago. Naturally it isn't complete. The roofs have gone and a good deal of the settlement has probably been washed out to sea, but what remains is remarkable: houses and connecting passages, their walls still standing to ceiling height, with stone-built cupboards and beds, the whole complex embedded in a mound of domestic rubbish. Still, we do not know much about the inhabitants' social organization or spiritual life. Likewise, Skara Brae is clearly an unusual place, and not only

The village of Skara Brae, looking out over the Bay of Skaill beyond. In Neolithic times the settlement was not on the sea's edge as it is today, but stood a little further back, sheltered behind sand dunes. It was these dunes that engulfed the settlement after its abandonment and preserved it until storms uncovered it once again in the nineteenth century.

because of the excellent preservation. Not many settlements were built as an agglomerated cluster of houses, and it can't be considered typical of Neolithic villages of northern and western Europe. Being made of stone, however, much has survived that has been lost at villages where timber frame buildings with wattle-and-daub infill were the norm. It is this that makes our experience of Skara Brae so vivid and engrossing.

The Settlement of Orkney

The Orkney Islands are separated from the Scottish mainland by less than 10 miles (16 kilometers) of open sea. The straits (known as the Pentland Firth) can often be rough, however, and the sea voyage is not always as comfortable as the short distance might suggest. Up to 14,000 years ago, the Orkneys weren't islands at all, but were joined to the Scottish mainland (and to each other) by a low-lying plain. It was the melting of the ice sheets and the consequent rise in sea-level that made the Orkneys a cluster of sixty to seventy islands and islets, large and small—some little more than isolated rocks.

The first signs of human presence are mesolithic flint scatters, but from around 3800 B.C. a new lifestyle emerged when farming was introduced from the Scottish mainland. This involved the transport to Orkney of cattle, sheep, pigs, and dogs, along with the all-important crop plants wheat and barley. The rafts or skin boats in which they arrived must have made the crossing a hazardous affair, though fishing had long been a part of the way of life around the Scottish coasts, and on a good day, the Orkney Islands are in fact clearly visible from Scotland.

These first Orkney farmers soon began to build houses that have left clear remains. They are in fact better known and better preserved than anything of the period in Britain or northern Europe. This is because they were built of stone. Orkney had some woodland and some timber that the first settlers could use, but unlike much of northern and western Europe, it wasn't a densely forested environment. It was always too cool and too exposed to western winds for temperate species such as oak, elm, and ash. The shortage of timber must have been a major headache for the early inhabitants, but it did have one fortunate outcome. In obliging them to build of stone, it ensured that some of their settlements would survive the ravages of time.

The Neolithic Village Today

Skara Brae is an exemplary survivor— a complete stone-built village, occupied from around 3100 to 2500 B.C. It stands on the shores of the Bay of Skaill on the west coast of the island called "Mainland," which is the largest of the Orkney group. This exposed, west-facing location is subject to fierce storms in winter, when powerful waves cast heavy rocks against the low cliffs, constantly nibbling away at their edges. Part of the Skara Brae settlement has been lost to the sea through storm action, most recently in 1925. Soon afterward, the present seawall was built to prevent further erosion. But this means we don't know how big the site was originally.

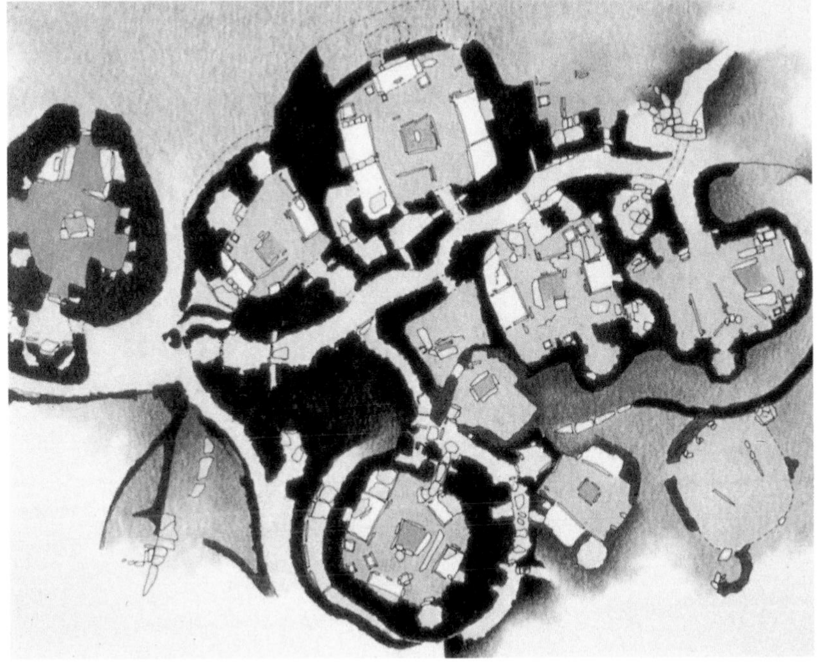

Plan of the Neolithic village of Skara Brae, showing the winding passages leading between the complex of stone-built houses. Beneath the extant houses (Phase II) are remains of earlier buildings (Phase I), though it is unlikely that the village was built in two simple phases; more likely, individual houses were demolished and rebuilt as need arose.

As it survives today, the settlement of Skara Brae consists of five houses of standard plan, two smaller rectangular spaces referred to as House 6, a free-standing "workshop" (House 8), and remains of two houses (9 and 10) built at a lower level and belonging to an earlier phase. In fact, there were several phases of occupation. The first village (Skara Brae I) was built on the site around 3100 B.C. The houses were smaller than those of the final phase, and had beds built into recesses in the side walls, rather than projecting box beds as in the later dwellings. Little of this early settlement can be seen today, since it was largely built over by the later settlement and most of it lies buried underneath the visible remains.

One theory suggests that the early village of Skara Brae was lived in for around three hundred years, at which point the occupants decided to rebuild the entire complex. There may have been a practical reason for this: the early village could have been damaged in one of the frequent storms that strike this coast. But it is much more likely that individual houses were demolished and rebuilt piecemeal, as need arose. Of the buildings we see today, House 5, for instance, seems to predate House 4, and House 1 was built before House 2. So we shouldn't think in terms of two distinct and separate phases, but of a gradual, organic development of Skara Brae during the six hundred or so years of its life.

Another theory that can be laid to rest is that the later stages of the village were intentionally sunk into a midden. "Midden" is essentially household rubbish that has been gathered together in a refuse heap and allowed to decompose. Some archaeologists have argued that the builders of Skara Brae piled up midden material around their houses. But new excavations at the

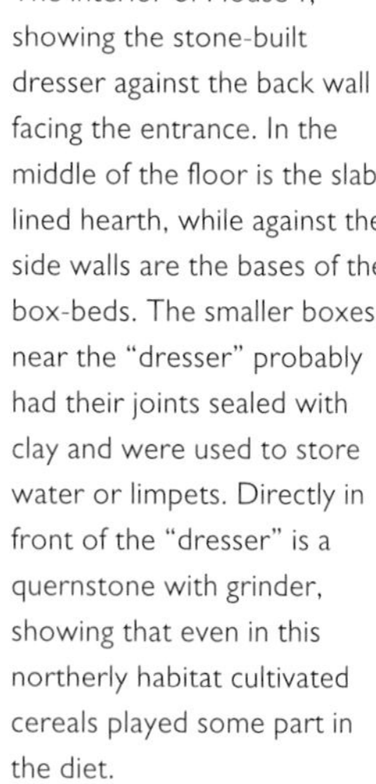

The interior of House I, showing the stone-built dresser against the back wall facing the entrance. In the middle of the floor is the slab-lined hearth, while against the side walls are the bases of the box-beds. The smaller boxes near the "dresser" probably had their joints sealed with clay and were used to store water or limpets. Directly in front of the "dresser" is a quernstone with grinder, showing that even in this northerly habitat cultivated cereals played some part in the diet.

Barnhouse settlement, another Neolithic settlement in Orkney, have shown it was encased not in midden material but in a jacket of turf. The reason for this was purely practical, since turf provides excellent draftproofing and thermal insulation against the rigors of an Orkney winter, especially the cold winds. This must have been the case at Skara Brae, too. But as houses were modified and rebuilt, the turf decayed and collapsed, steadily engulfing the village. Food remains and other debris became mixed in with the turf, creating the impression of midden. What had been turf packing around individual houses thus became a mound of organic matter, with houses embedded within it.

When complete, Skara Brae would have presented a strange, rather blank appearance to the outside world. The houses were built cheek-by-jowl, and even the passages that led between them were covered for protection against the elements. The sense of community must have been extremely powerful. The only access would have been by the narrow entrances at the ends of the passages—and even these were probably closed by stone doors at night. The entrance to the main passage, for example, was through a tiny opening less than 3 feet high and little over 18 inches (50 centimeters) wide. A few paces within it was a second substantial threshold, with the slots for a drawbar in the side walls. Security was important. After hours, when the inhabitants had retreated indoors, the only sign of life at Skara Brae would have been the smoke curling its way upward from holes in the cluster of turf-covered roofs.

A Skara Brae House

One of the best preserved of the Skara Brae houses is House 1. This is typical in plan and construction. Everything is built of stone—everything that has survived, that is. Stone slabs placed horizontally form the dry stone walls. Stone slabs balanced vertically on edge form special features such as beds and hearth. What we don't see are all the organics that would have made this house a home, the dwelling place of a family unit. Nor do we see the roof, which must have been supported on beams of timber or whalebone. The roof was probably made of turfs, laid carefully over the framework of supports. It certainly wasn't of stone, since if it had been the excavators of Skara Brae would have found material from the collapsed roof piled up on the house floors.

The central feature is the hearth, a square-shaped tray edged by upright stones. In recent centuries, peat was burned on Orkney hearths, but little of it would have been available in Skara Brae times (it only began to form in the Bronze Age). The Neolithic settlers must have burned dried turf or animal dung, or possibly driftwood or even dried seaweed collected from the beach. A good fire would certainly have been essential in the long Orkney winters.

The central position of the hearth is worth some thought. The main reason for the position was no doubt practical: beneath a smoke hole in the center of the roof, throwing heat evenly into all corners of the room, well away from the furniture arranged around the walls. But it is worth bearing

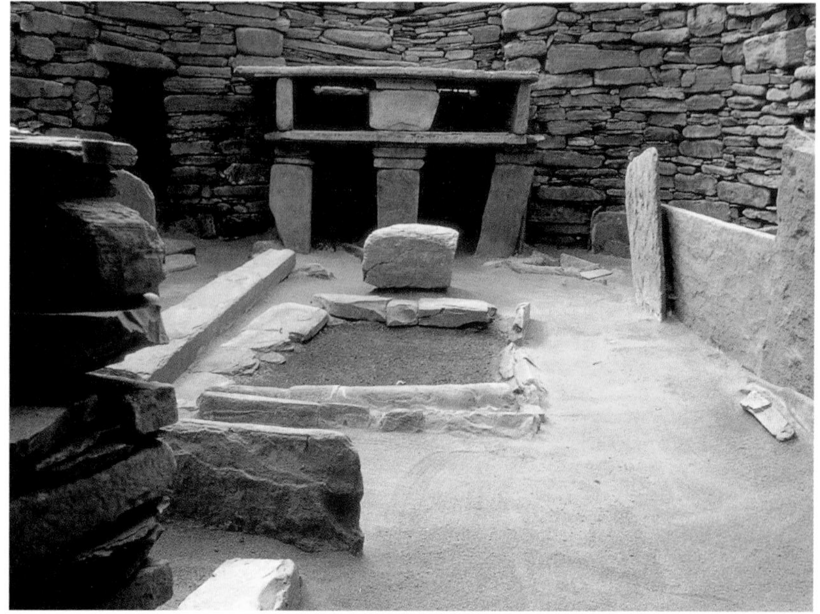

View into House 7 at Skara Brae, showing the stone-built "dresser" facing the main door. The stone slabs of the box-bed to the right are decorated with carvings, and just beneath it was a burial cist containing two female skeletons.

in mind that the Latin word for hearth is "focus," and the central hearths in the Skara Brae houses made them the focus of family life. The fire that burned in it was a source of light and heat, a means of cooking, and a symbol of domesticity.

It isn't the only symbolic feature of the Skara Brae houses. Indeed, the strict repeated layout of the houses—they all embody the same basic plan, with variations—suggests that they had a preordained idea of what a house should be like and what its various features meant. An obvious example is the stone-built cupboard called a "dresser," which was built against the wall opposite the main door. Each house had one of these, though the dressers in Houses 1 and 7 are the best preserved. The dresser in House 7 is especially well constructed, with stone uprights supporting two tiers of shelves, each consisting of a single flat stone slab laid lengthwise. Conventional wisdom has it that these dressers were for storage, but they weren't simply corner cupboards, tucked carefully out of the way. With serious intention they were placed directly opposite the house doors and would have been one of the first things a visitor saw when coming through the door. Maybe the shelves held specially treasured belongings, which were displayed here to show off the family's wealth. Maybe they held symbolic items, symbols of the ancestors or of the protector-deities who were supposed to look after the occupants' well-being. Unfortunately, the excavations that have been carried out at Skara Brae haven't thrown any light on this point.

Right in front of the dresser, in the most prominent position, was a stone seat. This may have been where the head of the household sat when receiving guests or presiding over the family.

Sleeping Arrangements

Door, hearth, seat, and "dresser" lie along the central axis of the house, dividing it into roughly symmetrical halves. The main features against the side walls were the beds. These look singularly uncomfortable today, since only the stone uprights remain. They formed a kind of tall sill around three sides, the back being formed by the house wall. In the house wall itself there is usually a recess or cupboard built into the thickness of the wall. Archaeologists have suggested that the bed's occupants kept their personal belongings here. Along the front face of the bed, at either corner, was a taller upright slab, which may have supported a curtain of cloth or animal skin. That would have made these enclosed or "box" beds, a common pattern in traditional houses before the days of central heating. The curtain would also have provided a measure of privacy, though here we must be careful not to impose our own twentieth-century values on prehistoric people. They certainly took steps to bar the house doors against outsiders, but whether they were concerned about privacy within the family we simply don't know.

NEOLITHIC HOUSES

Skara Brae is doubly exceptional in Neolithic northwest Europe: first, in being so well preserved, a fact it owes to the use of local building stone rather than timber or other perishable materials; and second, in being one of the very few examples in Britain of a Neolithic village with separate and identifiable houses.

Neolithic houses are better known in southern and central Europe. In the Balkans, they were generally small rectangular structures built of clay on a timber and wattle frame. They were often divided internally into two or more rooms and had built-in features such as hearths and ovens. Settlements in this part of Europe were long-lived and might comprise several dozen such houses. As the houses decayed and were rebuilt on or near the same spot, the clay from the walls of demolished structures built up to form settlement mounds or "tells," a feature that is also common in the Near East. Tells might be only a meter or so in height, but the largest of them are impressive artificial hills, sometimes spreading over many acres.

In temperate Europe, Neolithic houses were usually built of timber. At the beginning of the period, most of central Europe was heavily forested and suitable material was easily available. The earliest Neolithic houses in this part of Europe were long, rectangular structures, with massive posts to support the roof. They were grouped into clusters of four or five such houses (often along with subsidiary smaller buildings), and as the timbers rotted they were demolished and rebuilt. Unlike the tell sites of southeast Europe, however, these settlements didn't keep to the same location, but moved around the landscape. Furthermore, though the house walls were daubed with clay, most of the material (being organic) simply decayed away, leaving little trace. No settlement mound was left. That makes it much more difficult for archaeologists to detect these sites.

In northwest Europe, and in Britain in particular, evidence of Neolithic houses is even rarer. Post-holes of a few timber buildings have been found, but most occupation sites survive only as scatters of pottery and flint turned up in plowed fields. This has led archaeologists to conclude that British Neolithic settlements may have been much less fixed and substantial than was once thought. They think that communities moved frequently from site to site, leaving relatively ephemeral traces. Skara Brae, of course, is an exception to this pattern. But throughout much of Britain, the first regular villages do not appear until the Bronze Age.

We have looked at the basic structure of the box beds, but the people of Skara Brae probably didn't sleep on the ground. They may have had mattresses packed with straw or bracken, and probably used coverings of cloth or animal skin to keep warm. Sheepskin rugs wouldn't have been available, however, since the woolly sheep was a development of the Bronze Age. But there is no reason to doubt that the people of Skara Brae slept warm and cozy in their beds.

This isn't all we can deduce from the beds. One obvious question is how many people occupied each house, and how they were divided between the beds. Gordon Childe, the famous archaeologist who excavated at Skara Brae in the 1920s, made the observation that the larger of the beds was always the one on the right as seen from the doorway. A similar arrangement has been seen until quite recently on the remote Hebridean Islands off the west coast of Scotland. There, the larger bed went to the man and the smaller bed to the woman. If this was the case at Skara Brae, where did the children or elderly relatives sleep? We can imagine these houses occupied by families spanning at least two if not three generations. In some houses, Houses 1 and 7 for example, there are slab-edged areas adjacent to the box beds, nearer to the door. These may have been for children, though in one case you would have had to step over the bed to reach a cell built in the thickness of the wall—inconvenient if this cell was used as a lavatory!

House door at Skara Brae, looking outward and showing the paving, side walls, and ceiling of large flat slabs. Beyond the two irregular gray paving slabs can be seen the raised threshold; the moveable slab that served as a door was placed against this. The door was secured in position by a wooden bar, the ends of which fitted into sockets cut in the slabs of the side walls. (The right-hand socket is hidden in shadow in this view.)

Boxes and Cells

Boxes and cells are built-in as standard features of these houses. The boxes are formed of flat stone slabs set into the floor to form a square. House 1 has four of them, one at each of the front corners of the dresser, and two more tucked away in the corner to the left. Other houses also have three or four of these structures. The joints of the boxes were sealed with clay to make them watertight, a fact that gives rise to two alternative interpretations of their purpose. One is that they were simply for holding the family's freshwater supply. Drinking water would have been available to the villagers from streams close at hand; pottery vessels or animal skin containers could have been used to carry it. The other explanation for the boxes is that they were for softening limpets, which could be used as fish bait. Limpets are attractive food to fish, but only after they have been softened by immersion in water. It takes about a week to bring them to the desired state. We may imagine the people of Skara Brae using their boxes as limpet-softening tanks, keeping each batch separate so that they knew which were ready and which still had a few days to go. This could explain why each house has three or four small boxes rather than a single large tank.

The cells are more substantial but more enigmatic. They are basically rooms built within the thickness of the house walls. There seems to be no single simple explanation of their function. Some of them have drains beneath the floors and were probably indoor toilets. Others were storerooms. In one case, in House 5, a cell was built behind the dresser and would have been particularly difficult to get at. It may have been designed as a secure cupboard, though its contents are lost. Not so in one of the cells in House 1, which yielded a cache of 2,400 beads and pendants. The discovery of underfloor drains at Skara Brae deserves special emphasis. It is probably the oldest sewage system anywhere in the world.

Like all Skara Brae houses, House 1 was not rectangular but irregular in plan. It is hard to imagine an entire family living in this single space, but that is what archaeologists believe to have been the case. Our reaction is based largely on the fact that there is only a single main room, which would have made for little privacy.

One feature that is absent from House 1—and from every other Skara Brae house—is a window (the one in the back wall is modern). There must have been a smoke hole in the turf roof, which would have let in a small amount of light, but the house interiors must have been dark, lit only by torches or by the flickering fire light from the central hearth. Certainly little light would have come through the entrance door, since this opened out only onto a low, enclosed passage that ran between the houses.

Moving Through the Settlement

Let us for a moment imagine ourselves as Skara Brae villagers, getting up to go about the day's work. First of all, we must undo the house door. This was a slab of stone carefully shaped to fit the low entrance. It was held in place by a drawbar of wood or whalebone that pinned it securely against stone stops in the threshold and ceiling. Such a secure door shows there were limits to the communal ethos at Skara Brae; each family demanded a measure of independence and privacy (though it is also possible that animals were allowed to wander freely through the passages and the doors were to keep them out of the houses themselves).

The drawbar would be pushed back into the long slot specially made for this purpose in the thickness of the wall. Then, moving the stone door slab aside, we emerge into one of the sinuous, covered-in passages that transected the settlement. Only children would have been able to walk upright under these low ceilings. As we pass the doors of other houses, we can look in and see the same basic arrangement of furniture in each: a "dresser," displaying the treasured possessions, at the back; box beds with leather curtains to either side, and a smoking hearth in the center of the floor.

At length we reach the end of the passage, where it gives on to the outside world. Here again there is a door with a drawbar. We don't know how many entrances there were, as we don't know the original size of the village, because part of it has been destroyed by winter storms. The sole surviving entrance is on the western edge of the village and opens onto an area, paved with flat stone slabs, that has been labeled the "marketplace." It was really just a forecourt with no obvious special function. But it isn't actually the end of the village, since beyond it to the west lay the only free-standing structure of Skara Bare, the so-called workshop.

The Special Houses: 7 and 8

The "workshop," although known as "House 8," can hardly be considered an ordinary house. The construction is similar, to be sure, and there is a square central hearth, as in the houses. But there is no "dresser," no box beds, and no limpet tanks. Instead, there are several alcoves in the thickness of the walls and a semidetached annex on the south separated from the rest of the building by upright slabs. When Childe was here in the 1920s he found pieces of black chert scattered on the floor. Black chert was flaked by the villagers to make sharp-edged cutting tools. Further clues came from the annex, where a cluster of burnt volcanic stones had been left. Archaeologists interpret this evidence to mean that the people of Skara Brae had used House 8 as a workshop in which they prepared chert tools, sometimes heating the chert to make it easier to work. The heat was applied by means of the volcanic stones, which were roasted in a hearth or oven.

Was this the only function of House 8? Or did it also serve as a ceremonial meeting place for the whole village? In its position on the edge of the settlement, and its special furnishings, it resembles nothing so much as the kivas of the American Southwest. There, too, manufacturing debris is sometimes found.

There is another special building at Skara Brae: House 7. This has a number of features that suggest it wasn't an ordinary family dwelling, but a place of particular significance. First of all, as we approach the entrance we notice a small room in the thickness of the wall on the right. If we go inside, we find that this room controlled the drawbar that closed the door of the house. Hence, the entrance to House 7 was closed from the outside, not the inside, as if the aim was to lock things (or people?) in, rather than out. As archaeologist Colin Richards has remarked, it was a place that could be shut up and kept apart.

But that isn't the only special feature of House 7. There is a hearth in the left-hand doorjamb, just in front of the entrance. And inside, while House 7 has the standard equipment of beds and "dresser," there are several unusual elements. The most striking of these are on and under the right-hand bed. On the stone structure of the bed itself, there are a number of carvings. Similar carvings are scattered throughout Skara Brae, but are found mainly in the passages. The only other building with a significant number of carvings is House 8, and we have already seen that that had some special function or significance. But in House 7, what lay below the bed was even more surprising. What looked at first sight like the stone-paved floor of the bed proved to be the top of a burial cist containing skeletons of two mature women, laid out in a crouched position. These were the only burials discovered within the village of Skara Brae. A final special touch to House 7 was given by the cattle skull left lying on the left-hand bed.

Taken together, these features leave little doubt that House 7 was something more than an ordinary dwelling. But we can say little more. We don't know for sure, for instance, whether anybody lived there, or whether it was reserved for some kind of sacred or ritual use.

Eating at Skara Brae

At the time it was occupied, Skara Brae stood not on the edge of the sea, as it does today, but a little way inland, separated from the beach by an area of sand dunes. It was still a coastal settlement, however, and marine resources not surprisingly played a key part in the diet of the villagers. We know this was the case from materials found among the debris between houses, and from tools and other artifacts fashioned from animal bone. One of the most common food remains was limpet shells, but we aren't sure that the villagers ate these themselves. It is more likely that they used them as bait in fishing for cod and saithe. Although no fishhooks have been found, deep water fish such as these would have had to be caught with rod and line, probably mounted with a gorge made from a splinter of wood or bone rather than a fishhook. Bones of both species of fish have been found at Skara Brae. In order to catch them, the villagers would have needed to sail the coastal waters in boats, of which no trace survives. But they would in any case have used skin boats to travel between the scattered islands.

The villagers made use of other marine resources, including crabs and oysters. They also made artifacts from seal- and whalebone, though it is doubtful whether they actually hunted these creatures. Whales may have been washed up or stranded on the beach near the settlement from time to time, and no doubt the inhabitants made good use of the opportunity when it arose. Whalebone would have been a valuable alternative to timber for roof beams and bars. Whale and seal oil and blubber could have been used in lamps within the houses. Their skins would have made waterproof clothing.

Birds, too, were eaten by the villagers. Bones of gannet, great auk, shag, and guillemot have been found, along with fragments of eggshell, some of it from eider duck. On dry land, they hunted the occasional red deer and gathered the fungus known as puffballs, which have a cotton-wool interior that can be used to encourage blood-clotting in minor cuts. Fragments of ten puffballs were found in a waterlogged area of midden at Skara Brae.

But apart from making good use of their natural environment, the villagers of Skara Brae were farmers who grew crops of wheat and barley and raised herds of cattle, sheep, and a few pigs. The cereals were probably baked into bread or brewed as beer. They were grown in small fields, edged by boundary ditches; we know this because a field of the same period has been excavated at the Links of Noltland on Westray, one of the northernmost of the Orkney Islands.

What all this adds up to in terms of daily diet is hard to say. Animal bones and limpet shells were plentiful at Skara Brae, but plant foods must have played an equally important role, even though they are so rarely preserved. The puffballs and a few charred cereal grains are the only direct evidence. With the wealth of marine resources close at hand, however, the villagers probably enjoyed a relatively rich and varied diet, though the risk of seasonal shortages must have been ever present, and may have caused them anxious thoughts during the long winter nights.

Dying at Skara Brae

The people of Skara Brae didn't enjoy long lives. Without the benefits of modern medicine, some must have died prematurely from injury or disease. Childbirth was no doubt a hazardous time for women, and childhood illnesses probably carried off many offspring before they reached adulthood. We know this from studies of the skeletal material excavated from chambered tombs on Orkney that were in use at around the same time as the Skara Brae settlement. Isbister and Quanterness are two of the best-studied tombs, each containing several hundred burials. In both cases, little more than half the population reached adulthood. According to the specialists who analyzed these bone assemblages, few of the people buried there survived beyond thirty and none beyond fifty years old. Community "elders" would thus have been only middle-aged by modern reckoning.

The Orkney Islands have one of the greatest concentrations of Neolithic chambered tombs in western Europe. Almost eighty sites are known, not counting a number that must have been destroyed. They were built rather like the houses of Skara Brae, using the local flagstone to create chambers, passages, and facades, though with rubble (rather than turf) piled in the intervening spaces. Another difference is in the roofing of the burial chambers, where large stone slabs or corbelled vaults were used, rather than whalebone or timber. The tombs were built to last. They were also built to be seen, impressive dry-stone monuments placed often on hilltops.

There are so many chambered tombs in the Orkneys that some archaeologists have argued that each community would have had its own. The idea is that they continued in use over several centuries, with old interments pushed aside to make space for new bodies. The dry-stone passages were an essential part of the scheme, as they allowed continued access to the burial chamber long after the tomb was built. Tombs took on added importance as the resting places of the ancestors of the community. The fact that the bones of different individuals were not kept separate, but were deliberately mixed together, suggests that on death, the identity of the individual was swallowed up in the ancestors as a group. It is even possible that selected bones—skulls in particular—were brought out of the tombs from time to time to "participate" in rites and ceremonies.

Unfortunately, archaeologists know of no chambered tombs very close to Skara Brae. The nearest are two to three miles distant, at Holy Kirk and Vestra Fiold to the north, and Stones of Via to the south. We aren't able to say whether any of these was associated with Skara Brae, and we don't therefore know where the Skara Brae villagers buried their dead. But we may imagine a chambered tomb, now destroyed, which played a leading role in the spiritual life of the community. They may have gathered there from time to time for special ceremonies.

One feature that unites Skara Brae to the chambered tombs is the lack of an obvious social hierarchy. We have seen how most of the houses at Skara Brae are fairly similar to each other. Although there are differences in size, furnishing, and decoration, there is no individual house that is markedly larger and grander than the others. The same pattern is seen in the bones from the tombs, where the skeletons are mixed together without any sign of special treatment for privileged individuals. Both in tombs and settlements, among the dead and the living, it was the sense of community which was all-important.

Or so it seems. But was Neolithic Orkney really a society without hereditary leaders? Were decisions made communally, or by community elders who acquired their position simply by virtue of their age? It is a tempting scenario of a kind of golden age, but it isn't borne out by all the facts. Because, in the first place, not all the tombs are equal. They range in size from simple structures that may have taken fewer than 10,000 working hours to build, up to enormous mounds with impressive chambers such as the famous Maes Howe, which may have required 40,000 working hours to complete. Maes Howe was being built during the lifetime of Skara Brae, around 2800 B.C. Also roughly contemporary with Skara Brae are two ritual monuments of a different type: the stone circles of Ring of Brodgar and Stones of Stenness. Brodgar, Stenness, and Maes Howe all lie within a short distance of each other in the center of Mainland, the principal Orkney Island, and it is hard to avoid seeing the building of these structures as other than a centralization of some kind.

As we walk around Skara Brae today, however, it is the sense of togetherness that is most prominent. Here was a small community of fishers and farmers, self-sufficient in most things, perched on the very edge of Europe. It epitomizes a lifestyle where change was slow and distinctions of wealth and status were yet to achieve expression in homes and possessions.

Over the centuries, wind blew sand over the stone-built houses of Skara Brae, covering but protecting their contents. Eventually it was forgotten, buried beneath one of the many sand dunes along the west coast of Orkney. Until, that is, 1850, when violent storms stripped the sand from the dune, and

The Stones of Stenness on Orkney, showing three of the surviving uprights. The shapes taken by the stones follow the natural cleavage planes of the local rock.

Skara Brae was revealed once again to take its place as one of the most remarkable sites of prehistoric Europe.

Further Reading

The early excavations at Skara Brae are described by Gordon Childe in *Skara Brae: A Pictish Village in Orkney* (London: Kegan Paul, 1931). For the more recent investigations, see David Clarke, *The Neolithic Village at Skara Brae, Orkney. 1972–73 Excavations: An Interim Report* (Edinburgh: HMSO, 1976). David Clarke has also provided a useful guidebook (with P. Maguire), *Skara Brae: Northern Europe's Best Preserved Prehistoric Village* (Edinburgh: Historic Scotland, 1989). The evidence is reviewed and revised by Colin Richards in his article, "Skara Brae: Revisiting a Neolithic Village in Orkney" in *Scottish Archaeology: New Perceptions,* edited by William Hanson and Elizabeth Slater (Aberdeen: Aberdeen University Press, 1991). The best general introductions to Orkney prehistory, with details of Skara Brae and other sites, are *The Prehistory of Orkney,* edited by Colin Renfrew (Edinburgh: Edinburgh University Press, 2nd ed., 1990), and *Prehistoric Orkney* by Anna Ritchie (London: Batsford, 1995).

Further Viewing

A few finds from Skara Brae are displayed in the modest site museum, but the major collection is in the archaeology section of the National Museum of Scotland, Edinburgh. The Tankerness House Museum in Kirkwall, Orkney, has other material relating to Skara Brae and Orkney archaeology.

CHAPTER

EIGHT

Newgrange

C. 3200 B.C.

Art and burial

in Neolithic Ireland

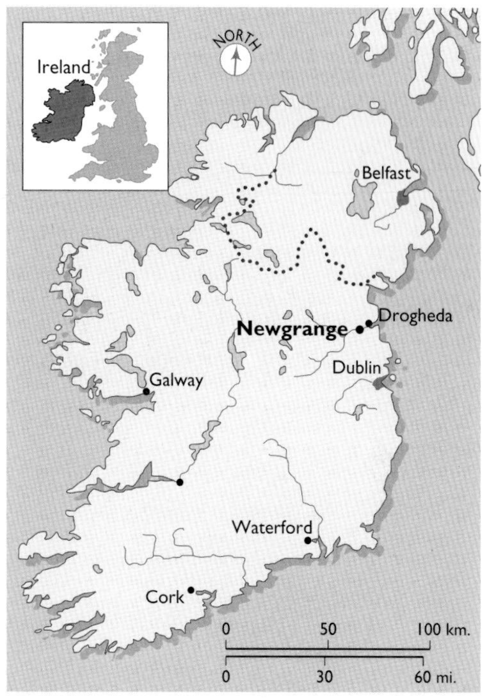

Newgrange, in the Boyne valley north of Dublin, is arguably the most famous archaeological site in Ireland—and deservedly so. This elaborate megalithic tomb, set within a carefully constructed mound measuring 260 feet (80 meters) across, has long surprised visitors with the ingenuity of its construction and the intricate designs pecked on its stones by the Neolithic builders.

It was constructed around 3200 B.C. and belongs to a class of monument known as a "passage grave," with a long passage leading to a burial chamber. Passage and chamber were covered by a large mound, though in some cases this has been lost, leaving only the skeleton of passage and chamber still visible. At Newgrange, however, internal structures and the covering mound survive in large measure intact.

Passage graves are found not only in Ireland but also in Britain, France, Iberia, and Scandinavia. Those of the Boyne valley in Ireland are among the most famous of all, both for their scale and their decoration—the pecked and incised designs known as "megalithic art." This particular stretch of the Boyne valley is in fact a Neolithic ritual complex that includes not only Newgrange but two other enormous passage graves (Dowth and Knowth) and a number of lesser structures. Knowth, indeed, is richer in art than Newgrange and has not one but two passage graves within its mound. But it is Newgrange that takes pride of place in the complex as a whole, with its long history of research, the excellence of its carvings, and its curious roof-box so carefully aligned on the winter solstice by the prehistoric builders.

Newgrange stands on a ridge overlooking the River Boyne to the south. It lies within the broad loop of river that gives the area its name: the "Bend of the Boyne." There is no doubt that the Neolithic builders chose carefully in placing their tomb here, in a prominent position on higher ground. For Newgrange is a monument made to be seen, a statement in stone proclaiming its message to the world. The message may be difficult for us to read today, five thousand years later, but its visual impact cannot be denied.

Reconstructing the Cairn

The principal elements of Newgrange are the mound, the passage leading to the chamber in its interior, and the impressive ring of megalithic kerbstones that runs around the foot of the mound. No fewer than a third of the stones are decorated with megalithic art. Yet today, viewed from a distance, the most striking feature of the site is surely the spectacular reconstructed facade.

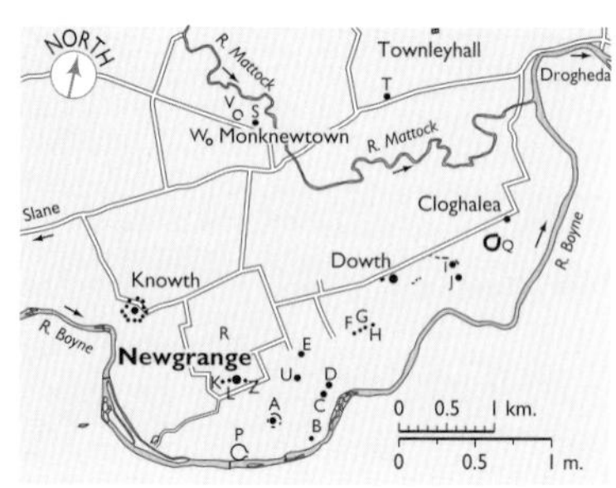

Prehistoric monuments in the Bend of the Boyne. Passage graves: Knowth, Dowth, Newgrange, and sites A, B, E, F, G, H, I, J, K, L, S, T, U, and Z. Enclosures: sites A, P, Q, and V. Standing stones: sites C and D. Site W is a prehistoric ritual pond (the Monknewtown ritual pond), 100 feet (30 meters) across and edged by a bank 7 feet (2 meters) high. It still holds water.

The gleaming white facade of Newgrange comes as a shock to those visitors more accustomed to seeing their prehistoric monuments in a state of romantic ruin. Newgrange too was overgrown and unkempt until the 1960s, with little provision for visitor access. Then, in 1961, the Irish State Tourist Board and the Office of Public Works decided to put matters on a proper footing. They purchased Newgrange, which became state property, and resolved to excavate and tidy up the site. As Ireland's premier prehistoric monument, the tourist board wanted to make it more presentable to the visiting public. But they also wanted to restore it, to straighten the leaning orthostats, and to stabilize the mound. Hence, one of the primary aims of the excavation was to gather information on the original appearance of Newgrange, so that the conservation and reconstruction work could be carried out as accurately as possible. (The true alignment of Newgrange is southeast–northwest, with the entrance opening in the middle of the southeast quadrant. For the purposes of simplicity we have here taken the liberty of mentally rotating the monument through 45° so that the main axis runs north–south, with the entrance in the southern side.)

The excavation was entrusted to Michael J. O'Kelly, professor of archaeology at University College, Cork. He and his team worked steadily from 1962 to 1975, concentrating mainly on the area around the entrance. Here they dug down to the old ground surface, removing the deep deposit of stones that had slipped off the mound as it decayed. It was careful examination of the layers of slip that led O'Kelly to imagine the reconstructed facade we see today. The key feature was a thin layer of white quartz blocks, resting directly on the old ground surface. Mixed in among the white quartz was a scatter of rounded gray granite boulders. This gray and white mixture spread over the whole area in front of the southern half of the mound, around the entrance, though it wasn't found in the small cutting made on the north side. O'Kelly decided that it was a collapsed facade, which hadn't extended right around the mound, but which had been specially designed to add grandeur to the key area around the entrance, making the southern aspect of the site—looking down toward the River Boyne—as impressive as possible.

The quartz and granite layer spread some 20 to 23 feet (6 to 7 meters) from the edge of the mound but was thickest around the kerb, tailing off gradually as it went further out. O'Kelly concluded that it must be the remains of a dry-stone wall or revetment that had stood on top of the ring of megalithic kerbstones. Engineers and archaeologists together studied the amount of material that had fallen and the size and height of the mound behind. They concluded that the dry-stone revetment had stood about 10 feet (3 meters) high and had had only a slight backward tilt—some 12 inches (30 centimeters) from top to bottom.

The eventual reconstruction gives Newgrange a striking, drumlike appearance, so far unparalleled at any other European burial mound of the period. In the reconstruction, the gray granite blocks have been randomly placed among the white quartz, but it is possible (assuming the reconstruction is broadly correct) that they originally formed a pattern. Perhaps they were arranged in spirals or lozenges, like the designs on the kerbstones.

Before we get too carried away by this idea, however, we have to consider the doubts and objections that some archaeologists have raised. It is hardly surprising that many people find such a dramatic reconstruction difficult to swallow. The best alternative theory is that the quartz and granite blocks had not fallen from a revetment but had been spread on the ground as a pavement in front of the entrance. According to this view, the mound itself had a more rounded profile, and it would certainly have been more stable than O'Kelly's near-vertical revetment. Or maybe the quartz and granite blocks were facing on the sloping surface of the mound itself, around the entrance, rather than a vertical wall. (Archaeologists have found evidence for that at Knowth nearby, and at Loughcrew, County Meath, another group of Irish passage graves.)

Whatever the truth of the matter, O'Kelly's reconstruction will stand for many decades—but only because the quartz and granite blocks are cemented into a concrete wall! The original revetment would soon have been pushed over as the mass of the mound material slipped and settled behind it. But if it ever really looked anything like this, it would certainly have made for a dramatic approach to Newgrange.

Art at the Edges

The brilliant whiteness of the revetment may at first draw the visitor's attention away from one of the key features of Newgrange: the ring of kerbstones

Newgrange today, as reconstructed following the 1962–1975 excavations by Michael O'Kelly. Note the line of kerbstones around the base of the tomb, one third of them decorated with pecked designs. Many archaeologists dispute the reconstruction, judging the face of the quartz walling too steep to have ever stood without the aid of cement (not used in the original construction). It is more likely that the quartz blocks and the granite blocks scattered among them were laid in a pavement in front of the entrance to the tomb. In the foreground and to the right can be seen standing stones of the Great Stone Circle that surrounds the monument.

around its base. There are ninety-seven of these, the largest of them 15 feet (4.5 meters) long and over three feet tall. None of them weighs less than a ton. Thirty-one of the kerbstones are decorated, with designs of lozenges, chevrons, zigzags, circles, and spirals the most common motifs. In most cases, the decoration has been picked or pecked into the stone. Where the marks are especially deep or broad, they have often been smoothed with a pebble. The most elaborate of all the designs are those executed in raised relief, where the background has been pecked away to leave the design standing out. This is the technique used on the massive entrance stone (K1) and on the elaborately decorated stone (K52) at the diametrically opposite point on the back of the mound. These were evidently positions of special significance. Most of the kerbstones have relatively simple designs—a few roughly pecked spirals, a couple of meandering or zigzag lines.

A surprising feature of the art was the way some of it had been carved on the back faces of the kerbstones where it could never have been visible once the mound was complete. These designs were probably carved before the stones were placed in position. By contrast some of the most heavily decorated stones—including K1 and K52—were evidently decorated after they had been put in position, for the decoration stops abruptly at ground level.

In a recent study, archaeologist Andrew Powell has shown how the builders of Newgrange laid out the ground plan of the mound. Powell argues that they used a standard unit of length measuring approximately 43 feet (13 meters), and proceeded to lay out six fixed points. They began with the entrance stone K1, the backstone of the chamber C8, and K52 at the back of the mound, thus establishing the main axis of the monument. The point where this line passes through C8 is well off-center, near to its right-hand edge, but is marked on C8 by two pairs of opposed triangles—a Neolithic surveyor's mark. It is interesting also that a vertical line appears in the decoration of both K1 and K52, as if to record a precise line of sight along the axis of the monument. These stones must have been among the first to be placed in position, and they must have been decorated—with their sight line—before the next stage of construction could begin.

The chamber backstone C8 lies one third of the way (c. 86 feet, two of Powell's units) from K1 to K52. The rest of the kerb was then laid out by taking arcs (measured in multiples of c. 43 feet) from K1 and K52. Arcs of three and five multiples gave the position of K67; arcs of four and five multiples allowed K77–78 and K21–22 to be positioned. This method of proceeding explains the almond-shaped plan of the final completed kerb.

The carved stones on the kerb clearly indicate points of special significance. A few of them relate to the laying out of the kerb, as just explained. On the other hand, most of them have nothing to do with Neolithic surveying but are concentrated in the southern sector of the mound, framing the entrance. Carvings at Newgrange weren't restricted to the kerb, however, but were also found on megalithic slabs in the passage and chamber, as we shall shortly see.

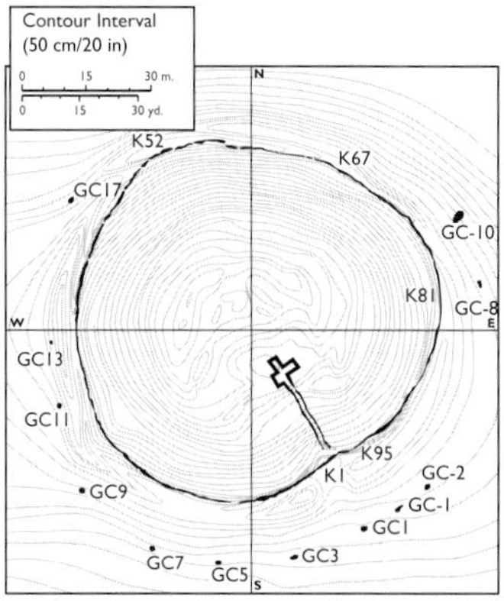

Plan of Newgrange showing the irregular shape of the mound within its surrounding kerb, and the cruciform passage grave opening from its southeastern side. Note the intentional "flattening" of the curvature on either side of the passage grave entrance, to create a more imposing facade. K1 is the entrance stone; other kerbstones are labeled K10, K20, and so on. Around the mound are the stones of the Great Stone Circle (GC1-17).

Entering the Tomb

Now that we have inspected the exterior of Newgrange it is time to go into the monument itself, making our way along the long passage to the cruciform burial chamber. We begin in front of the tomb entrance. Immediately facing us is the massive entrance stone. With its deeply carved spirals and lozenges in raised relief, it seems almost to challenge the viewer. The entrance stone forms part of the kerb that rings the mound; passing beyond it brings us within the kerb, into a small forecourt formed as the edges of the mound

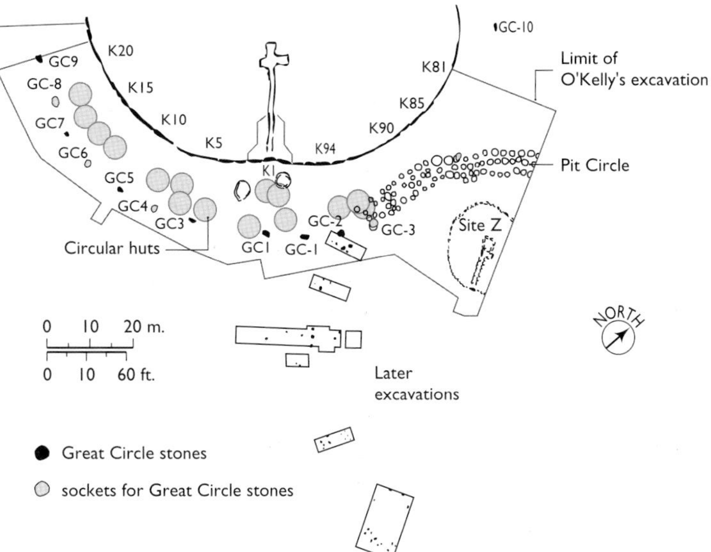

Plan of prehistoric features around the entrance to Newgrange. A smaller passage grave (Site Z) stands just 75 feet (23 meters) to the east of the main mound, while running between the two is the curving arc of pits and post-holes (labeled "Pit Circle") that may have been associated with ceremonial feasting on the site after the passage graves themselves had been blocked. The cluster of small circular huts in front of the facade of Newgrange belong to approximately the same period. The plan of Site Z and the Pit Circle have been laid out on the ground for the benefit of visitors.

The entrance stone at Newgrange, with the entrance to the passage grave beyond. The entrance stone, with its boldly carved spirals and lozenges, is one of the finest examples of Irish megalithic art. It may originally have been painted to heighten its effect.

swing inward toward the passage opening. The tall, curved limestone walls are modern work, to allow for visitor access; the "forecourt" behind the entrance stone was originally much narrower, the quartz walls continuing forward to the entrance stone to form a funnellike approach to the passage itself.

Immediately outside the present entrance, on the right, stands a large, flat slab, around 12 inches (30 centimeters) thick and carefully dressed into a roughly rectangular shape. This was the blocking stone, designed to fit snugly into the mouth of the passage. While the tomb was in use, it was probably removed only when new bodies, or new consignments of cremated bone, were carried into the chamber, or when people went into the tomb to perform rituals or ceremonies. We can't say for certain that they did so, but it seems quite probable that the chamber of Newgrange was the setting for a whole series of burials and perhaps for repeated, even regular rituals.

Finally, however, the decision was taken to close the tomb once and for all. The blocking stone was placed in position for the last time, and smaller blocks of stone were piled into the space in front of it. Within a few centuries, the surrounding cairn began to collapse and all trace of the entrance was buried. We don't know when it was rediscovered. In the early centuries A.D., gold coins and ornaments were left around the edges of the mound, probably as offerings to the spirits who were thought to dwell within. It became famous in early Irish literature as Brugh na Bóinne, the "house of the Boyne," the abode of various supernatural beings. Norsemen who invaded Ireland in the ninth century A.D. may have dug into Newgrange, but others think it lay undisturbed until 1699, when a local landowner came upon it accidentally while he was quarrying stone.

We are fortunate in having an account of the discovery of Newgrange in 1699 written very soon afterward by Edward Lhwyd, a Welsh scholar and antiquarian who happened to be touring Ireland in that year. Lhwyd came to hear of the discovery and made a visit to the site. Like later visitors, he was particularly struck by the decoration of Newgrange, including the entrance stone, which he described as "a very broad flat stone, rudely carved."

Beyond the entrance lies the passage, a tunnellike approach just under 60 feet (19 meters) long, leading to the burial chamber. The passage is built of upstanding megalithic slabs, known as "orthostats." There are twenty-one on the right-hand side and twenty-two on the left. It is roofed by capstones, the outermost pair of especially massive dimensions. The passage is lowest at its outer end—only 5 feet (1.5 meters) high. The visitor has to bend over to negotiate this sector. As we proceed along the passage, the roof steadily rises, until at the threshold to the chamber it reaches a height of 12 feet (3.6 meters). Just before the chamber is reached, however, a low lintel creates an obstacle and obliges us to bend over once again. This is the outer support for the great corbeled dome of the chamber roof. The visitor may well see it as simply a nuisance, impeding easy access to the chamber, but it is in fact remarkable evidence of the skill of the Neolithic builders, a structural necessity if the whole thing was not to collapse.

This was not the only structural precaution. Above the low lintel, within the body of the mound, the builders constructed a relieving arch across the line of the passage. It consisted of two long stones supporting a massive lintel.

Equally remarkable are the steps the builders took to protect the passage from water. Given the loose-packed nature of the mound makeup it was only to be expected that water would seep through it and trickle into the passage. This the builders were determined to avoid. So they carved a series of drainage channels around 2 inches (5 centimeters) wide and half an inch (1 centimeter) deep on the upper surface of several of the passage capstones. Being on the upper surface they are of course invisible today. But their pur-

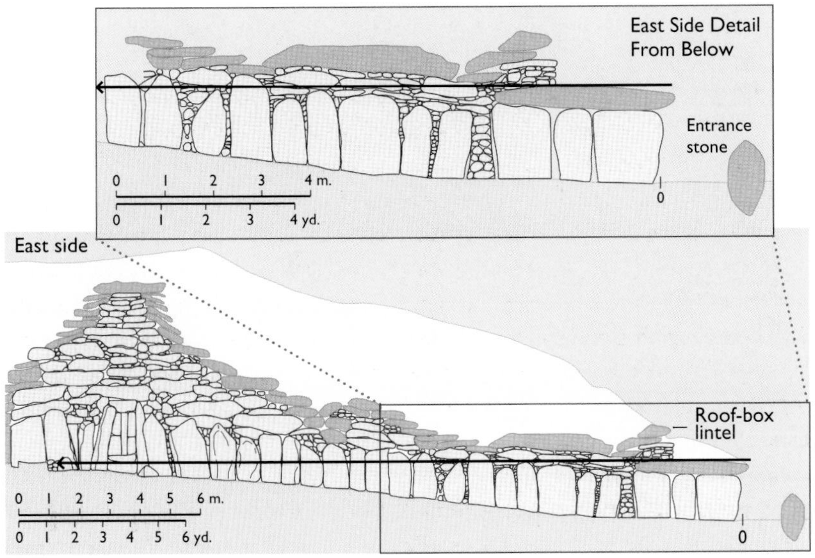

Cross-section through the passage and chamber at Newgrange. The arrow indicates the path of the sun's rays when, shortly after dawn at the midwinter solstice, sunlight shines directly through the roof box and down the passage to flood the floor of the burial chamber. The cross-section indicates how carefully the height of the roof box, the passage ceiling, and the chamber floor had to be coordinated by the prehistoric builders in order to achieve this effect.

pose is clear: to carry water away from the passage into the mound on either side. As a further precaution the builders packed a mixture of burnt soil and sea sand into the gaps between the stones, the burnt soil forming a kind of waterproof putty.

The Place of the Dead

The passage ends at the threshold to the chamber. Buried deep in the heart of the mound (though not quite at its center), this is the culmination of the whole edifice. It is of irregular cruciform plan, a central space giving on to three recesses, one at the far end (to the north) and one to either side (east and west). The lower walls are formed of megalithic slabs, like the passage we have just seen, but above these rises the glory of Newgrange, a lofty, corbel-vaulted roof soaring 20 feet (6 meters) above the chamber floor.

This isn't a true vault. In a true vault, stones or bricks are wedged together in an arclike arrangement in which the force of gravity prevents them from falling. The corbel vault is a less stable structure, in which each course of stones oversails the one below but is held in place by the mass of the mound behind

One of the most stunning features of Newgrange is the corbel-vaulted roof rising 20 feet (6 meters) above the floor of the burial chamber. It is constructed by overlapping successive courses of stone slabs so that the open space between them becomes smaller and smaller, until it is small enough to be closed by a single capping slab. The stones of each course lean slightly inward so as to lock against each other in a solid and stable structure. One recent theory holds that such a roof could only have been built by filling the chamber with sand, allowing the slabs to settle gently into position as the sand was drawn slowly away at the base. It is more likely that timber scaffolding was used, but whatever the precise technique this was a highly skilled constructional feat.

it. The weight of the mound material resting on the back of the stones prevents them from tipping forward. It was a major achievement to build such a structure, and still more impressive when we remember it has stood intact for five thousand years. How many of our modern office blocks, built of reinforced concrete to carefully engineered designs, will last so long?

We have noted already that the chamber takes the form of a central space (a continuation of the passage) surrounded by three recesses. The recesses played a key part in the burial rites and were equipped with stone basins, two (one

Inside Newgrange, looking toward the entrance passage from the alcove at the back of the burial chamber. On the left-hand slab is a finely executed triple spiral, part of the rich decoration of Newgrange that is found most notably on the stones of the outer kerb, but also on the stones of the passage and burial chamber.

above the other) in the east recess, one each in the west and end recesses. The basins were monolithic, formed of a single piece of stone, and those in the side recesses had a slightly dished upper surface edged by a low lip. The basin in the end recess was different in design, more like a flat-topped floor stone, but was smashed in the eighteenth century.

Early visitors to Newgrange remarked upon the quantity of bones in the chamber, but the human and animal remains had been seriously disturbed before modern archaeologists could record them. O'Kelly's excavation was able to throw new light on the subject by studying what was left in the trampled earth on the chamber floor. He divided the material into eighteen separate lots, depending on where they were found. Three of them (Lots 1, 7, and 15) were animal bones, but the remainder were human and were clustered around the edge of the basins in the east and west recesses. It looks as if all the human bone material was originally placed in the basins. Some of the bone was burned, suggesting the bodies had been cremated; burned material was especially abundant near the western recess. But overall, unburnt bone predominated. There was such a degree of disturbance, though, that it's difficult to know how much bone material has simply been lost since the tomb was opened in 1699. The specialist who analyzed the fragments found by O'Kelly was only able to say that at least three cremated and two unburned bodies were present, though there may have been many more than this originally.

Little seems to have been buried with the dead. We can't be sure what was there originally, since the tomb has been open for such a long time and so many visitors have crawled their way along the passage that a good deal must have been lost—either trampled underfoot or removed as souvenirs. As far as we know, however, only a few simple objects have ever been found within

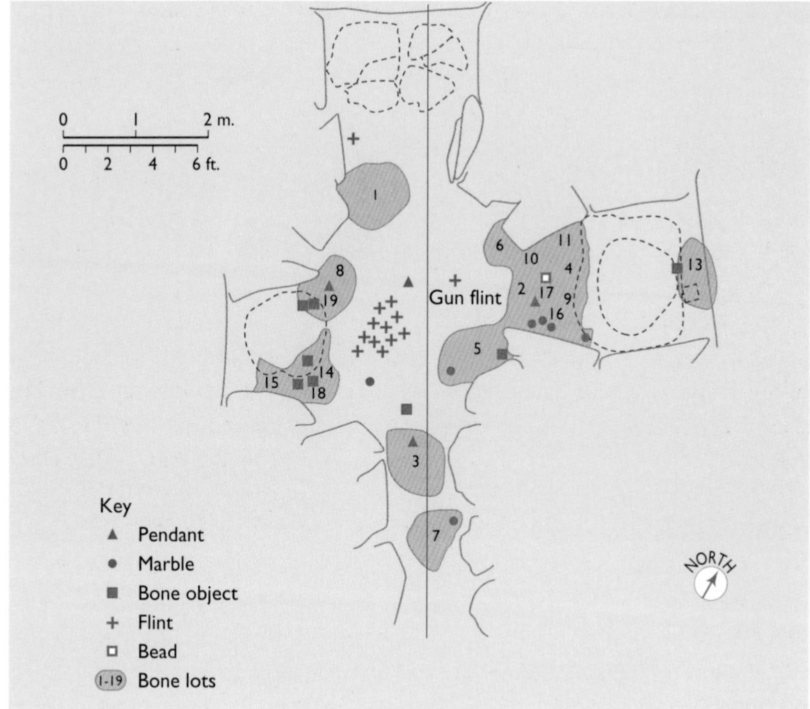

Plan of the cruciform burial chamber at Newgrange, showing the distribution of archaeological material. The shaded areas mark the position of bone material, divided by the excavator into eighteen lots (1–11 and 13–19; there was no lot 12), of which all except lots 1, 7, and 15 were human. This suggests that most of the burials had been placed in or around the large stone basins (indicated by dotted lines) in the western and eastern recesses. Other finds were scarce and consisted predominantly of simple objects such as bone pins. The gunflint is testimony to a more recent visitor.

Newgrange: pottery pendants, bone pins, and small spheres of chalk. The only really interesting object from the chamber was a stone lamp discovered in 1699. It serves to remind us that the interior of Newgrange would have been a dark and mysterious place to the people who built it, perhaps intentionally so.

Newgrange Art

Mention of light—or the lack of it—brings us naturally to the question of the art that decorates the walls of the passage and chamber. This is similar to that we have already seen on the kerbstones—shallow motifs pecked into the surface of the slabs and entirely abstract in nature.

We look at the art today with the aid of electric light, and it is important to remember that once the tomb was built it would have been almost completely dark, lit only by whatever daylight penetrated the passage or by lamps or torches that people may have carried. The flickering effect must have made the art look even more mysterious.

Sixteen of the passage orthostats carry decoration of some kind, though in some cases the designs would not have been visible once the tomb was complete. In one case, the decoration is on that part of the stone buried below the ground. There are also carvings on the passage capstones, though only on their upper surfaces, where again it would have been invisible. Quite why this is so is unclear. Maybe it was the carving of the art, rather than its display, that was considered important. Or perhaps the stones had been brought to Newgrange from another ritual monument. If that were the case, though, it is difficult to understand why some of the hidden carvings are so fresh.

Several of the chamber slabs also have pecked designs. The most splendid of all are on the underside of the roofstone in the east recess: a profusion of circles, spirals, zigzags, and lozenges. But even here, not all of them were made to be seen; they continue beyond the visible surface of the slab into the cairn around.

Parallels for the abstract art of Newgrange are known at other passage graves in Ireland, Brittany, and Iberia, and in parts of western Britain. Since very few of the motifs are representational, however, it is very difficult to say why they were carved and what they were for. One recent theory sees the art as "entoptic," the kind of abstract imagery which people experience as they enter a trance. This is an interesting idea, since it ties in with the possibility that certain people, ritual specialists perhaps, were in the habit of entering the tombs, not necessarily only for burial rites.

Whatever their specific cultural background, people entering trances tend to see a range of similar abstract shapes, such as chevrons, meanders, and spirals. These shapes are generated by the human neural system. In a recent study, Cambridge University archaeologist Jeremy Dronfield has proposed a strong statistical match between the art of Irish passage graves such as Newgrange and these neurally generated patterns. He suggests, from these results, that the Newgrange art (and that of Knowth) was inspired by the patterns that people see in trances.

One feature of these trance-states is particularly interesting. That is the common experience of traveling down a long passage, sometimes described as a spiral vortex. The prominent spirals on the entrance stone of Newgrange immediately spring to mind. Was the journey along the passage to the burial chamber at the end likened to the process of entering a trance? And was the purpose of entering a trance to make contact with the ancestors, whose bones were buried in the chamber? Or were the spirals themselves thought of as entrances to the other world?

All this is highly speculative, of course. Spirals and lozenges in themselves are pretty common elements of design, and some archaeologists find the trance-state theory far-fetched. Spirals, in particular, are found on different kinds of objects at various dates throughout the British Neolithic and Early Bronze Age. They need have no one specific meaning or connotation. But the trance-state theory is interesting, at the very least, in offering a new way of explaining both the abundance and prominence of the art in these tombs. The decorated stones would be still more striking in their original condition, picked out in paint (which they probably were, though all traces have vanished). There is no doubt they would have helped make Newgrange a still more impressive monument.

Sighting the Solstice

Another important clue to the meaning of Newgrange survives in the "roof box" built over the outer part of the passage. This came to light only gradually as archaeologists investigated the tomb and removed the overlying earth. For many years, visitors to Newgrange had noticed a slab protruding from the surface of the mound about 6 feet (2 meters) back from and 3 feet (1 meter) above the leading capstone of the passage. Those who inspected it more closely noticed that the outer edge of the stone was decorated with a frieze of crosses inscribed within a row of rectangles. It first came to light in the 1840s, when a local amateur cleared away the material that had accumulated in and around the tomb entrance. First thoughts were that the projecting stone was the lintel to a second chamber, and in 1874 an attempt was even made to dislodge it, though fortunately without success.

It was left to O'Kelly's more recent excavations to reveal the structure behind the decorated slab. When he and his team removed the surrounding earth they found what was the front of the structure we now call the "roof box," a slot built on top of the first and second capstones of the passage, sloping down toward the back. There it is aligned with the gap between the first and second capstones of the passage. The two stones are set at slightly different levels, so that this gap extends across the whole width of the passage (approximately three feet wide) and is around a 9 inches (20 centimeters) high.

Early theories were that this strange structure with its decorated outer edge and access into the passage was for placing offerings to the dead. We must remember that this would have been the only interconnecting shaft, once the outer entrance of the passage itself had been blocked. But even the "roof box" hadn't been left completely open. It had been closed by two blocks of quartz, which had left scratches on the capstone beneath. The blocks wouldn't have been difficult to move, however, and may have been placed and replaced several times throughout the year for special ceremonies. Maybe offerings were left there at these times (though if they were, they have left no recoverable trace). Or maybe the spirits of the dead were imagined to enter and leave through the roof box. This is quite possible, though of course we cannot be sure how the people who built the roof box either thought about it or used it.

The surprise came when O'Kelly discovered that the roof box was aligned on the midwinter sunrise. On 21 December 1969, the winter solstice, he waited within the chamber for the sun to rise above the eastern horizon. Fortunately it was a clear day, and at around 8:58 A.M. he saw a shaft of sunlight shine through the roof box right down the passage, flooding the floor of the burial chamber with light. There it remained for about fifteen minutes, until the southward movement of the sun extinguished the beam. It was a spectacular experience and testimony to the skill and planning of the tomb builders. To achieve this effect, they had to have taken careful sightings of the midwinter sun's rays and marked out their path on the ground. Passage and chamber must then have been built exactly on this alignment.

Direction of the sun's rays was one thing, but getting the vertical angle right was much more difficult. Newgrange is built on a gentle ridge, which means that the floor of the burial chamber is about 6 feet (2 meters) higher than the passage entrance. The roof box is almost 6 feet (2 meters) long and slopes downward toward the back. Ensuring that the sun's rays shone through the roof box to strike the chamber floor would have required great care on the part of the tomb builders. To do this they first marked the position of the passage and chamber on the hillside, in line with the winter solstice. (We have already seen how decorated stones may have been placed to mark out key positions—one of them being C8, the chamber backstone.) To determine the vertical height and the angle of slope of the roof box, they must have used wooden posts set into the ground along this line, marking on them the path of the sun's rays. Several years may have passed, surveying and refining the angles and declinations, especially when we remember that winter weather will often have obscured the sunrise altogether. It all goes to show how much care went into the planning and building of the tomb. These were no unskilled primitives, casually heaping together a mound of earth and stones, but consummate craftsmen with a precise design in mind.

The Newgrange roof box is unique. The trouble taken to get it right shows the importance placed on it. But we can only speculate on what exactly it meant. Ethnography shows us that midwinter rituals are often concerned with rebirth, with ensuring that the waning winter sun waxes strong again and brings another summer. That might have been the meaning here, too. But how did it relate to the burials in the chamber? It is tempting to speculate. Did the people who built Newgrange believe that some kind of rebirth took place when the dead were touched by the winter sun's rays? Did they patiently wait for a clear solstice, when the sky was unclouded and the sun's rays shone into the chamber, to complete the rites for the dead? Was it only then that they moved the bones—some burned, others not—from the center of the chamber to a final resting place in one of the side recesses? Archaeologists will often complain that such scenarios are entirely imaginary, with very little basis in evidence. Yet it is vital to recognize that elaborate beliefs and rituals lay behind the careful planning of many prehistoric monuments.

There are few more evocative sights than the midwinter solstice at Newgrange. Over a period of minutes, passage and chamber slowly fill with light, revealing details of design and decoration. Fortunately, visitors today don't need to wait for December to experience it, since a special system of lighting now re-creates the effect once every half hour or so during visiting hours!

The midwinter sunrise shining through the roof box and along the passage at Newgrange, as seen from within the tomb. For around fifteen minutes on this particular day, the sunlight floods the floor of the burial chamber. The alignment was evidently intentional on the part of the prehistoric builders, and may have been connected with a belief in rebirth or regeneration; the rebirth of the year at midwinter may have been a powerful metaphor for the fate of the dead.

After the Tomb

It will come as no surprise to learn that Newgrange is a complex site. The burial mound itself is only the most prominent of the archaeological features on this ridge. Another is the ring of standing stones that encircles the mound at a distance of 35 feet (10 meters) or so from the kerb. The arrangement isn't

THE BEND OF THE BOYNE

The Bend of the River Boyne encloses the greatest collection of prehistoric monuments in Ireland. Scattered along the valley floor and on the higher ground overlooking it to the north are remains of some forty burial mounds and other major constructions dating from the Neolithic period. Most famous of all are the three enormous sites of Knowth, Dowth, and Newgrange. These are circular mounds containing passage graves—one at Newgrange, but two each in the case of Dowth and Knowth. The mounds of Knowth and Newgrange are especially famous for their art—abstract designs pecked onto the stones—but are also united by a concern with solar alignment. The passage at Newgrange, facing south, is aligned on the midwinter sunrise. The two passages at Knowth face east and west, perhaps directed toward the spring and autumn equinoxes. The movements of the sun and the seasons were evidently so important to the builders of the tombs that they enshrined key alignments in their constructions.

Together, Knowth and Newgrange constitute the largest single collection of megalithic art in Europe, totaling between them well over two hundred of the three hundred–plus decorated stones from all the Boyne valley tombs. This in itself makes Knowth and Newgrange unusual. Add to that their size—both the scale of their mounds and the length of their passage graves—and we begin to appreciate their very special significance. But this is not all, for both are accompanied by smaller "satellite" passage graves. At Knowth, the principal tomb is surrounded by no fewer than seventeen smaller passage graves. In this case, the smaller tombs are grouped around the main mound, some of them almost touching its kerb. At Newgrange, three or perhaps four smaller passage graves are arranged in a linear fashion and share the same ridge, with Newgrange itself in the middle of the line.

Dowth, the third large mound of the Boyne valley group, is much less well known than the other two, and unlike them has not been excavated in recent years. Like Knowth, it is known to have two passage graves, but these

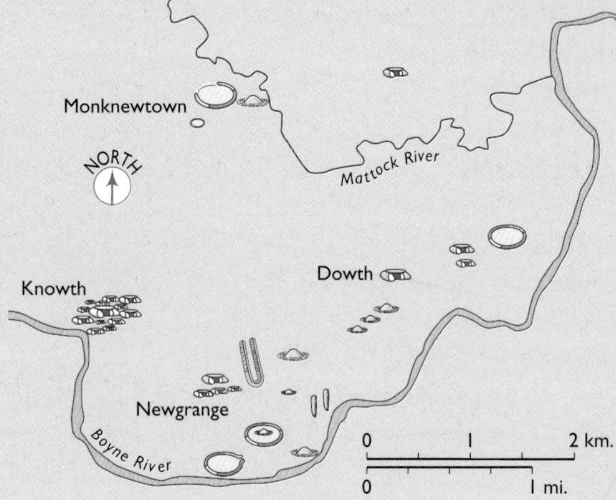

Passage graves and other prehistoric monuments in the Bend of the Boyne. The most recent discovery is the Newgrange cursus, a D-shaped enclosure a little to the east of the passage grave cemetery.

entirely circular, but neither is the mound. More significant is the fact that mound and circle have slightly different centers. They weren't laid out at the same time, but they are related. In fact the circle of stones—the so-called Great Stone Circle of Newgrange—is a key part of the later history of the monument, linked with what happened after it ceased to be used for burials.

From around 2800 B.C., new types of pottery made their appearance at Newgrange. One of these is Grooved Ware, a variety of decorated pottery also known from Britain, and especially common at ritual monuments such as henges. A couple of centuries later, a second new type of pottery appears: Beaker pottery, so-called from the characteristic shape of the vessels that are made in it. Beakers are also richly decorated with impressed and incised are much shorter in length than the passage graves of Knowth and Newgrange and open side by side from the west face of the mound. On the other hand, like Knowth and Newgrange, Dowth has many decorated stones in the passages and chambers and in the kerb that delimits the mound.

For a full appreciation of the Boyne valley tombs, however, we need not only to take account of the monuments themselves, but also to understand their setting. This means studying the changing appearance of the natural landscape, using techniques such as pollen and snail shell analysis. For the moment there is little solid evidence to go on, but we may imagine a wooded landscape at the beginning of the Neolithic, gradually cleared during the course of the fourth millennium B.C. as farming became established. The farmers lived in clusters of small houses. Remains of two separate groups of houses have been found directly on the site of the Knowth passage grave, and there were traces of a round wooden hut directly in front of the entrance to Newgrange. By 3200 B.C., when the great tombs of Knowth and Newgrange were built, the local people were pursuing a mixed economy of arable farming and livestock rearing. The only areas of forest that remained were on the valley floor and steeper slopes, the rest of the landscape having by this time been cleared and cultivated, perhaps even laid out as fields.

The passage graves weren't the only Neolithic monuments built in the Bend of the Boyne. Seven hundred years later, in the Late Neolithic, a whole new set of structures was built: circular embanked enclosures, similar to the henges of southern Britain. Four major examples are known from the Bend of the Boyne, and in contrast to the passage graves these were mainly positioned in low-lying locations. Two embanked enclosures lie near the river at the foot of the ridge below Newgrange itself (one around the small Passage Grave A). But the best known of the group is at Monknewtown, in the valley of the River Mattock to the north. Archaeologists excavating here found both Beaker and Grooved Ware pottery. Grooved Ware is also associated with henges in Britain, and its discovery here—and the form of the embanked enclosures—shows the strengths of the ideas and influences that must have been criss-crossing the Irish Sea during this period. There is even to the east of Newgrange a monument of "cursus" type, with parallel banks measuring over 330 feet (100 meters) in length. This too is a class of monument well known from southern Britain in the third millennium B.C.

By the time the embanked enclosures were built, the Boyne valley passage graves were no longer in use for burials. Ritual practices had changed, though the Boyne valley was still an important center. This came to an end around 2200 B.C., at the beginning of the Bronze Age, when the Bend in the Boyne seems finally to have lost its importance. There is no trace of Bronze Age settlement and only a handful of Bronze Age burials, almost as if the area were consciously off-limits. Yet the great mounds of Knowth, Dowth, and Newgrange didn't disappear. They remained, conspicuous yet mysterious, to become subjects of folklore and legend.

patterns, so that even small fragments can usually be identified as Beaker pottery. Yet another claim to fame is that Beakers are found throughout large areas of western Europe, as part of an international network of linkages and fashions that sprang up at this time. In many areas, Beakers also tie in with significant social changes.

For many years, archaeologists interpreted the first appearance of Beakers in Britain and Ireland as evidence of invasion—of new people arriving from the continent and driving off or enslaving the locals. But we now think of Beaker pottery, like Grooved Ware, as a fashion adopted by members of existing societies that were already abandoning some of their earlier traditions.

The advent of these new pottery styles at Newgrange is linked to several important changes. The first is the closure of the tomb, which seems to have happened at this time. It is even possible that in blocking the entrance they pulled down the quartz and granite facade whose remains we have already discussed. But this doesn't mark the end of ritual activity at Newgrange, and we may be sure that the blocked passage grave continued to exert a major fascination. In fact, a whole series of new structures were built at this time. One was a circle of pits, passing closest to the tomb just to the east of the entrance. This wasn't in fact a simple circle, like the outline of a house or a roofed building. In the first place, it was much larger, and in the second place, it was made up of roughly concentric rings of pits, four or five deep. The outer ring may indeed have held substantial timber posts (like a timber version of the Great Stone Circle), but the pits in the inner rings contained animal cremations, and the quantities of pig bone have led archaeologists to suggest that feasting took place here.

Nor was this the only new circular enclosure of this period. At about the same time, some 160 feet (50 meters) west of Newgrange, a smaller post circle was built, perhaps in this case a roofed structure. A similar building has recently been discovered at Knowth, with Grooved Ware pottery and evidence once again of feasting and rituals. And this isn't all. Two circular embankments were built on the river terrace below Newgrange, one surrounding an earlier small passage grave (Site A). On the ridge itself, a little to the east of Newgrange, a monument known as a "cursus" has been identified. This survives today only as shallow depressions marking a pair of parallel banks, around 330 feet (100 meters) long and 65 feet (20 meters) apart, linked at one end to make an elongated "U." Like the enclosures and pit circles, this "cursus" has close parallels in Late Neolithic Britain. In scale, all these monuments are dwarfed by the great passage grave, but they do demonstrate clearly how important a ritual center Newgrange remained in the centuries after the tomb itself had been blocked.

Alongside this ritual activity, the Beaker-users introduced a more domestic note at Newgrange. For they left remains of a small settlement of a dozen or so round houses arranged in a shallow arc, only 33 feet (10 meters) from the edge of the mound. The houses were 16 to 20 feet (5 to 6 meters) across, supported on timber posts set into the ground, and ran clockwise from a point just in front of the blocked entrance. When archaeologists excavated this settlement they found a range of domestic debris and tools that might have been used for metalworking.

This looks like an ordinary domestic settlement, and it could be taken to indicate a dramatic secularization of the Newgrange environs. But the people who lived in these round houses cannot have lost sight of the huge mound standing in their backyard. True, they no longer buried their dead within it, but they still may have revered it. Archaeologists think it was during the "Beaker period" at Newgrange that the Great Stone Circle was built. It was certainly in existence before the edges of the mound began to slip and spread.

Twelve stones from the circle are still visible. The circle must mean that Newgrange was still a place of special importance in the final centuries of the third millennium B.C.

Before descending the hill and leaving the site, the visitor should recall once again that Newgrange is not an isolated monument, but just one element in the Bend of the Boyne Neolithic complex. Part of the Knowth site, with its smaller satellite passage graves around a major tomb, is also open to the public, and Dowth has recently been purchased by the Irish government. A still more ambitious proposal would be a Boyne Valley archaeological park, where the whole complex, including earthwork enclosures and lesser monuments, would be accessible to visitors. As this is one of the most impressive collections of Neolithic monuments anywhere in Europe, we can only hope that the park one day becomes a reality.

Further Reading

The standard account of Newgrange was written by its excavator, Professor Michael O'Kelly—*Newgrange: Archaeology, Art and Legend* (London: Thames and Hudson, 1982). For the neighboring tomb of Knowth, see George Eogan's book in the same series, *Knowth and the Passage-Tombs of Ireland* (New York: Thames and Hudson, 1986). A concise but up-to-date account of the whole complex of monuments is provided by *Brú na Bóinne: Newgrange, Knowth, Dowth and the River Boyne* (Bray: Archaeology Ireland Ltd., 1997). Andrew Powell's study of Newgrange is published in the *Proceedings of the Prehistoric Society* 60 (1994) ("Newgrange—Science of Symbolism?" pp. 85–96). For Jeremy Dronfield's theory that the art of Newgrange is related to trance-states, see "Entering Alternative Realities: Cognition, Art and Architecture in Irish Passage-Tombs" (Cambridge Archaeological Journal 6, 1996, pp. 37–72). A general introduction to the prehistoric monuments of Ireland, with many illustrations, is provided by Peter Harbison's *Pre-Christian Ireland: From the First Settlers to the Early Celts* (New York: Thames and Hudson, 1988). For a more interpretative approach, concentrating on the social dimension, Gabriel Cooney and Eoin Grogan's *Irish Prehistory: A Social Perspective* (Dublin: Wordwell, 1994) can be warmly recommended.

Further Viewing

Interpretative reconstructions of Neolithic life and ritual can be seen in the new Brú na Bóinne Visitor Center, the starting point for a visit to Newgrange and Knowth. The finds from the Newgrange excavations are held in the National Museum of Ireland, Dublin.

CHAPTER

NINE

Stonehenge

c. 2950–1600 B.C.

The great stone circle of Salisbury Plain

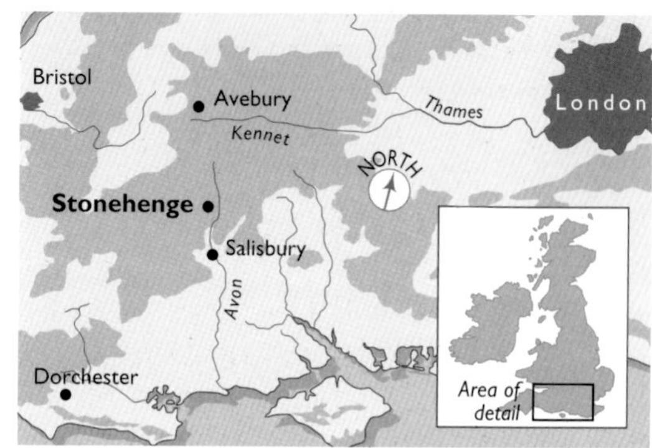

Stonehenge is without doubt the most famous prehistoric monument in Europe. The ring of stones standing on the open expanse of Salisbury Plain is an evocative image of wonder and mystery, immediately provoking the question of who built it, closely followed by how and why.

Stonehenge is both traditional and unique in British prehistory. It is traditional in that it falls within a whole class of monuments characterized by circular banks and ditches or by rings of standing stones. But it is unique in the size of the stones, the complexity of their arrangement, and the balancing of lintels on top of the uprights. Even that may be less distinctive than it first appears, for the methods used to fit the lintels to the uprights are clearly taken from carpentry, and it is likely that Stonehenge was a translation into stone of a timber circle.

The name itself is medieval in origin. The first element, "stone," is obvious enough, though the second, "henge," may derive either from Anglo-Saxon "hencg" (hinge, from the "hinging" or balancing of the lintels) or, in less savory fashion, from the Anglo-Saxon word for hanging, drawing on the resemblance between the Stonehenge trilithons and a medieval gallows. Stonehenge first appears in literature in the twelfth century, in the histories of Britain by Henry of Huntingdon and Geoffrey of Monmouth.

Henry was mystified by Stonehenge and knew neither how it had been built nor why. Geoffrey, by contrast, was less reticent and concocted or borrowed a legend attributing Stonehenge to Merlin, the famous magician in the story of King Arthur. Merlin, Geoffrey said, had used magic to transport the stones from Ireland (where giants had already set them up as a stone circle) to Salisbury Plain. As for the date of this event, he connected it with the wars between the British and the Anglo-Saxons at the time of the Anglo-Saxon invasions, that is to say, in the fifth century A.D.

Most of this is nonsense. Stonehenge is far older than the fifth century—4,500 rather than 1,500 years old, to be precise. Nor did magic play any part in its construction, though experts continue to debate the exact techniques that must have been used to raise the massive stones into position. Where there may be a hint of the truth in Geoffrey's account is in the idea that the stones were brought to Salisbury Plain from Ireland, where they were dismantled from an earlier stone circle. Intriguingly, modern analysis shows that some of the smaller stones at Stonehenge, the so-called bluestones, did come from the far west—though from Wales rather than Ireland. It is not impossible that they had originally been set up as a stone circle in south Wales, close to their source, and brought to Salisbury Plain at a later date. The builders of Stonehenge may have thought they were increasing the sanctity of their monument by reerecting within it a stone circle of especial sacredness which they had transported over a distance of more than 125 miles (200 kilometers).

Stonehenge as we see it today is sadly ruined. Many of the uprights have fallen and only a small section of the outer ring still retains its lintels. Yet it continues to impress. Artists of the eighteenth and nineteenth centuries painted Stonehenge under moody or stormy skies. Today, most archaeologists follow a more dispassionate approach, seeking to understand Stonehenge for what it was and is, but even they cannot ignore its emotional impact. And that is as it should be. Stonehenge was not built to be measured and analyzed, but to be appreciated, to form a dramatic setting for ceremonies and rituals, and to inspire feelings of awe.

The Stonehenge Sequence

Stonehenge is really not a single monument, but a whole series of monuments built on the same site, each incorporating the remains of its predecessors. In years, the entire sequence spans over a millennium. Those who made the final additions to Stonehenge were more distant in time from the first builders than we are from the soldiers who fought at the Battle of Hastings or the scribes who compiled the Domesday Book. Each generation came to view Stonehenge afresh in the light of a tradition and meaning that must have constantly changed, no less than the monument itself changed as new features were added and old ones rearranged. The Stonehenge we see today is hence not the result of a single unified plan, pursued doggedly from century to century.

Instead, it is a kind of palimpsest, a document on which earlier writings have been partially erased to make way for new ones. It is only by studying the partial erasures that archaeologists can learn how Stonehenge first came into existence, and what it looked like at each stage.

Much of the evidence comes from excavations. Not surprisingly, Stonehenge has been excavated on several occasions over the course of the last hundred years, but these have only recently been published. The most famous excavations were those by Colonel William Hawley, who between 1919 and 1926 stripped more than half the site, and the follow-up work (on a more cautious scale) by Richard Atkinson, Stuart Piggott, and John Stone in the 1950s. One of the trio, Richard Atkinson, published a short, popular account of Stonehenge that proposed a three-phase model of development, beginning with the ditch and bank and ending with the central stone settings and the avenue. Unfortunately, Atkinson died before he could complete a full account of the excavations. Over the past few years, however, a team of archaeologists has carried out a reanalysis of all the unpublished records and finds surviving from the explorations that have been carried out at Stonehenge during the twentieth century. Coupled with the rigorous application of radiocarbon dating, the recent study has given us a new and much sounder knowledge of the Stonehenge sequence.

The Stonehenge sequence as now understood begins way back in the ninth or eighth millennium B.C., in the Mesolithic period, long before the introduction of farming. In 1966, an exploratory excavation was made in advance of laying out part of the present parking lot. A line of three post-holes was discovered, which had once held massive upright timber posts, from 2.5 to 3 feet (0.8 to 1 meter) across. They were aligned on a possible tree hole. In 1988, a fourth post-hole was found a little further away. Settings of post-holes were already known from within the Stonehenge enclosure, and these new holes caused no great surprise until they were radiocarbon-dated to the ninth or eighth millennium B.C.

This, then, is a "pre-Stonehenge" phase. The Mesolithic posts are unlikely to have had any connection with the first phase of Stonehenge proper, which followed around five thousand years later. They must by then have long since decayed away. But the size of the posts suggests they were something special —not simply a hut or fence-line. Furthermore, the snail shells recovered from the post-holes were those of open-country species. Specialists have shown from other evidence that Salisbury Plain was covered by open woodland at this period, so the snail shells must mean that the area immediately around the post-holes had been intentionally cleared. It is tempting to think in terms of timber totem poles, with the tree as the focal point, though nothing like this has been found anywhere else in Britain at this early date. It certainly looks as though Stonehenge was a special location—and perhaps a special ritual location—long before the monument that we see today was built.

The Monument Develops

The sequence of Stonehenge proper began around 2950 B.C. with the digging of the bank and ditch. The ditch was cut into the chalk with the aid of antler picks, some of which were left lying in it. The material dug out was piled on both sides of the ditch, though mainly on the inner side, to create a bank. There were no stones in this stage of Stonehenge, just the circular enclosure limited by its bank and ditch, with breaks in the northeast for the main entrance (36 feet [11 meters] wide) and in the south for a secondary entrance around 10 feet (3 meters) wide. The northeast entrance retained its importance throughout the later history of Stonehenge.

The first phase of Stonehenge was completed by erecting a ring of substantial timber posts in holes cut into the tail of the chalk bank. There were fifty-six of these, and they are known as the "Aubrey Holes" after John Aubrey, the seventeenth-century antiquarian who first detected them as depressions in the grassy surface. But whatever their purpose, these timber posts weren't simply left to decay; they were intentionally removed. At the same time, parts of the ditch were filled in. It looks almost as if Stonehenge 1 were being dismantled or condemned.

There was no long period of neglect, however, for soon afterward a new series of post settings were set up, this time in the center of the site and in the northeastern entrance. We can't say exactly how these were arranged, since the center of Stonehenge has been so badly turned over by the erection of the sarsen uprights, and by repeated diggings since at least the seventeenth century. Nor do we know their exact date, though they fall broadly within the period 2900–2400 B.C. This is Stonehenge Phase 2, and once again no stones were involved, only timber structures. Whether these were simple uprights, decorated posts, or linteled structures like the later Stonehenge (or even roofed buildings) we shall probably never know.

There is little obvious trace today of Stonehenge 2. Stonehenge 3, by contrast, is the series of stone settings with which we are all familiar. It isn't just a single phase, but a sequence of modifications itself extending over almost a thousand years. In fact, such are the vagaries of archaeological dating that it overlaps with Phase 2 by a century and a half: Phase 2—the last of the timber settings—may run as late as 2400 B.C.; while the dating evidence suggests that the start of Phase 3 should be placed around 2550 B.C.

Stonehenge 3 began with the arrival of the bluestones from south Wales. These now stand among the massive sarsens, but that isn't the position in which they were originally set up. We know this because archaeologists have discovered two sets of holes, the so-called Q and R holes, which were dug to take them. These stone-holes show that the bluestones were originally erected as a pair of curving arcs, a bow-fronted arrangement facing northeastward toward the main entrance.

The famous Heelstone, just outside the main entrance, was set up at the same time. Another stone-hole exists below the turf just to the north of the Heelstone; so the Heelstone may not have been alone, but one of a pair with a narrow gap between them. Four more stones were erected just within the earlier bank and ditch of Stonehenge 1, the so-called Station stones.

Stonehenge stayed like this—a central setting of bluestones with larger stones around the inner edge of the ditch and in front of the entrance—for only a short time. It was then that the massive aggrandizement of Stonehenge took place. The bluestones are around 7 or 8 feet (2 meters) in height; substantial blocks of stone, but not enormous in size. After a relatively short interval the builders of Stonehenge decided to dismantle and remove them to make way for an entirely new structure, using sarsen stones of an altogether different scale.

Hence, the Stonehenge sarsens belong to a second stage of Phase 3, after the initial bluestone setting had been removed, not long, perhaps, after 2500 B.C. It was a huge undertaking. The largest of the sarsens is 30 feet (9 meters) long (8 feet of it buried below the ground), over four times as long as the average bluestone and ten times as heavy. Dragged all the way from the Marlborough Downs and weighing up to 45 tons (c. 40 metric tons), these were erected in the form of a continuous circle framing an oval setting of five massive trilithons, the most massive of all being the central trilithon facing toward the main entrance. When this was complete, and perhaps as an afterthought, the much smaller bluestones were brought back into the center of the site and erected as a circle within the sarsen circle, and as an oval (later a horseshoe) within the trilithon setting. Dwarfed by the sarsens, they added

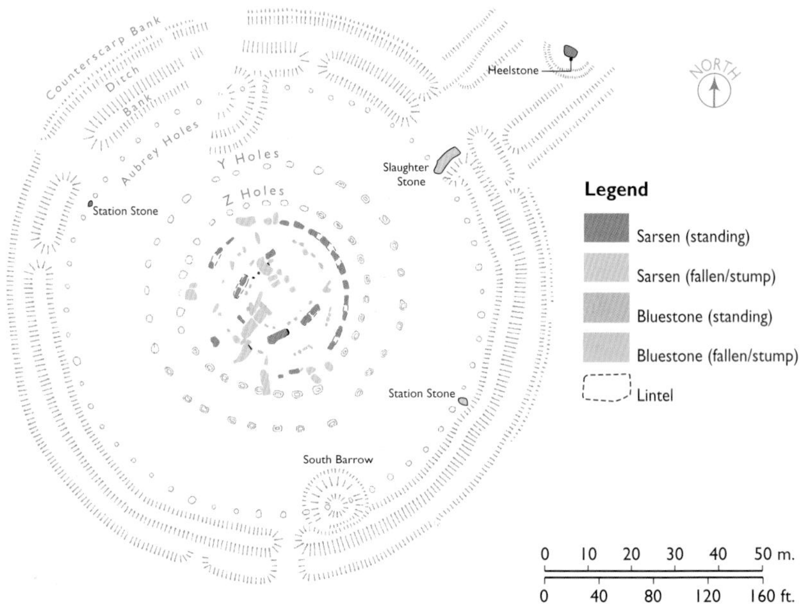

Plan of Stonehenge showing the principal features of the monument.

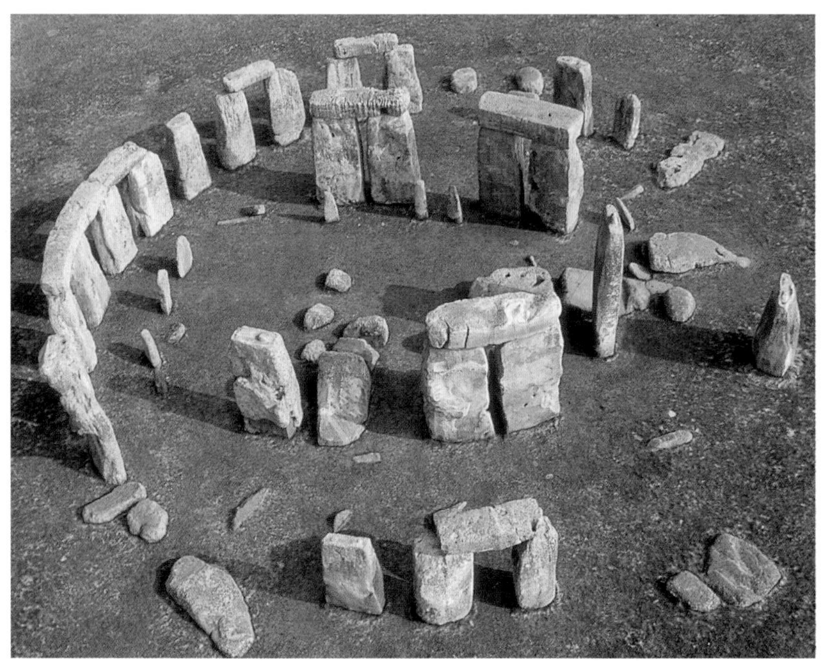

Center of Stonehenge from the air, showing the five massive trilithons (three of them standing complete with lintels), the incomplete outer circle of uprights and lintels, and between them the settings of smaller stones, the so-called bluestones. Note how the lintels of the outer circle are curved and jointed together with a rounded projecting tongue at the end of one lintel, engaging in a carefully shaped groove in the end of its neighbor.

little to the overall impact of Stonehenge 3, but we may guess they were too sacred to be disposed of.

A Tour of Stonehenge

With certain later additions and alterations, and a great deal of decay and demolition, this is the Stonehenge that greets the visitor today: a monument built and remodeled over 1,500 years. There was no single, predetermined design, but a series of ad hoc embellishments as new generations modified Stonehenge for their own purposes. The ceremonies and rituals probably changed, too. Stonehenge when first built may have had a very different meaning and use from Stonehenge of the sarsen circle.

A visit to Stonehenge naturally begins in the parking lot. This is the place where the line of post-holes was found, dating back 10,000 years. It is hard to imagine the scene as it must have been then, a clearing in woodland with tall timber posts, perhaps carved and colored into mythical beasts or fantastic shapes.

From the parking lot, a modern underpass takes the visitor beneath the road to the circle itself. But this is some distance from the original, Neolithic approach. To appreciate that, you have to make your way 160 feet (50 meters) along the roadside verge, to the place where a large leaning stone stands just within the perimeter fence. This is the famous "Heelstone," so-called from the legend that it bears the heelprint of a medieval friar at whom the Devil threw the stone. Here we are facing the main entrance to Stonehenge—the

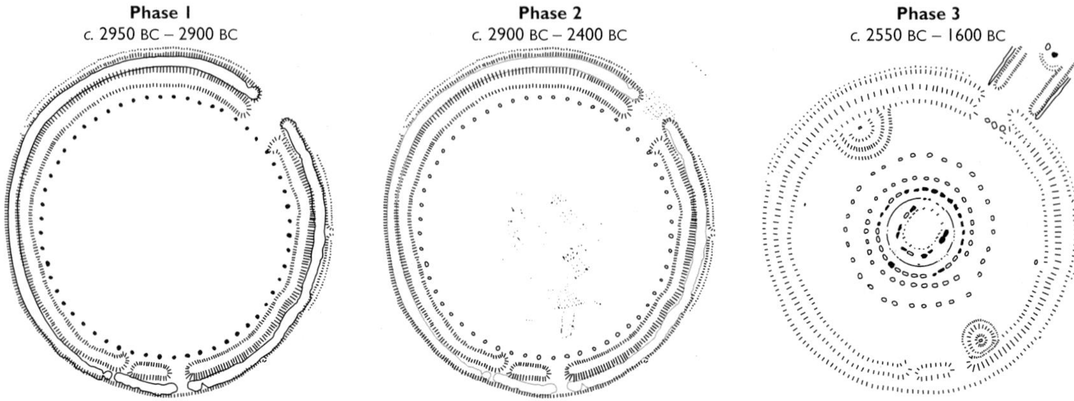

The three principal phases of Stonehenge, showing its transition from a simple bank and ditch backed by a line of postholes (the Aubrey Holes) in Phase 1; to a series of timber settings in Phase 2; and finally to the complex structures of Phase 3, when bluestones and sarsens were transported to the site and an embanked avenue leading up to the main entrance was added.

causeway across the early bank and ditch, with the tallest of the trilithons beyond. The Heelstone does indeed stand very near the main axis of the monument. And there is more to this than simple geometry. For at sunrise on midsummer's day, a person standing at the very center of Stonehenge sees the sun rising almost exactly over the Heelstone.

What the visitor doesn't see today is the large stone-hole found in 1979 just to the north of the Heelstone. Archaeologists think that this may once have held a similar stone, twin to the Heelstone. In fact, going back to the midsummer sunrise, the sun rises not directly over the Heelstone but slightly to its left. If the Heelstone's twin were still standing, then midsummer sunrise would be framed exactly between them.

Before leaving the Heelstone there is one more point to observe. To the right and left of the stone can be seen eroded linear banks, heading straight for the main entrance of Stonehenge. Turning now through 180°, we can see that these banks continue as a faint trace on the other side of the road, disappearing down the hill in a straight line. This is the Stonehenge avenue, a ceremonial approach flanked by banks and ditches about 40 feet (12 meters) apart, constructed during the third phase of the monument. It continues for almost a third of a mile (half a kilometer) in this direction, then makes a sharp turn to the right, runs straight for another half mile, before gently curving southeastward downhill toward the River Avon. We don't know what lay at the end of the avenue. There may have been another ritual site or perhaps a settlement. But we may imagine processions approaching Stonehenge along it, especially in the last straight section, mounting the gentle rise with the Heelstone and its twin directly ahead and Stonehenge itself on the slightly higher ground beyond. This is the way the builders of Stonehenge 3 designed their monument to be seen.

A Circuit of Stonehenge

The present arrangements lead the visitor into Stonehenge from the north. The path crosses the shallow scoop of the ditch and the low eroded chalk bank

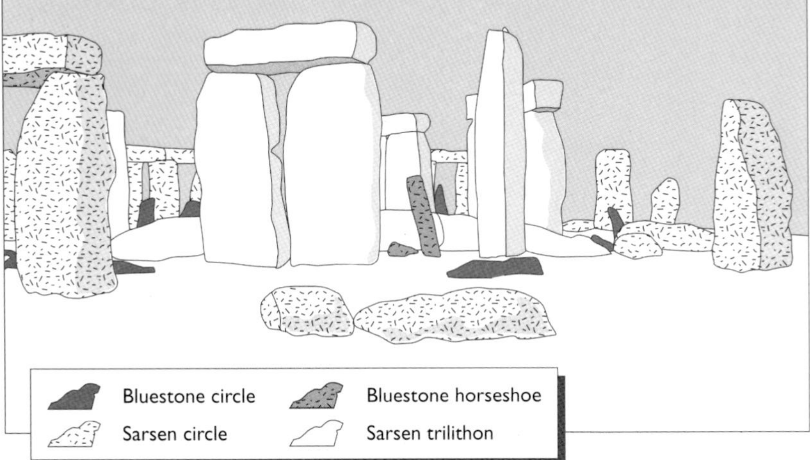

The central settings at Stonehenge viewed from the northwest. This view illustrates the ruined nature of the monument as it survives today. The number of recumbent or half-buried stones is particularly evident. The diagram identifies the different elements of the structure; the central horseshoe of five sarsen trilithons (three of them standing, the two others with one fallen and one upright); the sarsen circle, originally a continuous ring of uprights with lintels (though only seventeen of the thirty uprights are standing today, and only six of the lintels are in position); and the circle and horseshoe of bluestones, which echo the sarsen settings.

into the enclosure itself. There on the left is the core of the monument, at this distance a jumble of standing and fallen stones. As we walk around the circuit (for visitors are no longer allowed among the stones themselves) we begin to distinguish the various elements: the outer ring of sarsens, still standing on the northeast side, though only six of the original thirty lintels remain in place; the tall trilithons within the circle, three of the five still standing today; and between and among the sarsens, the much smaller bluestones. But it is the sarsens that are the dominant element.

As we look at the sarsens one of the most striking features is their shaping. In glancing sunlight many of the stones show distinct facets, traces of the pounding and grinding that must have gone on to turn rough blocks of stone to the right size and shape to fit the overall design of Stonehenge. For though the stones are rough and eroded, they are no misshapen boulders, but have been carefully tooled. It is hard to imagine how much time and effort went into their working, since the builders had no access to metal tools. But some evidence of the working survives. Every excavator of Stonehenge has encountered "the Stonehenge layer," a mass of stone chippings (mixed now with modern rubbish) showing that the shaping was done on site. There was a mea-

STONEHENGE AND THE DRUIDS

The connection of Stonehenge with the Druids lives strongly in the popular imagination, but in fact it dates back no further than the seventeenth century. The man responsible for this unfortunate link was antiquarian John Aubrey (1626–1697), but it was taken up with greatest vigor by William Stukeley (1687–1765). Stukeley saw Stonehenge as a Druidical temple, and despite the falsity and folly of the connection, his theory is one that has stuck. We know very little about the Druids, only what we are told by Classical writers such as Tacitus and Julius Caesar. They were the native priests of Gaul and Britain at the time the Romans conquered these territories in the first century B.C./A.D. But Stonehenge was by this date already 2,500 years old and had long been disused as a ritual center. There is not the slightest evidence to connect it with the historical Druids. Nor is there evidence that human sacrifice (a Druidical practice described in the Classical sources) was ever practiced at Stonehenge—a disappointment, alas, to those of a romantic disposition.

The only real connection between Stonehenge and the Druids is a modern one, and involves not the sinister priesthood of Caesar and Tacitus but the more genteel "Ancient Order of Druids," which was founded in 1781, and the still more recent "Church of the Universal Bond." It is the latter who have sought to celebrate the summer solstice each year at Stonehenge, at least since the early years of the present century. They dress in white robes for their ceremonies and have their own chants and rituals. Naturally, they are free to believe what they will about the stones, but they have no connection with the prehistoric communities who built Stonehenge.

sure of subtlety, too, in the design: note for instance how the uprights decrease in thickness toward the top. This is an intentional feature, known also to Classical Greek architects as "entasis." The Greeks discovered (presumably by trial and error) that a parallel-sided column appears to be leaning forward when looked at from below; entasis was used to remove this optical illusion. The builders of Stonehenge, two thousand years before, employed it no doubt for the same reason. The degree of curvature suggests they intended the stones to be seen from close up; we must imagine Stonehenge as a monument to be looked at from within, not only admired from afar.

Other features of Stonehenge may not be obvious at this distance. One such is the mortice and tenon system fitting the lintels on the uprights. Each upright had a pair of bosses or tenons projecting on its upper surface, which fit into a hollow or mortice cut into the underside at each end of each lintel. Furthermore, the ends of the lintels were alternately tongued and grooved, such that the tongue on one end of one lintel fit into the groove on the end of its neighbor. These devices helped to hold Stonehenge together. They are even more significant, however, in being derived from carpentry. They show us that Stonehenge is a version in stone of something that was usually built in timber. The circles of post-holes found at other henges—such as the nearby Woodhenge—may well have been the settings for smaller Stonehenges in timber.

One final detail that deserves mention is the axe and dagger carvings on some of the Stonehenge uprights. They can only be seen close-up and under special lighting conditions. Indeed, they weren't known about until the first of them was discovered by chance in 1953. Eight of the stones have shallow carvings of this type, most of them of flat axes of the Early Bronze Age

(c. 2200–1500 B.C.), though one shows a dagger. Since the sarsens themselves were erected around 2500 B.C. (or a little later), these carvings must have been added at a later date.

The path leads the visitor across the bank and ditch once again and around the edge of the enclosure. It passes by the four Station stones, which may have marked astronomical alignments, and leads us back toward the Heelstone. The main entrance to the Stonehenge enclosure can be seen from here, with the fallen stone, known as the "Slaughter Stone," lying prone within it. Romantics of the eighteenth and nineteenth centuries saw this as the stone on which the Druids sacrificed their hapless victims and imagined blood flowing into its many hollows. We know today that it was one of three stones erected across the causeway of Stonehenge in the third phase, to provide a fittingly monumental barrier at the main entrance to this imposing structure. It made clear that here, at the head of the avenue, you were entering the sacred place itself.

Building Stonehenge

This brief account of Stonehenge has so far concentrated on questions of what it is and when it was built. But it would be incomplete without some discussion of how it was built and why. And something must also be said of the well-known astronomical theories. Any explanation of how Stonehenge was

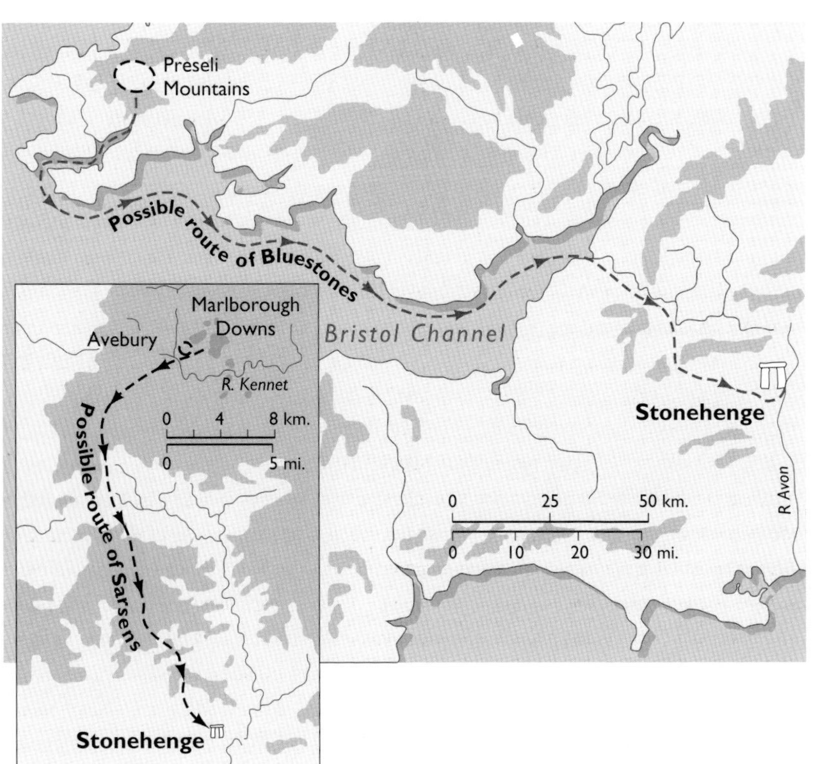

The probable routes by which the sarsens and bluestones were brought to Stonehenge. Note the importance of water transport in the case of the bluestones. The greatest difficulty came in moving the stones over land, especially where steep slopes or rough country was encountered. The sarsens would have posed particular problems, weighing up to 45 tons apiece. The route suggested here is much longer than the direct route but would have avoided the steepest gradients. Transport may have involved a sledge and rollers, perhaps even a purpose-built timber trackway, but the pulling power was provided by humans.

built divides naturally into two parts: first, how were the stones brought to the site and from where? And second, how were they erected?

The stones used at Stonehenge fall (as we have seen) into two groups: the large sarsens and the smaller bluestones. The name "sarsen" is given to a kind of sandstone that formed on the chalky bed of the sea that covered this region of southern England 70 million years ago. It is amazingly tough, which means it has withstood the ravages of time and tempest, but must have been extremely difficult for the Neolithic builders of Stonehenge (and Avebury) to work. Sarsen blocks occur in natural scatters on the chalk downs, such as the Marlborough Downs 18 miles (30 kilometers) north of Stonehenge. Each of the massive sarsens must have been dragged that distance, probably on a timber sledge, crossing the Vale of Pewsey only by an incredible effort of will and muscle power.

The bluestones are more of an enigma. They are much smaller than the sarsens and would have been easier to transport, but they come from much further away—from the Preseli Mountains of southwest Wales, about 130 miles (210 kilometers) distant. Why on earth were they brought all that way? There is nothing particularly special about their appearance. They are in fact not a single kind of stone but a mixed bag of rhyolite, spotted dolerite, volcanic ash, and sandstone. They aren't especially striking in appearance; the description "blue" scarcely applies, nor are they particularly fine-grained or easily worked.

It was in 1923 that the Welsh origin of the bluestones was first established. How they got to Stonehenge is altogether more problematic. If they were brought by human action then we need to explain why. But is there any alternative? Some geologists have put forward the theory that glaciers brought the bluestones to Salisbury Plain, but glaciologists have dismissed this as impossible. It seems, then, that for some compelling reason, the builders of Stonehenge brought the bluestones, mainly by sea and river transport, all the way from south Wales. And the most persuasive explanation for this behavior is that there was something especially sacred about the bluestones. Maybe they were already standing as a circle in south Wales, which the builders of Stonehenge simply demolished and transferred to Salisbury Plain? The suggestion (if true) is very close to Geoffrey of Monmouth's story of Merlin bringing the "Giant's Round" by magic from Ireland.

There are almost as many theories about how Stonehenge was built as there are stones at the site. Early writers invoked the power of magic; the feat seemed too incredible to explain in any other way. Yet somehow the massive 45-ton (40–metric ton) sarsens were raised into position, and the huge lintels placed across them. This can only have been done using ramps and rollers, but the weight of the largest stones must have made it difficult to avoid crushing and collapsing any of the timber or earthen supports. What is clear is the accuracy and expertise of the builders. The holes for the stones were dug to precise measurements for the lower ends of the uprights, each one tailor-

The midsummer sunrise axis of Stonehenge, looking from above the center of the monument out toward the avenue. On the edge of the modern road can be seen the Heelstone, originally one of a pair of standing stones framing the entrance to Stonehenge. To its right (and more faintly to its left) can be seen the slight depression marking the position of the ditches of the avenue, which continues in a straight line away from Stonehenge, downhill into Stonehenge Bottom, where it turns sharply right and begins heading for the River Avon. In line with the Heelstone and just within the Stonehenge ditch can be seen the fallen Slaughter Stone, one of an original three stones that stood here to mark the inner entrance to Stonehenge, on the inside edge of the ditch. To the right of the Slaughter Stone a row of concrete markers indicates the position of the Aubrey Holes.

made for a snug fit. Extreme caution and control must have been exercised as the stones were lowered into their holes, so that they didn't slip or topple under their own weight. The positioning of the uprights had to be exact if the lintels were to fit properly. The lintels themselves must have been raised either on a timber crib or scaffold, or on an earthen ramp. In the absence of either cranes or pulleys, it was an amazing and highly skilled undertaking. The whole monument must have resembled a building site while work was in progress, the bluestones stacked carefully to one side awaiting their eventual reerection, and much of the central area perhaps engulfed in massive earthen and timber ramps.

Rites and Rituals

When at last it was complete, for what was Stonehenge used? This is a key question that, alas, we still cannot answer. We know that during Phase 2, cremation burials were deposited at Stonehenge. But there is nothing to show that these are the bones of sacrificed individuals. There is simply no evidence for human sacrifice at Stonehenge, despite popular imaginings.

In its final phase, if not before, Stonehenge became linked with the sun. A careful sighting line was set up by the builders, passing between two of the three stones in the entrance to the enclosure, then out between the Heelstone and its partner in the avenue beyond. Previously, the main axis of the monument had been aligned slightly to the north of the most northerly sunrise (the summer solstice), but by this modest shift of axis Stonehenge 3 was brought

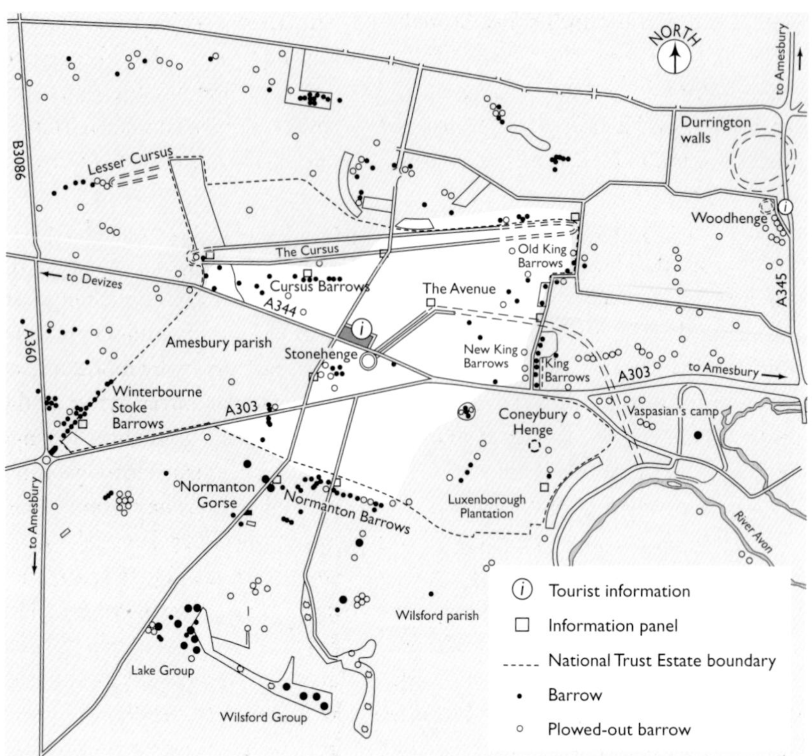

(right) Stonehenge in its prehistoric landscape. Note the avenue leading down to the River Avon and the cemeteries of Bronze Age burial mounds laid out on the skyline to south, north, and east of Stonehenge (the pale area shows the limit of visibility from Stonehenge). The Cursus and Lesser Cursus are probably contemporary with the first phase of Stonehenge, and Durrington Walls and Woodhenge with the second or early part of the third phase (c. 2800–2200 B.C.). Excavations at Woodhenge in the 1920s revealed a pattern of concentric timber post circles within an enclosing bank and ditch. Some have interpreted this as remains of a roofed building, but it may have prefigured (on a smaller scale and in timber) the sarsen settings of Stonehenge 3, which incorporate a number of carpentry features such as mortise and tenon joints.

directly into line. So it was that each year at dawn on midsummer day, a person standing at the center of Stonehenge could have looked along this line, between the stones, and witnessed the sunrise that marked the middle of the year (always assuming, of course, that there were no clouds). Such sightings must have had significance for the builders of Stonehenge, but they can hardly have been the main reason for its construction, nor could they explain why it took the form it did. Other theories—that stones of Stonehenge were also aligned with lunar or stellar events, or could be used to predict eclipses—are intriguing but simply don't stand up to careful scrutiny.

Stonehenge in the Bronze Age

Stonehenge does not stand in splendid isolation. Looking out from the circle, the eye catches the telltale humps of clusters of burial mounds, especially to the east, on King's Barrow Ridge, and to the south on Normanton Down. These are only the most obvious of a whole series of Early Bronze Age burial mounds, which make the area around Stonehenge an enormous funerary focus.

Until recently, archaeologists believed that the sarsen structures at Stonehenge themselves belonged to the Early Bronze Age. The new dating, however, shows that the stone settings are a Late Neolithic phenomenon. But that does not mean that Stonehenge was abandoned in the Bronze Age. Far from it. As the burial mounds show, Stonehenge remained a major ritual focus, a place near which people chose to be buried throughout much of the second millennium B.C. There were even modifications to the monument itself—the enigmatic Y and Z holes, a double ring of stone-holes outside the sarsen circle, possibly intended for a new setting of bluestones, but one that was never completed.

In the Early Bronze Age, then, Stonehenge stood within a landscape of burial mounds. The most famous of all is the Bush Barrow, one of the group standing on Normanton Down, which can be seen from Stonehenge. In 1808, a local antiquary, William Cunnington, excavated this prominent mound using local workmen. The excavation was careless and cursory by modern standards, but Cunnington was rewarded by a spectacular burial lying at the center of the barrow. On the chest of the skeleton was a gold-sheet lozenge bearing a decoration of engraved lines. Nearby was a smaller lozenge and a belt hook cover of gold. To one side of the body lay a polished stone macehead, its wooden shaft ornamented with bone fittings. Cunnington's workmen also discovered thousands of tiny gold nails, so small, indeed, that they threw many of them away before they realized what they were—intricate decorations from the wooden hilt of a bronze dagger.

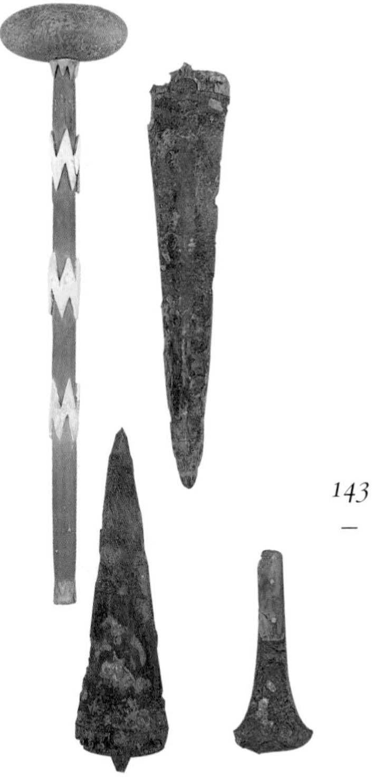

(above, and facing page) Objects excavated by William Cunnington in 1808 from the Bush Barrow, one of a group of Bronze Age burial mounds visible on the skyline south of Stonehenge. The importance of the individual buried here is illustrated by the rich trappings interred with the deceased: three bronze daggers; a stone macehead with a bronze fitting and zigzag bone handle mounts (the wooden shaft is modern); and a gold lozenge-shaped chest ornament, a second smaller gold lozenge, and a gold belt-hook cover. Dating to around 2000 B.C., the richness of this grave assemblage shows that Stonehenge remained a place of great importance in the Early Bronze Age, since powerful individuals were still choosing to be buried near it.

The individual laid to rest under Bush Barrow was evidently someone of special importance. His richly furnished grave illustrates the allure of being buried near to Stonehenge in the Early Bronze Age. As we have seen, it is only one of many Bronze Age burial mounds in the Stonehenge area, some of them visible from Stonehenge itself.

Among the most accessible of these burial mounds for the modern visitor are those at Winterbourne Stoke crossroads, a mile and a half (two and a half kilometers) west of Stonehenge. The apex of this cemetery of mounds is a Neolithic long barrow tucked into the corner of the field nearest the modern road junction. It dates from around 3500 B.C., but the other mounds in this cemetery were built during the course of the Early Bronze Age, between 2200 and 1500 B.C. They have an obvious common feature: they are circular in plan. In other respects, however, they show considerable variety in their construction. Alongside "ordinary" round barrows—inverted bowl-shaped structures with surrounding ditches— are small barrows standing at the center of a large circular ditch (known as "disk barrows"), and two barrows that aren't mounds at all, but hollows surrounded by circular banks (known as "pond barrows").

By the time the last barrows were built, the landscape around Stonehenge had undergone a significant transformation. During the early third millennium, the period of Stonehenge 1 and 2, the monument stood within open grassland, not unlike today. From the Stonehenge 3 period down to the end of the Early Bronze Age (c. 1500 B.C.), cultivation began to encroach on the grassland, and for the first time small farmsteads may have appeared within the purview of the circle. Thus the ritual monument found itself increasingly close to secular concerns. Yet the process didn't continue. There is no evidence

The Winterbourne Stoke barrow cemetery, 1.2 miles (2 kilometers) west of Stonehenge. The earliest element is a Neolithic long barrow (to the north of the triangular woodland). In the Early Bronze Age this became the focus of a cemetery of round barrows, several laid out in line with the main axis of the Neolithic long mound, others in a less regular line alongside it. The barrows themselves fall into a number of distinct types, including "bell" barrows, where a space or berm is left between the barrow and its encircling ditch; "disk" barrows, where the mound is reduced to a modest protuberance in the center of the ditched circle; and "pond" barrows where there is no mound at all, but instead a shallow pond-like scoop within a circular bank. The Winterbourne Stoke cemetery is another example of the ritual importance of the Stonehenge area in the Early Bronze Age.

that Stonehenge was still in active use after 1000 B.C., but the field systems were abandoned at the same time. Stonehenge was left in solitary splendor, a half-forgotten monument to a bygone age. Today, in the late twentieth century, as archaeologists apply new techniques and gather new information, we are beginning to understand it better and better. Yet it would be a sad day—and one happily still far distant—were Stonehenge ever to lose its mystique.

Further Reading

As may be expected, Stonehenge is well served in both the popular and professional literature. The now-classic older acount is *Stonehenge* by Richard Atkinson (Harmondsworth: Penguin, 1979). It can be supplemented by Aubrey Burl's *The Stonehenge People* (London: Dent, 1987) and Julian Richards's *Stonehenge* (London: Batsford, 1991). For the colorful history of the site, from antiquarians to the twentieth century, see Christopher Chippindale, *Stonehenge Complete,* 2nd ed. (New York: Thames and Hudson, 1994). None of these books takes account of the recent reassessment of the dates and phases of Stonehenge. For that, the reader must consult the detailed specialist report, *Stonehenge in Its Landscape* by Rosamund Cleal, Karen Walker, and Rebecca Montague (London: English Heritage, 1995), or "The Structural History of Stonehenge," by Andrew J. Lawson in *Science and Stonehenge*, edited by Barry Cunliffe and Colin Renfrew (Oxford: Oxford University Press for the British Academy, 1997, pp. 15–37).

Further Viewing

Material from excavations at Stonehenge is displayed in the Salisbury and South Wiltshire Museum, which is in King's House in the cathedral close at Salisbury. Important collections from neighboring sites, including impressive gold ornaments from the Bush Barrow, can also be seen in the museum of the Wiltshire Archaeological and Natural History Society at Devizes.

CHAPTER

TEN

Valcamonica

c. 8000–16 B.C.

Prehistoric rock art in northern Italy

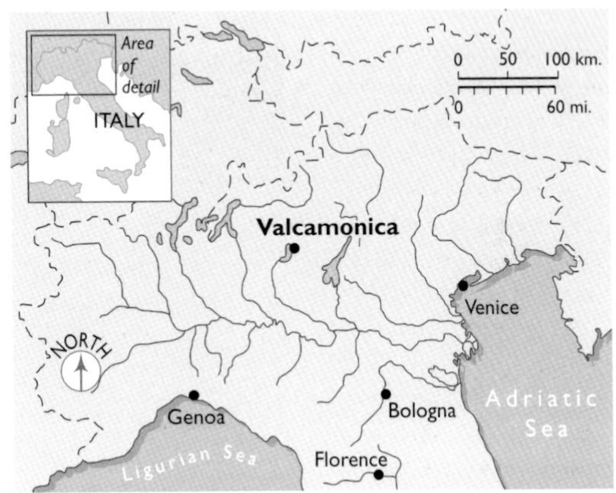

The Valcamonica, a picturesque north Italian valley, has the largest collection of prehistoric rock art in Europe. As many as 300,000 carved figures have been found here, dating from just after the last Ice Age to the High Middle Ages. It is a remarkable concentration of carvings, especially notable for its relatively remote location. For the visitor, it has the additional attraction of its mountainous setting in the heart of the north Italian lakes.

The Italian lakes have been a popular tourist destination since the nineteenth century. They were painted and visited as part of the "Grand Tour of Europe" by wealthy British and Americans. The Valcamonica (Camonica valley) lies rather outside the most popular areas, which are centered on Lakes Como and Garda. It lies, in fact, roughly halfway between them. Alpine glaciers plowed their way through this terrain some tens of thousands of years ago. When they retreated, they left a curving valley, flanked by mountains to either side and drained by the River Oglio. The Oglio eventually makes its way into the Chiese and thence into the Po, a short distance upstream of Mantua. There comes a point, however, where its southward course is hindered by a barrier of moraine (clay and stones dropped by the melting glacier), and the river expands to form Lake Iseo, 15 miles (24 kilometers) long and less than 3 miles (5 kilometers) wide.

General view across the Camonica valley.

Road and railway coming north from Brescia head direct for the town of Iseo, a small holiday resort on the lake's southeastern shore. They avoid the marshy land at the southern end of the lake, where remains of prehistoric timber pile dwellings have been found. They follow the steep eastern side of the lake as they travel north, passing through tunnels before debouching into the beautiful Valcamonica itself.

The valley takes its name from the Camuni, a native people whom the Romans encountered as they extended their control over the Alpine region. The area was officially absorbed into the empire in 16 B.C., long after the lowlands to the south. The Roman historian Cassius Dio, writing over two hundred years after the event, gives us the laconic notice, "The Camuni and Vennii, Alpine tribes, took up arms against the Romans, but were conquered and subdued by Publius Silius." It must have been a very uneven contest, the might of Rome pitted against a small valley community. The Camuni dutifully took their place ten years later on the victory monument erected near Monaco to commemorate the Alpine conquests of Augustus; they come second in a list of forty-five conquered Alpine tribes.

By the time the Romans subjugated the Camuni they were masters of the Mediterranean, from the Euphrates River to the Atlantic coasts of Spain and Portugal. It may at first seem surprising that a people who had conquered such mighty overseas powers as Egypt and Syria hadn't dealt with such near-neighbors as the Camuni rather sooner. The reason lies in the remoteness of the Valcamonica. From the south, the traveler has to negotiate the steep cliff-

VALCAMONICA AND THE ICEMAN

The prehistory of the Italian Alps was brought dramatically back into the spotlight of publicity in 1991 by the discovery of the so-called Iceman. Two German mountaineers vacationing in the Italian Tyrol were descending after a morning's climb near Similaun when they noticed a brown object protruding from the ice. It proved to be the body of a man, perfectly preserved by the freezing conditions. It was so well preserved that it wasn't thought to be more than twenty or thirty years old—the consequence of a modern climbing accident. Only when specialists began to examine the body and the objects found with it, including a copper axe still mounted in its wooden handle, did they realize the true antiquity and importance of their find. This was confirmed when radiocarbon dates showed that the Similaun man had lived and died around 3500 B.C.

Thus Similaun man belongs to the period when engravings were being made in the Valcamonica, and it is natural to ask whether there were any connections between the two. Similaun itself lies on the Austrian–Italian border, so much so indeed that the body was thought first to be in Austrian territory, until official surveyors from both countries decided otherwise. This is of course a high Alpine area, largely covered by snow and ice even in summer, and very different from the lowland Valcamonica. But nobody could have lived in the Similaun region and the man who died there 5,500 years ago must have come from a lowland community and been hunting in the Alps when he got into difficulties and died. Maybe he was overtaken by a prolonged blizzard and was simply unable to make it to shelter.

The main clue to the Iceman's home was provided by the copper axe he had been carrying. This was found near the body and can be paralleled exactly in carvings on statue-menhirs in the Val Venosta, only 12 miles (20 kilometers) south of Similaun. The Val Venosta penetrates deep into the heart of the Alps, and it is easy to imagine the Iceman living in one of the villages there, leaving from time to time to spend a few days hunting in the high mountains around the edge of the glaciers. It was on one of these hunting expeditions that he came to grief.

The Val Venosta—the Iceman's home—is over 40 miles (70 kilometers) from Valcamonica as the crow flies, even further if we follow the deep mountain valleys and difficult passes that connect the two. But though the Val Venosta has no rock carvings to compare with those of Valcamonica, the carved statue-menhirs from the Val Venosta show that this was, during the late fourth millennium, part of the same ritual world. Thus the Iceman takes his place in the study of the Valcamonica, reminding us that these rock carvings were the work of real individuals and bringing us face to face with somebody who lived, not far away, at about that time.

The discovery of the Alpine "Iceman" (Similaun Man) at 10,500 feet (3,200 meters) on the Austrian-Italian border in September 1991. Radiocarbon dates indicate that this man perished here between 3550 and 3300 B.C., and a CT scan carried out on the body at Innsbruck suggests he was at least forty and probably closer to fifty years old at the time of death. The body was accompanied by hunting gear, and remains of clothing had also been preserved for over 5,000 years by being frozen within the ice. The exceptional preservation brings us a vivid if somewhat macabre encounter with a particular prehistoric individual.

(facing page, top) Area I of the Great Rock of Naquane. Among the many images are huntsmen or warriors with spears and small shields raised aloft, deer with impressive antlers, and solid rectangles with projecting poles. These last have been termed "paddles," though what they actually represent is far from certain. The projecting pole sometimes terminates in a rounded knob, and occasionally (though not on this panel) in a hollow ring, which suggests it is a handle. Anati, struck by the prominence of "paddle" motifs and their apparent association with a whole range of different "scenes," interpreted them as magical objects ensuring victory in battle and success in the hunt. The reality may be more prosaic, though, on the other hand, it is possible that many or most of the Naquane figures have some magical or mythological significance.

(facing page, bottom) Stags are especially numerous in Area V of the Great Rock of Naquane. A number of superpositionings can be seen (where one figure has been carved over another), and these have provided valuable evidence in the attempt to divide the Camonica art into chronological phases. Anati has noted fifty cases of superpositioning on the Naquane rock.

sides overlooking Lake Iseo, a journey that the modern road and railway make with the help of tunnels and bridges. Nor is it a particularly good route northward, toward the main Alpine passes, since it ends at a kind of T-junction where passes east and west lead to adjacent valleys. The Valcamonica was thus an area easily ignored; by no means cut off from outside contact but away from the main routes, and its inhabitants left throughout much of history and prehistory to lead their own lives undisturbed.

Traveling up the Valcamonica one passes Cividate Comune, the principal Roman center, with remains of a medieval castle and nunnery and an archaeological museum. Next comes Castello di Breno, with a Neolithic settlement and Iron Age cemetery, testifying to the long prehistoric occupation of the valley. But the real excitement of Valcamonica comes at the next town, Capo di Ponte, for it is on the rock surfaces around here that thousands of prehistoric carvings have been found. The major concentration is now protected within the Parco Nazionale delle Incisioni Rupestri, and here too is the Centro Camuno di Studi Preistorici, where research on the art has been in progress for over thirty years. The study of the Valcamonica rock art has indeed played a major role in developing new techniques and approaches for the reading and interpretation of rock art in general.

The visitor impatient to understand what all the fuss is about has simply to pay an entrance fee and walk a little way down the main path into the park. There, in front of a small farmhouse, is one of the most impressive monuments of prehistoric Europe: the Great Rock of Naquane, covered with over a thousand carved figures. Dozens of different groups can be made out: here an armed and armored warrior on horseback; there a "labyrinth"; on the left, men and dogs hunt deer; on the right, there are upright weaving looms and processions of figures. Everyday life, indoor and outdoor pursuits, ritual scenes and enigmatic symbols are all represented in this magnificent palimpsest of images. And palimpsest it clearly is, for aside from the crowding and strange juxtapositioning of the different figures, some have been carved on top of others. They weren't all made at the same time. The dating of the art is a subject we shall return to below. Suffice it to say here that the Great Rock of Naquane shows an accumulation of images stretching over two thousand years, but even this is only a fraction of the entire time-range of the Valcamonica carvings.

When Was It Found?

The rediscovery of the Valcamonica rock art has been described as "one of the major archaeological adventures of our century." This is the verdict of Emmanuel Anati, the Italian archaeologist who has been chiefly responsible for its study over the past three decades. It isn't that the art wasn't known earlier; but it wasn't really understood, nor its archaeological importance really appreciated, until the twentieth century.

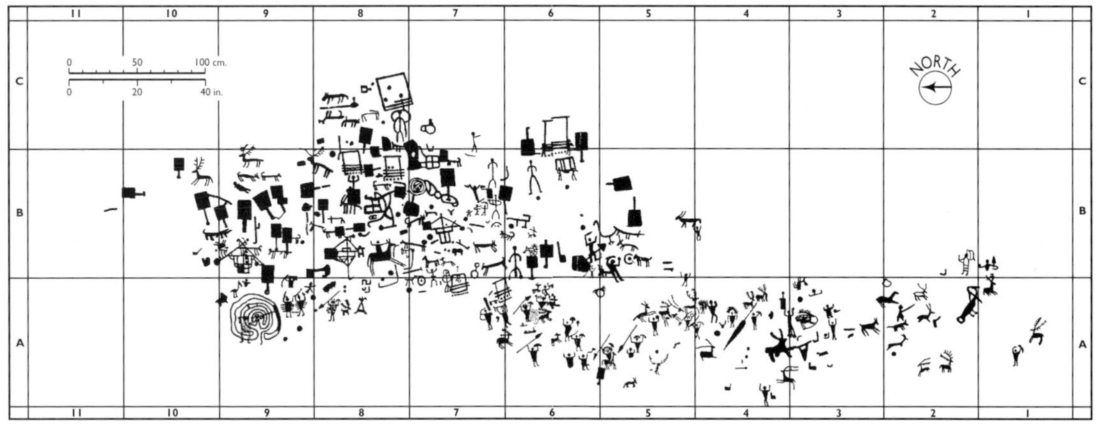

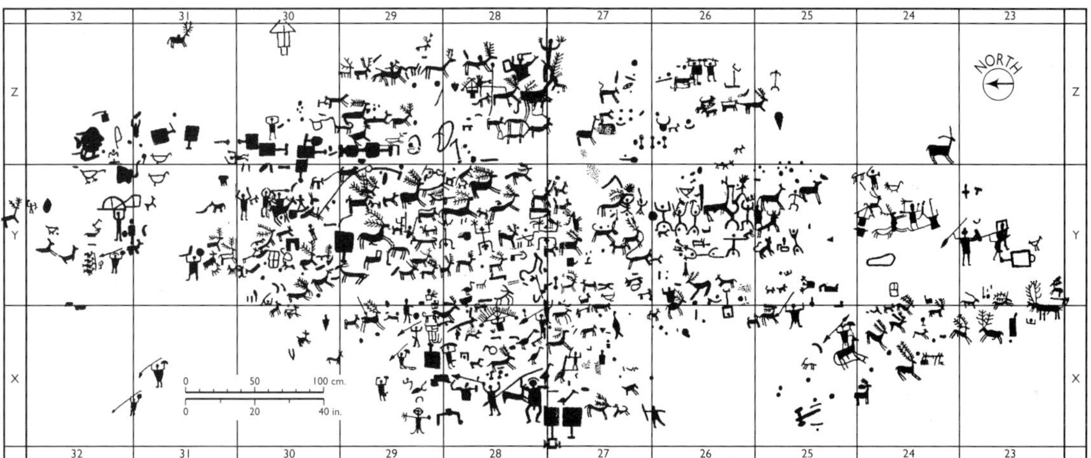

The story of the rediscovery begins in 1908, when Gualtero Laeng, a citizen of Brescia, announced the discovery of a decorated rock at Massi di Cemmo, across the River Oglio from Capo di Ponte. What he had found was in fact one of the less typical examples of Camonica art, carved not on a rock face but on a boulder that had fallen from the cliffs above. On this the prehistoric inhabitants of Valcamonica had carved groups of deer, cattle, and daggers. Despite its importance, Laeng's announcement wasn't followed up for over twenty years. Then in 1930 two archaeologists made separate visits to Valcamonica to inspect and publish Laeng's boulder. As Anati has pointed out, the irony was not only that they both chose to go there at about the same time, but also that they competed to record the same boulder yet failed to notice a second decorated boulder a mere 50 feet (15 meters) away. And at 7 feet (2 meters) tall it wasn't exactly inconspicuous, although the carvings themselves were covered by moss. It was only when one of the researchers, Giovanni Marro, returned to the site a year later that he discovered there were two decorated boulders at Massi di Cemmo.

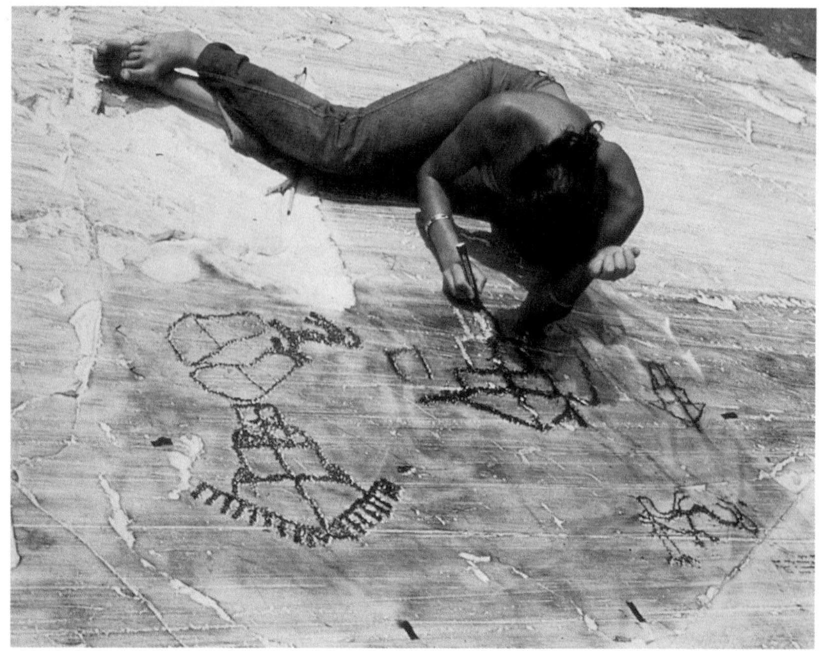

Recording the Camonica rock art: a polythene sheet is laid over the rock surface, and the carvings are then traced in ink, using different colors for different phases or features.

Marro and his colleagues made further explorations and discoveries of rock art around Capo di Ponte during the course of the 1930s. But it was only in the 1950s that the study of Valcamonica rock art began to be put on a proper footing. A key name is that of Emanuele Suss, who compiled a map of the carvings in the Naquane area. This was based on a field survey so thorough and comprehensive that only six new sites have been added by later research. But it was limited to the Naquane area near Capo di Ponte and showed nothing of the overall extent of Valcamonica art. This was to be the life's work of Emmanuel Anati, the second key name, and the man who brought the real importance of Valcamonica to the attention of the wider world.

Anati first visited Valcamonica in 1956 and made an annual field study during the following years. With a team of students and volunteers he would focus each year on a new area or rock surface. There were two parts to the operation. First, the team would strip away grass and moss from likely rock surfaces, revealing the engravings beneath. Then they would record the carvings, tracing the designs on polythene sheets laid directly over the rock faces. It was slow and painstaking work, but little by little it yielded spectacular results. By 1964, 30,000 carvings had been found; by 1995, the total had risen to 300,000, making Valcamonica the richest European rock art site. Many of these discoveries have been in other parts of the valley, away from the original finds at Massi di Cemmo and Capo di Ponte. Rock art is now known throughout almost the whole Valcamonica, beginning as far south as Darfo and Boario Terme. In altitude it stretches from the edges of the valley floor to the higher slopes, in all cases taking advantage of rock faces polished smooth by the glaciers that plowed through the valley some tens of thousands of years ago. These smoothed rock faces made ideal panels for the prehistoric artists who lived and worked here once the ice sheets had gone.

How Old Is It?

Finding the Valcamonica art was one thing. Dating it and understanding it were quite different, and much more difficult, enterprises. The interpretation of the art is still subject to much speculation and debate. The question of dating, however, has now been settled, at least in its broad outlines.

The key to dating the art is superimposition. This relies on the fact that the Valcamonica artists did not hesitate to add new engravings alongside, or even on top of earlier carvings. The results can be a confused mass of images crowded onto a single rock face. In his study of these surfaces, Anati soon came to realize that where one image overlapped another, it was possible to distinguish which of them was the earlier. This is because they are carved to different depths, the later carvings often obliterating parts of earlier figures. Anati also recognized that the images had often been made in groups—a herd of deer, a pair of fighting warriors, a cluster of daggers, for example—and that the occasional overlaps between individual elements afforded a means of establishing the order in which the different groups had been carved.

Anati's analysis of Boulder 1 at Massi di Cemmo is a good example of the technique. It isn't as crowded as some, but it is clear at first glance that not all of the figures could have been carved at the same time. Some of them overlap, and others have been almost obliterated by later additions to the panel. Anati has used these features to divide the images on the Massi di Cemmo boulder into four successive phases. First, toward the top left of the stone, came a group of deer with curving antlers. Only one of these survives, but traces of the curved antlers of the others were left when the deer were recarved with straight antlers in the second phase. At the same time a group of hornless quadrupeds (possibly elk) was added in the center and toward the right-hand side of the stone. In the third phase, a scatter of mountain goats, some with conspicuous curved horns, was carved across the whole of the surface. On the left-hand side the artists seem intentionally to have avoided the herd of deer, which must still have been evident, but elsewhere they carved them between and across the earlier figures. The same is true of the fourth and final phase, in which a group of triangular-bladed daggers with narrow hilts overlay and obliterated parts of the earlier carvings.

Unpicking this kind of palimpsest has given Anati a chronological scheme applicable to all the Valcamonica art. It shows (as we might have expected) that certain images are found only in particular phases. The changes no doubt reflect changes in the life of the valley's inhabitants, in the landscape and fauna, and in what they chose to represent. This is how palimpsests such as that on the Cemmo boulder make themselves so useful to the archaeologist. But

The distribution of known rock art sites in the Camonica valley.

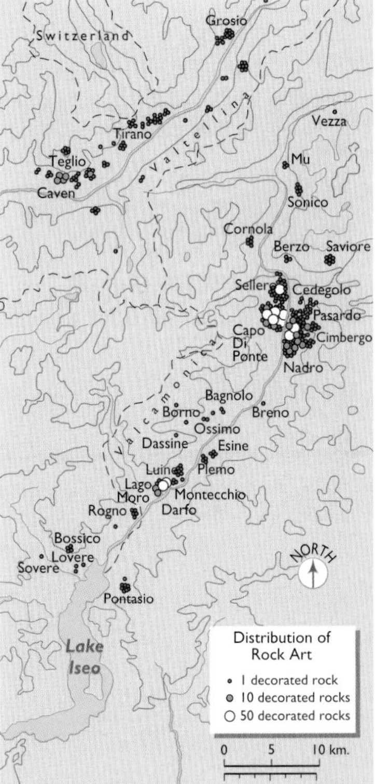

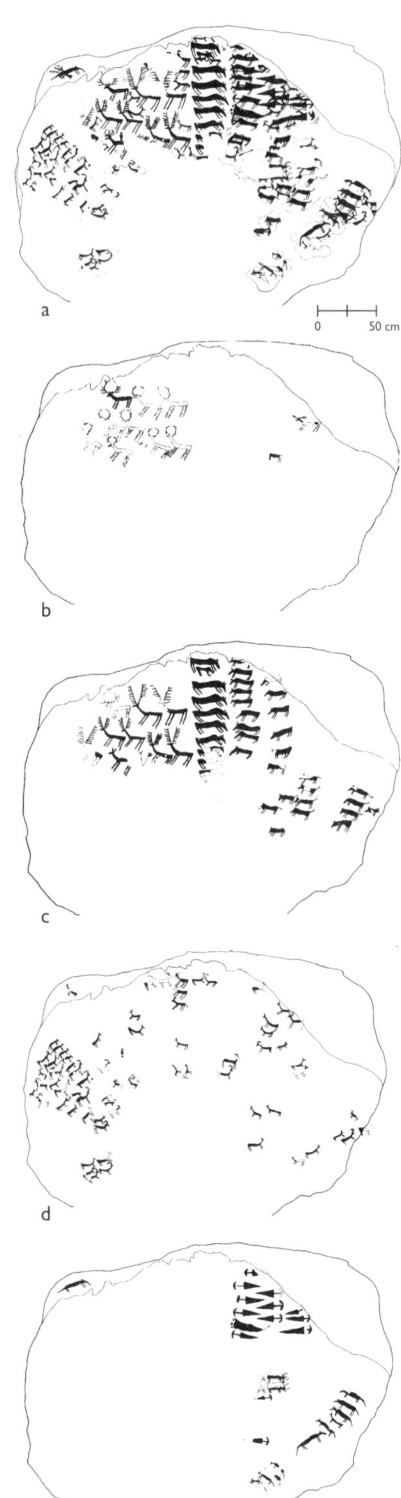

before we look further at the dating, we must say more about the palimpsests themselves. Why on earth did the artists carve all these designs on the same block? Why didn't they avoid surfaces that were already carved and go for new pristine rock surfaces instead? The point is given added weight by the practice of superimposition, where the earlier designs must physically have been in the way of the new images the artist was trying to engrave.

In answering the question, we must first consider how the images were made. They were pecked rather than scratched into the Permian sandstone. At Luine, near Boario Terme in the south of the valley, a small sanctuary was excavated adjacent to a decorated rock surface. Within the layers of deposit, archaeologists found roughly shaped tools of quartz, quartzite, and conglomerate, which had been used for making the engravings. Where new images were carved over old ones, however, there must have been some way of distinguishing the new design. The most likely method is color. Today, we see the art as a maze of shapes and lines pecked into the smooth rock surface —except, that is, where modern paint has been added to make them more visible. Painting was also part of the original technique. We know this because Anati and his colleagues found quantities of coloring materials in their excavations between and around the decorated boulders at Massi di Cemmo.

The overlaying of new art on old makes more sense when we realize it was painted. In some cases the artists may have repainted the earlier designs alongside the new ones they had made. Other old designs were probably ignored. This still doesn't explain why they simply didn't choose an unused rock surface. The answer must be that some surfaces were considered especially suitable or especially sacred (a feature found also in Paleolithic art: *see* Lascaux, chapter 2). The larger surfaces were obviously special, since they were few and far between in the valley as a whole. There are not many rock surfaces in Valcamonica the size of the Great Rock of Naquane. Other surfaces may have been considered sacred because they were associated with mythological events; or, indeed, simply because they had been decorated by earlier generations of valley-dwellers. We shall return to this point when we consider what the Valcamonica rock art means.

After several years' research, Anati has divided the Valcamonica rock art into six successive stages or periods, the four discussed above preceded by Proto-Camunian and followed by Post-Camunian. These are derived from the pattern of superimpositions, differences in the degree of weathering of different images, and a broad understanding of stylistic changes and changes in choice of subject. Elk, for example, are depicted in the earliest period, but then disappear from the art—at the same moment, presumably, that they disappeared from the valley, driven to extinction by local hunters.

The elk belong to what Anati terms the "Proto-Camunian" period. This falls between the retreat of the Alpine glaciers some 10,000 years ago and the beginnings of farming in the Neolithic period, around 5500 B.C. Two of Anati's rock art styles (Periods I and II) belong to the Neolithic. They are characterized by the appearance of domestic animals such as dogs and cattle, alongside the plow. The next phase, Period III, is itself divided into two. Period IIIA is one of the most interesting of all the Valcamonica phases, since it includes triangular copper daggers and the first wheeled vehicles. The dagger engravings have direct parallels on the statue-menhirs of the Alpine region, upright stones carved in the stylized likeness of a human being with a belt and (sometimes) a dagger. The kind of dagger they show is that of the north Italian Remedello culture, which belongs to the so-called Copper Age or Chalcolithic period (c. 3500–2500 B.C.). The Valcamonica daggers are probably of broadly the same age.

Period IIIB in the Valcamonica art corresponds roughly to the Bronze Age, and Period IV to the Iron Age, up to the Roman conquest of the valley in 16 B.C. Warriors and warfare play an increasingly prominent part in these later scenes, though there are also representations of hunting and houses, as well as the enigmatic "maps." In these it seems as though the Valcamonica artists were actually drawing plans of their fields and settlements on the rock surfaces, notably in the complex engraving at Bedolina. The "map" interpretation is all the more convincing from the location of the Bedolina carving, on the crest of the plateau high above Capo di Ponte. It is tempting to think that the Bronze Age artist simply drew what he or she could see, looking out over the valley: a pattern of rectangular fields linked by trackways or canals. In the dots within the fields the artist may even have marked individual trees. Photographs or drawings do not do justice to this intricate design; in order to appreciate the Bedolina panel, we must bear in mind that it measures more than 13 feet (4 meters) across and over 6 feet (2 meters) high.

In Period IV we are on the threshold of written history. This is brought home by the carving of short inscriptions on many of the rock panels. The inscriptions use the north Etruscan script, borrowed from the literate peoples to the south, but the language is the local Camunian.

The final period, Anati's "Post-Camunian," opens with the Roman conquest in 16 B.C. The Romans themselves have left few traces in the rock art of Valcamonica. Some of them seem, however, to have "rediscovered" the art. One of the rock surfaces at Luine, near Boario Terme, has the Latin word "mucro" (dagger) scratched alongside a carving of a Copper Age dagger, which must already have been three thousand years old. The final additions to the Valcamonica rock art corpus were made by the medieval inhabitants of the valley, who chose some of the rock faces to carve scenes and objects relevant to their own experience of everyday life. They bring to an end a practice which we now know to be at least 8,000 years old.

(facing page) Boulder I at Massi di Cemmo, showing (a) the totality of prehistoric carvings on this rock and (b-e) the four phases into which Anati has divided the carvings. Note how in some of the phases artists avoided earlier carvings, while in others (notably the triangular daggers of period IV) they deliberately carved over and between the earlier images. In Anati's scheme, wild animals such as deer and elk are characteristic of the earliest Camonica art, with daggers somewhat later. This is supported by the sequence of carving on the Massi di Cemmo boulder (daggers carved over elk), though hunting of deer and other wild animals has remained an important pursuit down to the present day, and many depictions of wild fauna in Valcamonica belong to the later phases.

What Does It Mean?

Recording the art is relatively easy compared with the difficulty of discovering its meaning. The question can be divided into two distinct parts. First, why is there such a concentration of rock carvings in this particular valley? And second, what do the signs, scenes, and symbols mean?

To the first question we have no sure answer. Valcamonica is not unique in that other Alpine valleys also have prehistoric rock art. The most famous of them is the so-called Vallée des Merveilles on the French side of the frontier, at the foot of Mont Bégo. This is a truly remote site, far from any modern road and around 6,500–8,000 feet (2,000–2,500 meters) above sea level. Such a high altitude valley is in sharp contrast to Valcamonica, where the valley floor slopes from 1,600 feet (500 meters) in the north to a mere 600 feet (200 meters) in the south. Mont Bégo also has many fewer engravings than Valcamonica (a mere 40,000, compared with over 300,000 in Valcamonica), and they fall within a more restricted time period: the Chalcolithic and Early and Middle Bronze Age (c. 3300–1500 B.C.). In contrast to Valcamonica, there is little likelihood that any community ever lived in this remote upland location. The Mont Bégo art, though similar in style to Period III art from Valcamonica, was probably carved by people who visited the area during the summer months. It may have been a place of special sanctity, where Bronze Age pilgrims came to make contact with the gods. In many religions the gods are thought to live on high mountains. Alternatively, the sky may be their dwelling-place, and mountains take on significance as the closest humans can come to them. Whatever the precise rationale, the carvings suggest that Mont Bégo was a place

The rock-carved "map" at Bedolina. The enclosures (mostly rectangular) might indicate fields, and the spots within them may even be individual trees. The lines linking the "fields" could be trackways or canals, or simply property boundaries. The interpretation of the Bedolina composition as a map is made all the more persuasive by its location high up on the slopes looking out over the valley. It is tempting to think that the artist or artists were simply drawing what they could see laid out before them. We must be cautious about reading too much into this theory, however, for we do not know what the scene represents, or if it is indeed intended to be a portrayal of the landscape.

Scene of human figures with upraised arms adjacent to a prominent rayed "sun-disk." Anati suggests that this may show a solar cult in progress, with people worshipping the sun. As so often in Valcamonica rock art, however, there are many enigmatic features to the scene, including the rectangle with projecting staff, the various dots (some isolated, others linked together), and the schematic animals (?) at the left-hand side. Despite Anati's attempts to provide a chronology for the art, we still cannot say for sure whether all the elements of a rock panel such as this are contemporary and belong together.

of special sacredness for prehistoric communities of the surrounding lowlands, a quality that was enhanced by its very remoteness.

Stylistically, key phases of the Valcamonica art (notably Period III) are very similar to that of Mont Bégo, but the location is very different. Valcamonica is something of a remote backwater, a segment of valley without good connections either north or south. But it was an inhabited valley throughout the period when the art was being made. Unlike Mont Bégo, the art was no great distance from the farms and villages of the local people. We need not envisage any lengthy and hazardous summer pilgrimages, though that doesn't of course rule out the idea that rituals and ceremonies, seasonal or otherwise, were carried out at key locations such as the Great Rock of Naquane.

What we simply can't explain is why the Valcamonica art is restricted to this particular valley. Why are there no similar concentrations in the adjacent valleys, which lead into Lake Garda, Lake Como, and Lake Maggiore? There is no evidence that people from these valleys came to worship in the Valcamonica (though that cannot be entirely ruled out). Does the presence of the rock art itself suggest that Valcamonica was in some way more sacred than the other valleys? More likely we are dealing here with a local tradition, one of those peculiarities that enclosed valley communities develop through relative isolation from their neighbors. If so, it was a remarkably rich and vigorous tradition, lasting from the time when hunter-gatherers first moved into the area at the end of the last Ice Age to the Roman conquest several thousand years later.

Anati has pointed to many features that suggest the Valcamonica engravings had a religious or ritual significance. A large number of carvings seem, it is true, to show images from daily life, such as plowing, or animals, warriors,

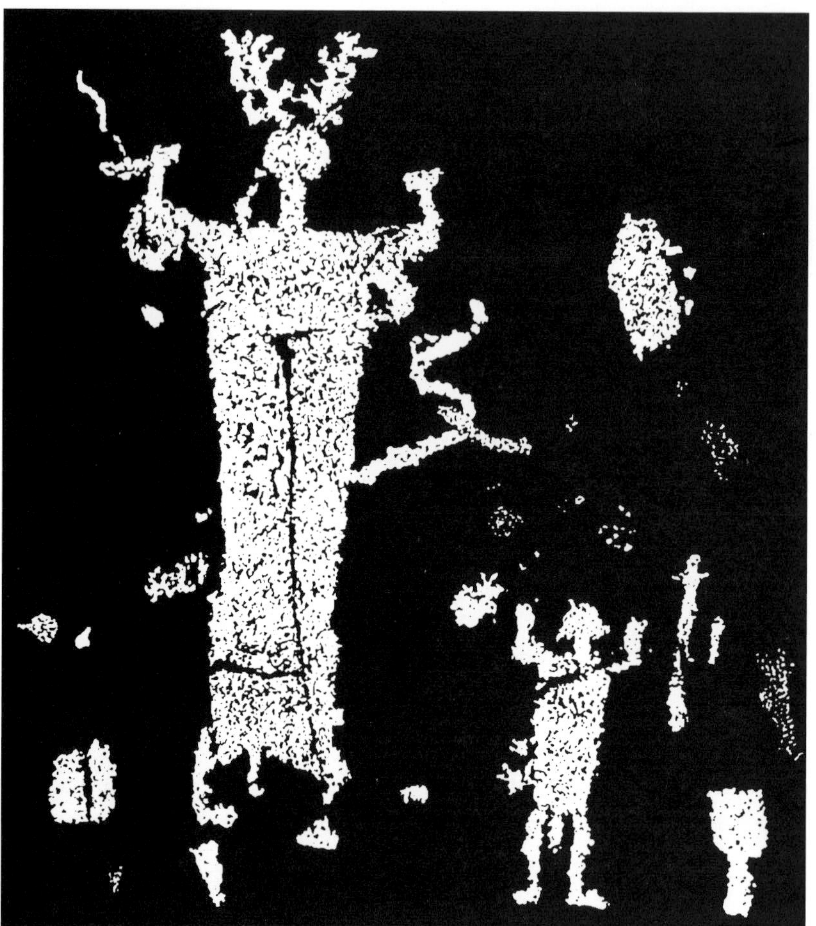

Group of figures from Zurla in the Camonica valley. Anati assigns the principal figures to Period IV in his chronological scheme, which would mean mid-first millennium B.C. By this time Celtic peoples had made their appearance in northern Italy (moving in from north of the Alps), and some archaeologists have interpreted the large figure with stag antlers and upraised arms as the Celtic god Cernunnos. The smaller figure might then be a worshipper, but this interpretation is thrown into doubt by the fact that both figures have upraised arms. Surely both are engaged in the same activity, be it worship, dancing, or simply greeting? In many parts of the world, rock art has a strong mythological component, and the figures shown here may well be taken from myths (whether Celtic or indigenous) that were current in Valcamonica at this time.

or the famous "maps," but even these may have had ritual meaning. There are also numerous abstract symbols and disembodied features such as carved "footprints." Anati interprets the latter as marks of worship or reverence, but this of course is highly subjective. He is much more convincing when it comes to the scenes portraying sun disks accompanied by small human figures. A good example is Rock 59 at Coren del Valento, where a rayed sun disk is surrounded by human figures with upraised arms. Anati interprets this scene, and others like it, as evidence of a prehistoric sun cult in the Valcamonica. Elsewhere he sees representations of deities or idols, especially on the standing stones or "statue-menhirs," which were set up during the Chalcolithic period. At Zurla is a later scene with a large figure with stag antlers and upraised arms, and a similar, smaller figure, without antlers, alongside it. The smaller figure may be a worshipper, and the larger one has been interpreted as the Celtic god Cernunnos. Austrian archaeologist Ludwig Pauli sees this scene as evidence that Celtic religious ideas from the Po plain gradually infiltrated the Valcamonica during the first millennium B.C.

Is all the Valcamonica rock art ritual in intent? This seems likely, though we don't know what the rituals were nor the mythologies that lay behind them. Thus the warrior scenes may be ritual or mythological combats, the four-wheeled carts may be ritual carts (like the hearse placed in the Hochdorf grave), and the plowing scenes may be connected with fertility rites. But it is important not to go too far with this kind of explanation. Anati thinks the small crescent-shaped decorations on the gable end of a building carved at Coren del Valento make this a special ritual hut. It is just as likely, perhaps even more so, that this is merely an ordinary building. The crescent shapes may be ritual bull's horns, as Anati suggests, but they don't make the building a temple.

There is one final argument in favor of the Valcamonica art being ritual in nature. This is the practice of superimposition that we touched on above. If the art was intended simply as decoration, we would have expected the artists to choose fresh rock surfaces for their scenes. That they returned to the same surfaces time and time again suggests that these had some special significance. They may well have been sacred places, hallowed by mythological associations. The Valcamonica rock art, like a rainbow's end, tempts even the soberest archaeologist to think in these terms, but the crock of gold, the real meaning of the art, remains elusive.

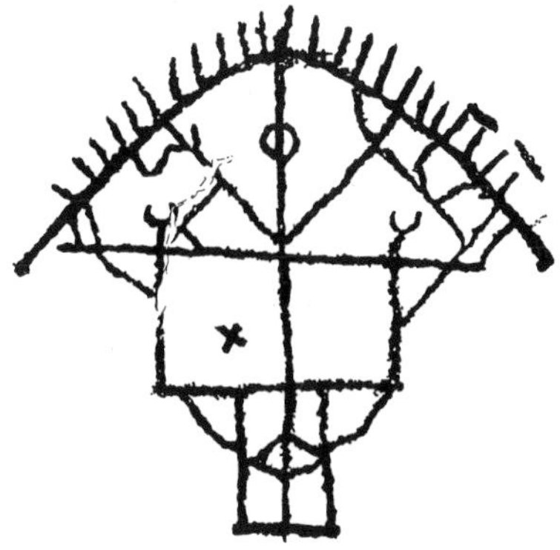

Depiction of a "hut" at Coren del Valento. Anati interprets this as a ritual structure on the basis of the "bulls' horns" motif shown on the long beam that marks the bottom of the roof space. There are a number of these "hut" carvings in the Camonica valley, and several of them have the same top-heavy structure with narrow base and oversailing upper stories. It is perhaps logical to see the rectilinear and oblique lines as the timber frame of the house, and the forest of lines on top of the roof as either gable ornaments or an indication of roofing material. Despite the occasional decorative elements (such as the bulls' horns in this example), there is little about these "huts" to convince us that they are special-purpose ritual structures. They raise once again the important question as to whether the Valcamonica artists were depicting features from everyday life, or whether these are scenes from legend or mythology.

Further Reading

The key publications on Valcamonica are by Emmanuel Anati, the leading expert on the art and the director of the Centro Camuni di Studi Preistorici. His *Evoluzione e stile nell'arte rupestre camuna* (Capo di Ponte: Edizioni del Centro, 1975) is one of the cornerstones for studying the chronology of the engravings. Also useful (and in English) are his *Camonica Valley* (London: Cape, 1965) and more up-to-date *Valcamonica Rock Art: A New History for Europe* (Capo di Ponte: Edizioni del Centro, 1994). A convenient general survey of Alpine archaeology is provided by Ludwig Pauli, *The Alps: Archaeology and Early History* (London: Thames and Hudson, 1984). The standard popular account of the Similaun body and its possible significance is *The Man in the Ice* by Konrad Spindler (New York: Harmony Books, 1994).

Further Viewing

Four areas of Valcamonica rock art are open for public viewing: the Parco Communale di Luine at Darfo-Boario Terme; the Riserva Regionale delle Incisioni Rupestri de Ceti, Cimbergo, Paspardo; the Parco Nationale delle Incisioni Rupestri di Naquane at Capo di Ponte; and the Parco di Sellero.

CHAPTER

ELEVEN

Biskupin

C. 730 B.C.

A timber township in northern Poland

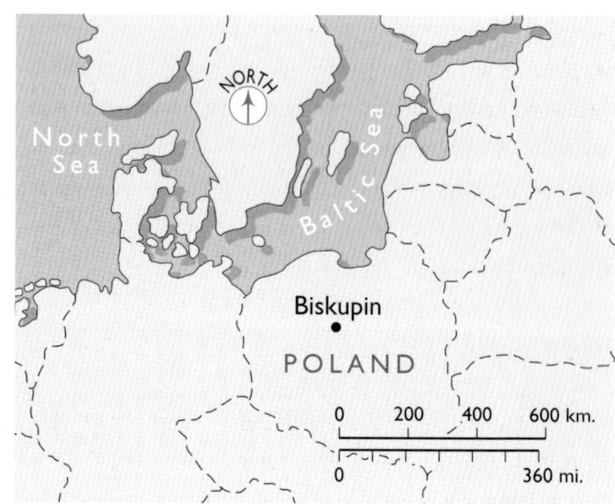

Biskupin, an Iron Age town in northern Poland, is one of those archaeological sites made famous by its remarkable preservation. A whole timber-built town, complete with terraced houses of standardized plan, corduroy tree-trunk roads, and hefty wooden defenses, has been saved from decay by the conserving properties of a moist environment. The site lies on a low peninsula on the edge of one of the many lakes that dot this region of Poland. They were formed as the last ice sheets melted, spreading an impermeable deposit of clay over the landscape, with low relief provided by moraines and lakes and peat bogs in the marshy hollows. It is a bleak landscape today, especially in winter, but its very bleakness has proved a blessing to archaeologists. In other parts of Europe, peatlands have been systematically drained and turned to fields or pastures, or the peat itself has been cut for fuel. This has happened in northern Poland, too, but more slowly than elsewhere, and some of the sites that might have been destroyed have escaped for archaeologists to find and visitors to enjoy today.

Not without justice is Biskupin labeled "the Polish Pompeii." For alongside the remains of roads and buildings, there were hundreds of artifacts of perishable materials such as birch-bark fishing floats and wooden plow-parts. In its day, Biskupin was far from unique. It was just one of many fortified settlements built along the river and lake-edges of this region of Poland. It wasn't even among the largest: Biskupin's 4 acres (1.5 hectares) is relatively small compared with the 15 acres (6 hectares) of nearby Sobiejuchy. But Sobiejuchy was built on higher land, and only around the edges of the settlement, where it disappears into the lake, are wooden timbers preserved. It is no rival for Biskupin.

The visitor to Biskupin approaches the site by car from Poznan, the nearest big town. It is possible to reach by bus (with many changes) or in summer by means of a narrow gauge railway, but car is by far the most practical. The journey takes you across the glacially moulded terrain, broken by lakes, but generally treeless today. An effort of imagination is necessary to think back to a time when the landscape was densely forested and 80,000 trees could be felled to build Biskupin, and 30,000 more when the settlement burned down and had to be rebuilt. Multiplying this to take account of Biskupin's neighbors—the larger Sobiejuchy among them—gives an indication of the massive deforestation they involved. The north Polish landscape has probably never been the same since.

The Discovery

It was an overactive nightlife that led to the discovery of Biskupin. Walenty Szwajcer was a young teacher in Znin, the local town, in the early 1930s. His frequenting of local bars didn't amuse the school authorities, and when his comrades gave him the title "Count of the Night" the authorities decided to act. To remove him from the temptations of Znin they sent Szwajcer to Biskupin, a small and rather benighted village some 6 miles (10 kilometers) to the southeast.

Szwajcer had been teaching in Biskupin for a year when in the summer of 1933 he noticed oak stakes visible under water on the edge of the nearby lake. They lay beside a peninsula where he took his pupils for school outings and where a Polish ruler had built a bathhouse in the thirteenth century. Szwajcer knew of the Alpine lake villages that had been discovered in Switzerland in the 1850s, and was excited by the thought that this could be the Polish equivalent. It was a long hot summer, and irrigation work on the River Gasawka had lowered the level of the lake by several feet. It was this that exposed the timbers and gave archaeologists their chance. The schoolchildren playing on the peninsula came across pieces of pottery that Szwajcer thought must be very old, but it was when he learned of discoveries made by the landowner that his suspicions were confirmed. In digging for peat on the peninsula, the landowner had found valuable objects that he took into the local town to sell. When Szwajcer visited the diggings he saw not valuables but a mass of preserved timber and a scatter of prehistoric pottery.

Szwajcer wrote to a professor of archaeology at the University of Poznan to tell him of the finds and was rewarded by a visit from Jozef Kostrzewski, a leading archaeologist and specialist in prehistory. Kostrzewski had been in

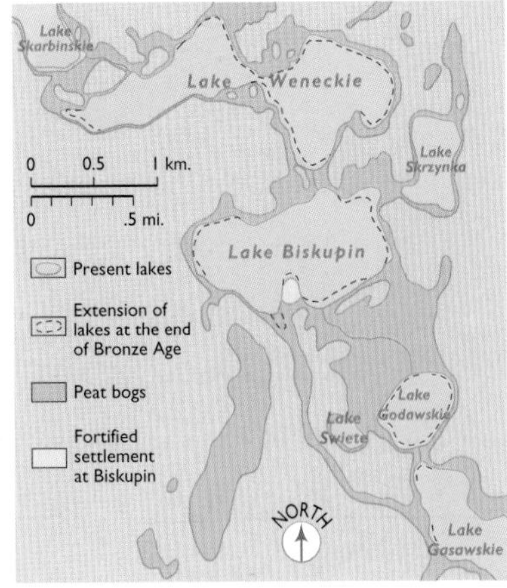

Biskupin in its prehistoric environment. The settlement stood on a low promontory projecting into a lake, with peat bogs providing further natural protection on the landward side.

the area a few years before, in 1925, but had noticed nothing of significance. This time, thanks to Szwajcer, his visit was amply rewarded. As soon as he saw the woodwork and pottery revealed by the turf diggings he realized their significance and was able to date the site (from the pottery) to the Early Iron Age "Lusatian" culture, around 700–500 B.C.

There was little money available for Polish archaeology in the 1930s, but Kostrzewski was able to persuade his university of the importance of Biskupin, and in June 1934 sent his assistant, Zdzislaw Rajewski, with three trained assistants and thirty laborers, to begin excavations. An initial cutting of only a little over 100 square feet (10 square meters) was enlarged to 4,000 square feet (370 square meters), revealing floors and wall stubs of seven houses and yielding a mass of pottery, bone, and wooden objects. Rajewski returned with a larger team in 1935, and the operation grew until war broke out in 1939. The excavators worked by stripping topsoil from large areas of the site and then planning the finds and structures they had revealed. The latest technology was employed. The Polish army lent the archaeologists three observation balloons, which took spectacular overhead photographs of the excavations. Adjacent to the site itself, a suite of laboratories was built for processing the finds, with sleeping accommodation attached. Millions of objects were processed in these laboratories. They became a center for the study not only of the artifacts but also of the animal bones and plant remains. Divers searched the lake bed around the site, recovering many more finds. One of the most notable was a dugout canoe, made from a single hollowed-out tree-trunk. Around the site itself a protective dam was built, to shield the excavations from flooding.

Plan of the Biskupin settlement, showing the regimented street plan and the standardized houses. The circles (filled or open) indicate the position of hearths within the houses. The settlement was bounded by a timber rampart and breakwater, with a single entrance (marked by a gate tower) in the southwest.

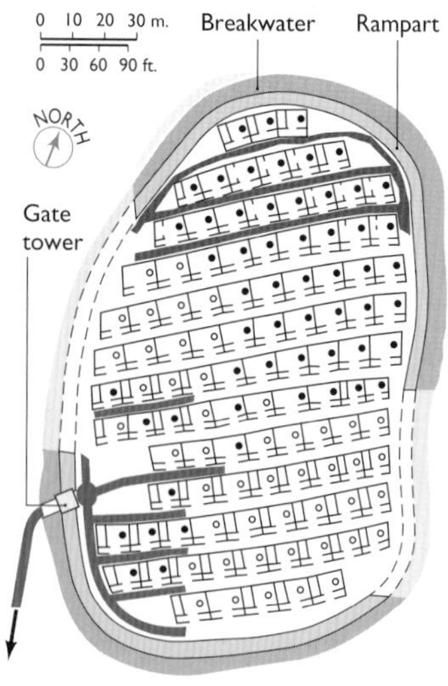

The Reconstruction of Biskupin

Reconstruction went hand-in-hand with excavation. Biskupin soon became a Polish national symbol. Artists visited it and painted imaginary reconstructions; as early as 1936 there were attempts to reconstruct some of the buildings themselves on the site. In that year, two houses and part of the wall were rebuilt, using the same materials as the original and the same building techniques. Not a single iron nail was allowed. By 1939 the excavators had discovered that the original settlement had been linked to the mainland by a wooden bridge. They imagined the site as an island surrounded by water. The idea also took root that Biskupin had been destroyed by a Scythian assault, and in 1939 a rather improbable reenactment took place, when "Scythians" in dugout canoes attacked the reconstructed rampart.

Events like these heightened Biskupin's popularity and helped to attract money for the ambitious excavations. By the time war broke out in September 1939, around half the site had been excavated and no fewer than 400,000 people had visited it. Less successful were attempts to preserve the timbers. Once exposed to the air and allowed to dry out, they quickly began to shrink and distort, and ultimately to decay. At first, the excavators tried to retard this process

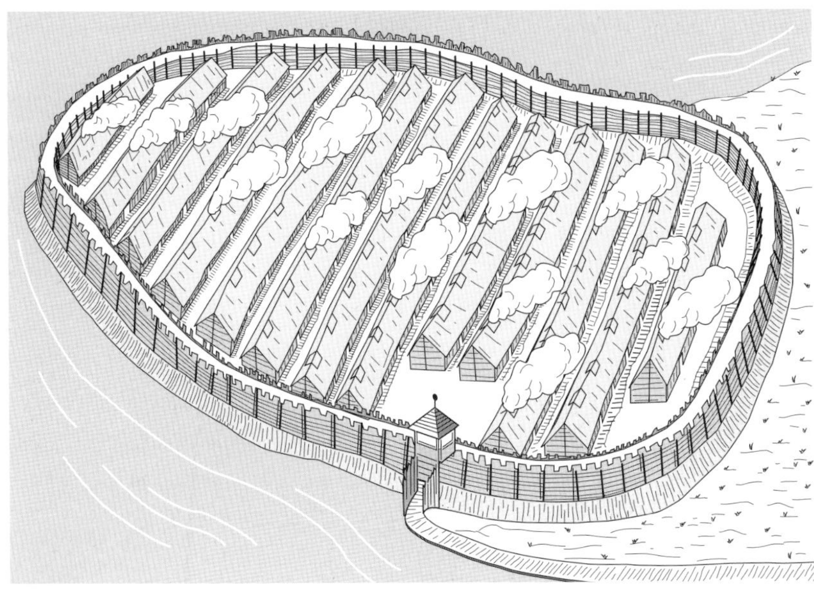

Reconstruction of the Biskupin settlement as it may have appeared c. 700 B.C. The neatly organized houses clustered within the tight perimeter wall and surrounded by lake and bog make a striking impression, testimony both to community planning and the quest for security.

by covering up again what they had excavated. Later, chemical treatments were tried, but even these were not entirely successful. Techniques developed to cope with small finds of wood or other perishable materials could not easily be applied to an entire waterlogged settlement. As a result, what the visitor sees today is not so much the ancient preserved woodwork but the reconstructed timbers of the protective wall with its distinctive gate-tower, and the tree-trunk roads and thatched, terraced houses in the interior.

The reconstructions seen at Biskupin today date from the late 1940s, replacing those that were destroyed or damaged by the occupying German forces or by simple neglect during the Second World War. When Poland recovered its independence in 1945, the restoration of Biskupin, its most famous archaeological site, was made a priority. Rajewski turned the place into a field school for a new generation of Polish archaeologists, involving excavations in the morning and lectures in the afternoon. Excavations continued into the 1960s, but with diminishing returns, and the new philosophy argued that efforts should be directed toward researching and conserving what had already been found, rather than uncovering new areas of the site. Even so, at the present day no less than 75 percent of the Biskupin settlement has been excavated, though much has been covered over again in an effort to prolong the survival of the fragile timbers.

A Visit to the Site

The number of visitors to Biskupin has steadily grown since 1945. A museum to display the major finds was opened in 1950 and replaced by a new and better building in 1986. Efforts have been made to restore parts of the original

Excavations in progress at Biskupin in the 1930s. At top right can be seen the broad curving sweep of the breakwater and rampart, and within the rampart the corduroy roads (built of split logs laid edge to edge) and houses are visible. Several of the houses appear as paler rectangles marked by a central circular stone-built hearth. During and after the Second World War until the 1960s, excavation continued in the central and southern parts of Biskupin, uncovering the remains of the main gate toward the bottom left of this photo.

forested landscape, and in a reservation near the site there is a herd of tarpans, small Polish horses similar to those whose animal bones were discovered in the Iron Age settlement. It is the site itself, however, that is the focus of attention and interest.

As visitors leave the museum and make their way along the peninsula they see before them the reconstructed timber gateway that dominates the whole complex. Soon they are walking across dry land that was peat bog when Biskupin was built. It is recent geological cores that have shown that the early excavators were wrong when they envisaged the settlement surrounded by water even on the landward side. The peat bog was nevertheless a significant barrier, and Biskupin in the Early Iron Age was effectively a low marshy island, rising only two or three feet above the peat to the south or the waters of the lake on the other sides; ideal for defense, but not the driest or most pleasant place to settle.

The modern path follows the line of the original timber bridge, built of oak and 400 feet (120 meters) long. The bridge skirted the edge of the settlement as it approached the gate in the middle of the west side. This sector has not been reconstructed, so visitors must imagine for themselves the tall timber rampart that once stood here. The point is an important one, since it shows how the bridge led people, whether friend or foe, under the lee of the rampart for some considerable distance, giving ample opportunity for arrivals to be identified and for the heavy timber gates to be swung closed if necessary. Any attacker using the bridge would also have been exposed to missiles fired from the rampart, and the narrow, open-sided bridge would have afforded little opportunity for shelter or escape.

There is no question that defense was prominent in the minds of the people of Biskupin. If any doubt remained, it would be dispelled by the gateway itself. The entrance itself was 10 feet (3 meters) wide and closed by a heavy, two-leaved oak door. The leaves themselves were discovered in 1939, lying where they had fallen, braced by cross-timbers and pivoting on rounded posts. A touch of ordinariness was added by the wooden kennel, complete with dog skeleton, found just inside it: an Iron Age guard dog!

Above the gate itself stands the reconstructed timber tower with two superimposed galleries topped by a thatched roof. In times of hostility the

WETLAND PREHISTORY

One of the greatest problems facing archaeologists is the disappearance through decay of most of the artifacts that were made and used by the prehistoric communities archaeologists seek to study. What they are left with are potsherds, stone tools, and animal bones, and metals for the later periods. But these preserved remains represent only a fraction of what there must once have been. Textiles, wooden objects, basketry—all are gone leaving very little trace. The same applies to buildings. Archaeologists are accustomed to making what they can of post-holes and pits in the ground. The timber structures themselves have long since vanished. It is this that gives waterlogged sites their very special importance. For here are preserved all those organic materials that are lacking at dry land sites.

In Europe, the study of waterlogged prehistoric settlements goes back to the nineteenth century. The crucial event in this story was the dry winter of 1853–1854, and its impact on the Swiss lakes. Water levels fell, revealing a mass of timber posts embedded in the floor of Lake Zurich, just beyond the present shoreline. The local schoolmaster called in Dr. Ferdinand Keller, president of the Antiquarian Society of Zurich, who recognized them as the remains of timber houses dating to the Neolithic and Bronze Age. Keller spent several years investigating the Swiss lake-dwellings, calling in specialists to help with particular aspects of the work. An amazing range of objects was recovered, not only the houses and their palisades, but dugout canoes, clothing and textiles, basketry, and food remains. Here at last was an opportunity to see just how prehistoric Europeans actually lived.

Keller's work in the Swiss lakes encouraged archaeologists in neighboring lands to investigate their own lakes and bogs, where similar discoveries were made. It also encouraged the first attempts at fully underwater archaeology, using a primitive wetsuit, as early as August 1854. By the end of the 1930s, archaeologists had explored waterlogged sites in other parts of the Alps, in the British Isles, and in northern Europe. But the spectacular discoveries at Biskupin set new standards, both in the wealth of finds and in the rigorous way they were studied.

The settlement viewed from the west across the shallow waters of Lake Biskupin. The amazing preservation of the waterlogged timbers encouraged attempts to reconstruct parts of the site as early as 1936. The visitor today sees reconstructions of the main gate on the western edge of the settlement, two rows of terraced houses flanking a corduroy street in the interior, and a length of defensive rampart on the eastern side (visible in the background of this photograph, with a rectangular opening forming the modern visitor exit). Maintaining these timber reconstructions in good repair is one of the key current management problems at Biskupin.

open-fronted galleries would have been manned by archers and spear-throwers to protect the gate from frontal attack. Spear- and arrowheads of animal horn have been discovered in the excavations, as were piles of stones (to be used as missiles) placed every few yards along the line of the rampart. The gate tower was also an impressive symbol of community pride, the only feature to break the otherwise level skyline of the encircling timber stockade.

Short lengths of reconstructed stockade stand to either side of the gate tower, but for a better idea of the original defenses it is necessary to cross to the far side of Biskupin, where a longer length has been rebuilt. It consists of two separate elements.

The first of these is a kind of breakwater, at or below water level around the entire perimeter of the original settlement. Rows and rows of oak and pine stakes had been driven into the lake bed at an angle of 45°, leaning back against the sloping shoreline. This in itself was an enormous undertaking, requiring around 35,000 stakes, each of which needed to be felled, trimmed, transported to the site, and hammered into the lake mud. But it was an essential preliminary to the building of the settlement, for without it the lake waters lapping against the promontory would steadily have undermined the perimeter stockade.

The rampart itself was built a short distance behind the breakwater. It enclosed the entire settlement in a ring of timber-work 1,500 feet (450 meters) long and originally some 20 feet (6 meters) high. The rampart was built in box-type fashion in two stages. The first stage, at ground level, consisted of oak log foundations 10–12 feet (3–3.5 meters) square. Above these was a system of smaller boxes, each around three feet square. Thus from front to back the rampart consisted of three lines of three-foot-square boxes, inter-

The reconstructed main gate at Biskupin. Many of the details are conjectural, but such a gate tower would have made both an imposing symbol of community and a powerful protection for the gate. In the foreground can be seen the corduroy road, which is the modern visitor access to the site, and behind this, at the base of the reconstructed timber rampart, are the wooden stakes of the breakwater.

One of the heavy twin oak leaves of the main gate, discovered during excavations in 1939. At the far side is the rounded projecting pole that formed the pivot on which the gate rotated. Note also the waterlogged conditions that are the reason for the amazing preservation of these 2,700-year-old timbers.

locked at the corners in log cabin manner, plastered with clay to protect them from fire, then filled with sand and earth to create a solid structure. Along the top was a walkway for the defenders, protected by a timber screen or stockade along its outer edge. The amount of timber and effort that went into these structures is clear evidence of the need the Biskupin people felt for defense.

Within the Walls

Biskupin was an orderly and tightly organized community. We can read this at a glance from the plan. Terraced rows of uniform houses, almost identical in size and layout, front onto a series of parallel streets that run across the site from one side to the other. It resembles nothing so much as a nineteenth-century estate of industrial workers' cottages. Space was at a premium on the small promontory. This explains the tightly packed arrangement, with only one open area, just inside the gate. Every other available piece of land was built on. And developed not haphazardly, but according to a preconceived master plan.

A key feature of the plan was the layout of streets. These are of what is termed "corduroy" construction, a name normally associated today with cloth but essentially meaning ribbed. In the case of Biskupin, the streets consisted of split logs of oak and pine, laid edge to edge and covered with sand and earth to provide a smooth surface. The excavators found remains of two- and four-wheeled carts, but the streets themselves were so narrow that they wouldn't have had room to pass or turn. This may not have been a problem, since the authorities capable of planning such a rigidly laid-out settlement would no doubt have imposed a strict, one-way traffic system.

The broadest of the roads was a continuous loop running just inside the rampart. Eleven narrower parallel streets ran transversely across the settlement, joining the perimeter road. The whole settlement is so tightly packed, the streets so narrow, that it must have been a claustrophobic environment. Still more so when we recall that eight hundred people are thought to have lived in this confined space.

It was along the transverse streets that the houses were arranged. They measured around 25 by 30 feet (8 by 9 meters) and had a uniform, two-roomed plan. Two rows of houses have been reconstructed. On entering one of the houses by a door in the middle of the street frontage, visitors find themselves in a wide but shallow entrance hall. Here the family kept pigs and perhaps cattle, too, in winter. It must have made Biskupin a smelly place to live. A second door immediately ahead leads into the main living room, which also provided cooking and sleeping quarters. Internal details are standardized, just like the houses themselves. On the left was a communal bed; on the right a circular hearth, built of clay and stones. Above the hearth was a spit and behind it were shelves and containers. Finally, in the roof space above there was a loft for storage.

A Biskupin house, showing the stone-built central hearth, the timber floor of the main rectangular room, and (to the right of this) the broad shallow entrance hall fronting onto the street. Stubs of two timber posts mark the position of the original front door. Almost every house at Biskupin followed this standardized plan.

The construction of the houses is no less remarkable than their regularity. Once again, timber was employed throughout, using slots and grooves rather than iron nails to hold the structures together. The key elements were the upright posts, with slots cut into their sides. Into these slots the ends of the horizontal wall-timbers were inserted. The builders packed clay and moss to fill any cracks and keep out the bitter winter weather. Roofs were steeply pitched and thatched with reeds, a readily available commodity in this lakeside setting. Even so, the quantities required were enormous. Each house needed around 5½ tons (5 metric tons) of reed thatch, and the whole settlement would have needed 550 tons (500 metric tons) or more. Similar calculations can be done for the woodwork. They suggest that over 250 mature trees went to make a single house, rising to over 27,000 for all the houses in the settlement, and perhaps 75,000 trees if we include the roads, rampart, and breakwater as well. Huge swathes of forest and reed bed must have been cut down to build Biskupin. It may have been a winter task, taking advantage of the frozen lake. We can imagine men and cattle, year after year, dragging loads of timber across the ice, until at last the plan was completed and each Biskupin family was provided with a standardized housing module.

Life at Iron Age Biskupin

One hundred and two houses of the same size and plan: what does this tell us about the social organization of Biskupin? It presents us, in fact, with a kind of paradox. On the one hand, the disciplined and regimented settlement plan strongly suggests the operation of a powerful central authority. Some ruler or supreme council must have ordered the work. On the other hand, all the houses are the same. Where are the mansions or palaces of the leading families?

The solution must be that even community leaders had only ordinary-sized houses. There must have been a strongly egalitarian social ethos. This is not the same as saying that there were no social divisions. Biskupin must have had its leaders, the people who planned the settlement, apportioned the construction work, and allocated the houses. Only they didn't mark their special status by the houses they lived in. If we look at burials, for instance, we get a very different picture. The cemetery of Biskupin itself has never been found, but in contemporary cemeteries elsewhere in the region a small number of richly furnished graves stand out against the mass of ordinary burials. These rich graves are the clearest trace of the social elite, which must have organized projects such as the building of Biskupin and controled daily life within its crowded confines.

Antler digging tool (*below*), antler spear-heads, and decorated pottery vessel (*facing page*) from Biskupin. Enormous numbers of smaller objects were found during the excavations, many of them of perishable materials such as wood that would not have survived in the dry conditions common at most archaeological sites.

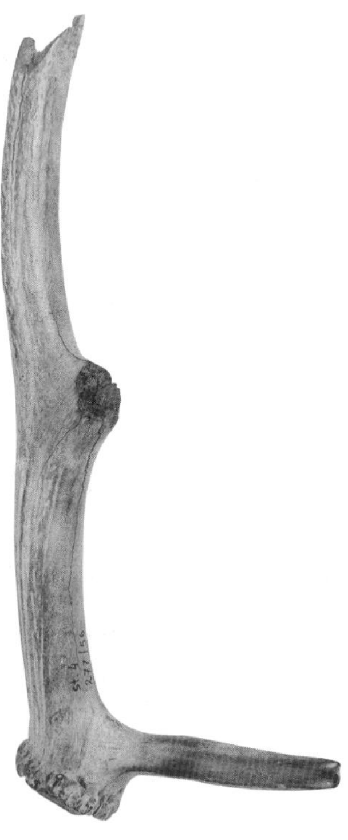

What that daily life consisted of is shown by remains discovered at the site and by studies of its landscape setting. Some of the finds have already been mentioned—weapons and wagons. The most abundant material, however, was pottery, including black, glossy-faced vessels sometimes decorated with geometric patterns or (more rarely) with animal scenes. The geometric scenes probably borrow their designs from the textiles that were woven at the settlement. Evidence for weaving comes from wooden loom frames and pottery rings, which served as weights for the vertical threads on the upright looms. Archaeologists think the pottery itself was made by women, arguing this from the size of the fingerprints which they sometimes left accidentally in the soft clay before firing.

Alongside the black, glossy-faced pottery are thicker and cruder vessels used for storage and cooking. The excellent preservation of organic remains at Biskupin tells us much about what they ate and how they farmed the land. Cereals were crucial, notably four species of wheat and two of barley. They may have been baked into bread or boiled as gruel. The drier land around Biskupin is excellent cereal-growing country, and remains of wooden plows and bronze and iron sickles or reaping knives show how the crops were grown and harvested. There were many other edible plants as well: peas, beans, lentils, and turnips, together with flax for linen cloth, lilac for dyeing, and knot-grass for medicinal purposes.

Animals, too, had a place in the economy. Cattle were most important, kept perhaps for their milk as much as for meat. They were a small-sized variety, reaching little over three feet in height. Horses also were small, not much larger than the modern tarpans kept in the enclosure near the site museum. Despite their size, they were probably ridden. Pigs were no doubt kept for eating—they may have spent the summers rooting around in what remained of the local woodland. Sheep and goat could have provided milk and wool as well as meat.

Hunting and fishing also played a part in the economy. Almost 10 percent of the animal bones were from hunted species such as wild boar, red deer, hare, and beaver (the latter valued mainly for their skins). People fished using nets suspended from bark floats on the waters of the lake, or with rods and lines armed with bronze fishhooks. Archaeologists have identified an area in the middle of the settlement as a fishermen's quarter from the density of fishing equipment found there, mainly in the outer rooms of the houses.

Another specialized pursuit was bronze-casting. Only a few of the Biskupin houses had direct evidence of bronze-working, but the products were found scattered throughout the whole settlement—tools such as sickles and knives, and ornaments including bracelets and necklaces with delicate incised designs. Other ornaments came from far afield and must have been brought to Biskupin by occasional traders or visitors: glass beads from the south and amber from the Baltic shores to the north. Biskupin was clearly linked into a network of long-distance trade routes that spanned the continent of Europe carrying raw materials and luxury manufactures.

No account of daily life at Biskupin would be complete without further mention of the extraordinary wealth of wooden objects. At most sites of this antiquity, they have perished without trace long ago. At Biskupin, wooden plows, hoes, spoons, whisks, troughs, and tubs enable us to complete the picture of ordinary objects and everyday life in the Early European Iron Age.

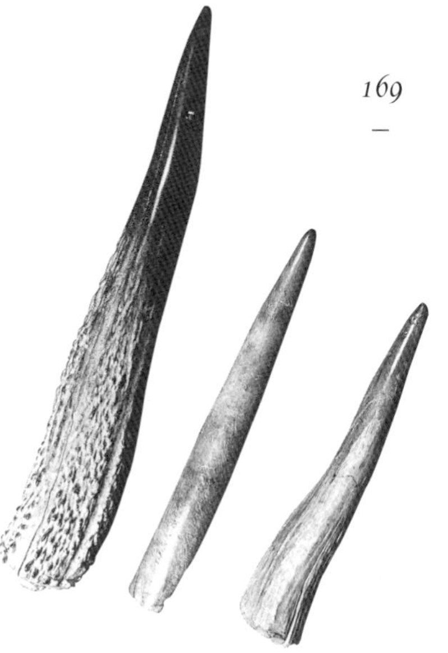

The History of a Settlement

Biskupin provides a rare and unique glimpse into the past, but how does it fit into the history of European society? We have already seen how in 1933, Professor Jozef Kostrzewski identified the pottery as that of the Lusatian culture, which flourished in much of central and northern Europe from c. 1200–400 B.C. Some archaeologists have speculated that the settlements and cemeteries of the Lusatian culture are those of early Slavs. This is a tempting equation to make, but one which is also difficult to support or deny.

Biskupin is one of many fortified settlements of the Lusatian culture. The appearance of fortifications indicates that warfare and insecurity were on the increase, perhaps the consequence of a growth in population. Too many people coveting too little land naturally leads to competition and hostility.

Biskupin itself was built in the eighth century B.C., probably in the 730s B.C. We know this from tree-ring sequences in the oak timbers used to build the rampart, the breakwater, and some of the houses. Most of the trees used in these structures were felled in the winter of 738–737 B.C., but felling continued down to 722 B.C. This makes it over two hundred years older than Kostrzewski initially thought.

The original settlement may have taken ten or twenty years to build. Some time later—perhaps after only a few decades—it burned down. A new Biskupin rose on the ruins, but it too was destroyed after perhaps a hundred years. In its third and final phase, Biskupin was a smaller and poorer settlement, without a defensive rampart. After a short occupation the people left to settle elsewhere.

The successive destructions of Biskupin have fired the imagination of romantically minded archaeologists who saw in them evidence of hostile attack. Two enemies have been proposed: Lusatian neighbors, some of them living in fortified settlements only 6–9 miles (10–15 kilometers) away; and the fearsome Scythians, a warlike people from the Ukrainian steppes who, some maintain, burned and looted their way across this part of Poland in the fifth century B.C. The new tree-ring dates from Biskupin rule out the Scythians, and despite claims to the contrary, there are no good grounds for thinking they ever made an appearance in the Biskupin area. Local warfare, on the other hand, might well have played a part in one or the other of Biskupin's conflagrations. It is not hard to see, however, that the close-packed timber buildings must have posed an enormous fire risk, even without enemy action, and it is possible that, at the end of the day, Biskupin simply burned down by accident.

The final hand in the early history of Biskupin was played by the lake itself. The water level had been rising steadily since the settlement was founded, and in its final phases the house floors were raised above ground level to avoid seasonal flooding. The lake continued to rise, however, and eventually forced the inhabitants to leave. For several centuries the site itself was under water, and lake-bed sands were laid across it. Only in the Middle Ages did the peninsula emerge from the waters again.

Further Reading

The primary accounts of excavations at Biskupin were published in specialist Polish archaeological journals and are not easily accessible. For the English reader, there is the invaluable short guide by Zdzislaw Rajewski, *Biskupin, A Fortified Settlement Dating from 500 b.c.* (Poznan: Wydawnictwo Poznanskie, 1980). There is also a special feature in the May 1984 issue of the magazine *Popular Archaeology* (pp. 9–40), coinciding with the Biskupin Exhibition being held in London at that time. The new dendrochronological dating was published by Tomasz Wazny in his short article, "Dendrochronological Dating of the Lusatian Culture Settlement at Biskupin, Poland —first results," *Newswarp* 14 (1993), pp. 3–5. For a recent study of the environmental setting, see Władystaw Niewiarowski et al., "Biskupin Fortified Settlement and Its Environment in the Light of New Environmental and Archaeological Studies," in *The Wetland Revolution in Prehistory,* edited by Bryony Coles (Exeter: The Prehistoric Society, 1992, pp. 81–92). A wide-ranging survey of wetland archaeology is provided by Bryony and John Coles in *People of the Wetlands: Bogs, Bodies and Lake-dwellers* (New York: Thames and Hudson, 1989).

Further Viewing

The site museum at Biskupin displays some finds from the excavations, but the bulk of the material is in the State Archaeological Museum (Panstwowe Muzeum Archeologiczne), in Warsaw.

CHAPTER

TWELVE

Hochdorf

c. 550 B.C.

A chieftain's grave

in southern Germany

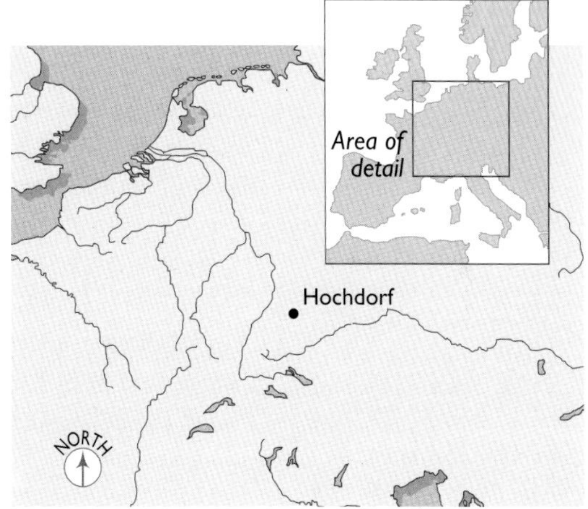

Hochdorf is one of the most recent and spectacular prehistoric tombs to be excavated in Europe. Its discovery came as something of a surprise. Several richly furnished graves of Celtic rulers had been found in eastern France and southwestern Germany, beginning in the 1870s. Most famous of all were the Hohmichele grave on the Danube excavated in 1937, and the Vix mound in Burgundy investigated in 1953. The latter was furnished with a huge bronze krater (mixing bowl) of Greek manufacture, the largest Greek metal vessel to have survived from ancient times. The Hohmichele grave was equally spectacular, even though the central burial had been robbed in antiquity.

Hohmichele and Vix were both conspicuous burial mounds, but few would have imagined that the barely visible rise at Hochdorf held a still greater discovery. It was Renate Leibfried, an archaeologist from the town, who alerted the regional archaeological service in 1977. Ten years earlier, in 1968, she had noticed stones being brought up by a plow in an otherwise stone-free soil when she was looking for a Roman villa. It was only in February 1977 that further plowing revealed a whole ring of stones, and Leibfried realized that this was no Roman or medieval ruin but a large Iron Age tumulus. Alarmed that it was steadily being plowed away, and fearing that the central burial chamber would soon also be destroyed, the regional archaeological service decided to mount a full rescue excavation.

The service entrusted the task to Jörg Biel, a prehistoric archaeologist who had been working for them since 1972. He had considerable experience at excavating sites in the region, but none of them remotely compared with what he was to find at Hochdorf. Excavations began on 5 June 1978. When they ended in November the following year, Biel and his team had made the discovery of a lifetime: an undisturbed grave chamber with an astonishing richness of furnishings—bronzes, gold, remains of drinking horns, and a four-wheeled wagon. Even some of the original wood and textiles had survived, preserved by the special microclimate created within the carefully sealed timber chamber. Among it all, on a bronze couch, lay the skeleton of a south German chieftain who had died at approximately forty years old, buried here with all his finery in about 550 B.C.

Plan of the Hochdorf burial mound. At the center is the rectangular timber chamber (1) within its pit (2). Around the pit is spread the upcast material that was dug out of it (3), and in this is a subsidiary burial (Grave 3). The ceremonial approach-way starts from the northern side of the mound and is flanked by drystone walls (4); the entrance itself (5) was blocked once the burial was complete. Around the perimeter of the mound a ring of timber posts (6) was erected, and the edge was marked or reinforced by a timber fence or palisade (7) and by a layer of stones (8). Around the edge there were also a number of subsidiary burials (Grave 2, Grave 4). Beneath the mound, archaeologists discovered pits (9, 10, 11) with debris from the manufacture of grave furnishings (including goldwork) on the site.

The Chamber

The chamber in which the burial lay was a double-skinned affair made of massive oak timbers. The outer skin was of split oak logs, their curved sides facing inward. In the middle of this structure, the tomb-builders had created a more carefully finished chamber of squared oak timbers. The timbers of the inner chamber overlapped at the corner in the manner of a log cabin, though only the lowermost lengths of timber were preserved in the moist earth.

The floor of the inner chamber was made of smooth oak planks, but the roof was more difficult to interpret since it had long since collapsed and decayed and there were few clues. Biel eventually concluded that it too had been multiskinned. The inner chamber had had its own roof of squared oak timbers, creating a sealed box. The mound-builders had then piled stones around and over it, almost filling the outer chamber. To finish the job they laid a double-skin roof of split oak trunks, a further layer of stones, another timber roof, and more stones on top of that.

By the end of this process the Celtic chieftain within his central chamber was enclosed by four layers of oak roofing and over 55 tons (50 metric tons) of stones. The intention must have been to give the maximum possible protection to the burial and its rich grave goods. However distinguished the deceased, and however strong the sanctions and beliefs forbidding disturbance of the dead, the bronze and precious metal must have presented a tempting target for potential tomb-robbers. Other Celtic graves were certainly robbed in antiquity. Some were looted not long after they were closed: at the Magdalenenberg, the tomb-robbers' abandoned spades were shown by tree-rings to be only forty-seven years younger than the burial chamber they had been used to rob. The extra precautions adopted in the Hochdorf tomb seem to have worked, however, since what Biel and his colleagues found was an intact grave, undisturbed since the initial burial over 2,500 years ago.

The open chamber within the primary mound, shortly before the burial. The stone walling forms a ceremonial entrance to the processional way leading to the chamber. On the near edge of the primary mound, to the right of the entrance, were two pits containing workshop debris from the manufacture of grave goods; a third, similar pit lay beneath the mound just within the ceremonial entrance.

The completed mound in its final form, as re-created at the site itself. The primary phase is now entirely hidden beneath the large secondary mound. A rough stone edging runs around the foot of the mound, with a ring of stout timber posts immediately outside it (and perhaps a fence). A marker stone stands over the burial chamber.

The Furnishings

When Biel began digging into the central grave pit in 1978, he was confronted by a mass of stones. These were the fallen remains of the stone-packing that had been placed above and around the timber chamber. With great care, the layers of stone were removed, until at length buried objects began to appear beneath them: first the rim of a large bronze vessel in the northwest corner and a 6-foot (2-meter) length of bronze sheet against the west wall; then in the eastern part of the chamber, remains of a timber wagon covered with iron sheeting. For Biel, these were the first unmistakable signs of what he was about to discover.

Conservation of the finds was a major headache, and once he had dug down into the chamber Biel arranged for some of the major elements to be removed in blocks for more detailed excavation in the laboratory. Conservation became even more crucial when organic materials began to be discovered at the bottom of the chamber. There were some five hundred samples of ancient textiles, not to mention animal skins and plant remains.

By the end of the excavation, Biel had gathered sufficient information to reconstruct the original layout of the grave chamber. It was an extraordinary

Reconstruction of the Hochdorf burial chamber. To the right, the body of the dead man lies on the bronze couch, with the top of the bronze cauldron just visible near the foot end. On the left is the four-wheeled wagon, on which a horse harness and a bronze dinner service are piled. Nine drinking horns hang on the far wall of the chamber; the one by the dead man's head is of iron decorated with bands of gold.

One of the most extraordinary finds from the Hochdorf burial chamber was the bronze couch on which the dead man was lying. Made of six separate metal sheets riveted together, it is supported by cast bronze legs in the form of human figurines. Between their feet are metal wheels that would have allowed this cumbersome piece of furniture to be moved. The back of the couch is decorated with scenes of sword-wielding warriors and four-wheeled wagons.

picture. The long bronze sheet against the west wall proved to be a decorated bronze couch on which the body of the dead man had been laid. It came out of the ground twisted and discolored, but careful conservation revealed a stylish piece of furniture 9 feet (3 meters) long with curving ends, made of two separate sheets of bronze riveted together and supported on a system of wheels so that it could be moved around. Bronze figures of female dancers with raised hands formed the feet. The back was decorated with a punched-dot design of sword-wielding warriors fighting or dancing, flanked at either end by four-wheeled wagons pulled by pairs of horses. A wagon of just this kind (minus the horses) was found within the grave. Traces of textiles and animal hairs were found on the seat of the couch, showing that it had either had padded upholstery or been covered with cushions, blankets, or skins.

The dead man himself was richly attired with gold-decorated shoes, a gold neckring, and massive gold bracelets on his right arm. There were gold serpentine brooches to fasten clothing, a gold-decorated belt around the waist, with a gold dagger sheath and iron dagger with decorated gold hilt. Not without justice did Biel, writing in *Antiquity,* describe the body as "virtually covered with gold ornaments." In all, the grave contained a pound (half a kilogram) of gold.

Less valuable but no less remarkable was the conical hat that had slipped from the dead man's head and lay against the curved inner corner of the couch. It was made of two pieces of birch bark stitched together. The uppermost piece had been decorated with finely punched concentric designs. The stone statue from the nearby Hirschlanden tumulus shows a person wearing just such a hat.

The dead ruler's personal belongings were completed by a wooden comb and iron razor placed beside his head, fish-hooks and a nailcutter in a cloth pouch on his chest, and a leather quiver filled with iron- and bronze-tipped arrows, which was hung over the back of the couch. The head of the man himself was supported on a cushion filled with aromatic herbs.

But this wasn't all that was placed in the grave. For a start, there was the great bronze cauldron, around three feet in diameter, which was positioned at the foot of the couch. This was fitted with cast-bronze lions and massive bronze handles around the rim, and was the work of Greek craftsmen. The likeliest origin is not Greece itself, but a workshop in one of the Greek colonies of southern Italy or Sicily. Sometime in its life one of the lions had been damaged or lost and replaced by a locally made copy of superior craftsmanship. What did the cauldron contain? There is no certain answer, though Udelgard Körber-Grohne from Stuttgart University did analyze the half-inch-thick peat-like deposit in the bottom. She concluded that it had contained not wine (as might have been expected in a Greek-made bronze vessel) but a drink made with honey. Mead is the obvious candidate. Whatever the liquid was, it was probably ladled out using the embossed gold bowl found within the cauldron, and drunk from the nine decorated drinking horns that hung on the south-

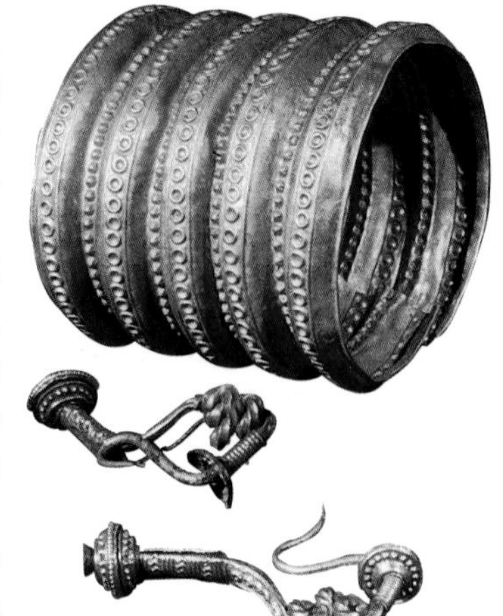

Gold ornaments from the Hochdorf grave include the armring with embossed decoration that the dead man was wearing on his right forearm, and two gold serpentine pins used to fix the man's outer clothing in position. The armring and pins (along with other gold ornaments from the burial) were decorated using the same punches, and were probably manufactured specifically for the burial in a special workshop on the site.

Replica of the four-wheeled wagon found in the Hochdorf grave. The body of the wagon, the ten-spoked wheels, and the long draught pole were sheathed in decorated iron sheet. This had decayed and broken into thousands of corroded fragments. Piecing them together to allow this accurate reconstruction to be built was a major work of conservation.

ern wall of the grave chamber. All this goes to show that while the Hochdorf chieftain appreciated Greek bronzeware, he had not yet adopted Greek wine nor Greek tableware.

The third major element that Biel found in the grave, after the couch and the cauldron, was the splendid four-wheeled wagon. This was encased in embossed sheet iron and had to be reconstructed from the thousands of tiny fragments into which the metal had decayed. In contrast to Scythian burials of the same period, the horses that pulled the wagon had not been placed in the grave, though their equipment was: yoke and harness for two horses. There was a long wooden pole, decorated with a spiral band of bronze, for directing the horses. Also piled on the wagon were the dead man's dinner service, comprising three shallow bronze bowls and nine bronze dishes. The number nine corresponds with the number of drinking horns hung on the southern wall, and suggests it was a number of special significance, though quite what significance we cannot now say.

The final touch to the burial chamber was given by floor and wall coverings. A coarse-weave carpet had been laid on the floor and finer fabrics nailed to the timber walls. The wall coverings had been pinned together with bronze brooches, and fragments of the cloth still adhered to the corroded bronze. They may well have been brightly colored. Had they survived better, they might have given us an impression of how a south German chieftain's residence would have looked in the sixth-century B.C. Above all, however, the Hochdorf grave speaks to us of the belief in an afterlife held by this leader and his society, a belief that led them to make the grave a comfortable dwelling for the dead man, complete with the luxury feasting equipment so crucial to the social standing of Celtic aristocrats.

One thing that is very clear is the peaceful nature of the grave goods. There is hunting and fishing equipment, but no weapons of war. This doesn't mean the Hochdorf chieftain himself was a man of peace, but it does suggest his power was not dependent on his success as a fierce warrior.

The Body, the Mound, and the Funeral Rites

The body of the Celtic chieftain had been reduced to a skeleton; none of the flesh or hair remained. It was still possible, however, to draw a number of conclusions about the dead man himself and the treatment his body had received before burial. First, he was around forty when he died, though the cause of death cannot now be determined. He was by no means an old man, though in prehistoric societies, where disease was rife, only the fortunate few could expect to live their full natural span. Anthropologists studying the Hochdorf skeleton calculated that the dead man stood over 6 feet (almost 2 meters) tall, well above average for his place and time.

Still more exciting was evidence that the body had been embalmed before burial. Most of this was indirect; there was nothing to show what method had

WHO WERE THE CELTS?

The word "Celtic" derives from ancient Greek writers who described the peoples living north of Massilia (modern Marseille, on the south coast of France) as Celts; the Romans usually referred to them as "Galli" or Gauls. They were found in modern France and in central Europe north of the Alps; in the third century B.C. a group of Celts ("Galatai") even crossed into Asia Minor. In later centuries the story becomes confused, however, and when the Romans invaded Gaul in the first century B.C. they made a clear distinction between the peoples of their new province and those living east of the Rhine, whom they called Germans. It is clear, indeed, that there was no Celtic people as such—they never called themselves Celts—but that this was a term used, often vaguely or inaccurately, by Greek and Roman writers to refer to certain "barbarian" neighbors. The word Celtic is nonetheless still used by many archaeologists as shorthand for the peoples who occupied most of Europe north of the Alps in the first millennium B.C., and it is used in that sense here.) Only in the sixteenth and seventeenth centuries A.D. did writers begin to describe the inhabitants of Ireland and parts of Britain as Celtic.)

been used. But Biel is confident that the body must have been conserved in some way, since vegetation had begun to grow on the exposed soil at the bottom of the grave pit, showing it had been left open for at least four weeks and perhaps longer. The body must somehow have been preserved during this time. Another tantalizing clue is provided by the fact that the body had lost its hair before it was placed on the bronze couch. How do we know this, when only the skeleton survives? The answer lies in the hairs that were found adhering to the couch. These were animal hairs, from the rug or hide placed beneath the body, but there was not a single human hair. Hair loss is a common consequence of preservation treatments. Neither were there any traces of fly larvae, which suggests that the body was treated immediately after death, before decomposition had set in. Was it covered in honey or immersed in salt? We shall probably never know. Nor do we know exactly why it was treated in this way. Egyptian mummification was based on a belief that survival after death was dependent on the physical preservation of the body. In the Hochdorf case, the intention may merely have been to keep the deceased in reasonable repair while the burial mound was completed and arrangements could be made for the funeral.

The building of the mound began with the digging of the pit for the burial chamber. This measured 36 by 36 feet (11 by 11 meters) and was some 8 feet (2.5 meters) deep. Within this the timber chambers were constructed, one inside the other. Once these were complete—or perhaps in parallel with them—work began on the surrounding mound. The material for the mound must have been stripped from around its foot. The mound-builders began with turf, piling this up to make a primary mound 130 feet (40 meters) across, reaching up to the lip of the burial chamber, which was still open to the sky awaiting its occupant. Then on the northern edge of this turf mound they built a ceremonial entrance facade, a pair of hefty stone walls with a ramp between them leading up onto the turf mound.

Nearby, special workshops were set up to manufacture the grave goods. We know this since traces of the artisans' activities were found within the turf mound. All the gold objects, save the neckring, were made here. Once the artisans had completed their work they carefully gathered up the debris that remained (including unfinished gold objects) and buried it in three shallow pits within the mound, so that what was intended for the dead would not be touched by the living.

At last, the day of the funeral arrived. We can only guess what happened, using the scanty archaeological traces available. It was probably a public affair, with subjects and relatives of the dead ruler playing the part either of participants or onlookers in the ceremony. The rich grave fittings were probably carried in procession, through the ceremonial gateway and up the sloping side of the mound to the lip of the burial chamber. There, waiting attendants lowered them into the grave and placed them carefully in their preordained positions in the chamber. The great bronze vessel with its lion mounts and the

HALLSTATT PRINCELY CENTERS

The Hohenasperg near Hochdorf is one of several hilltop fortresses that seem to have been centers of power during the seventh and sixth centuries B.C. Medieval and Renaissance rebuilding at the Hohenasperg removed all trace of the prehistoric arrangements. But for an idea of the original appearance of one of these Hallstatt centers we can look southward to the Heuneburg on the banks of the Danube. Here a flat-topped plateau overlooking the river became the site of a remarkable Iron Age fortress, with imports from the Classical world and even a fortification wall of Greek construction —mud-brick on a stone foundation, with projecting rectangular towers at regular intervals. Within the defenses, in one corner of the enclosure, German archaeologists have uncovered remains of rectangular buildings that seem to have been divided into separate sectors, one for workshops, another for living areas. Such a tightly organized settlement plan betrays the presence of a strong central organization. The rulers of the Heuneburg (like those of other Hallstatt centers) were buried in impressively furnished grave-chambers in mounds nearby, such as the famous Hohmichele mound at the foot of the Heuneburg itself.

The importance of foreign craft goods—and possibly foreign craftsmen—in the functioning of such centers was underlined by the discovery of an Etruscan ceramic mold showing the head of a Silenus figure (Silenus being a character from Classical mythology). The mold would have been used for casting a Silenus head at the base of a bronze vessel-handle. This suggests that craftsmen at the Heuneburg were casting bronze vessels of Italian type, though whether the craftsmen themselves were locals or Italians, this object alone cannot tell us.

Finds such as this are eye-catching and suggestive, but they don't mean that the Heuneburg—or the other Hallstatt hillforts—were dependent for their survival on Mediterranean trade. It is better to think of them as powerful local centers, linked to long- distance trade networks that brought them profitable contacts with a whole range of neighboring peoples.

The Heuneburg on the Upper Danube. This is the best known of the Hallstatt "princely centers" of the sixth century B.C. Although the Heuneburg is only half the size of the princely center nearest to Hochdorf, the Hohenasperg (8 acres [3.2 hectares] as compared with the latter's 15 acres [6 hectares]), the discoveries made here in 1963–1979 have provided the fullest picture yet available of the nature and function of these centers.

decorated bronze couch would have been brought in in their turn and placed in the grave. Last of all came the body itself, richly dressed and ornamented, carried perhaps on the splendid four-wheeled wagon. This would have been pulled by horses or men up the slope of the mound and then unloaded of its cargo at the graveside. The dead body was laid carefully on the bronze couch and strewn with flowers, then the wagon was lowered into the grave and bronze vessels and other objects placed upon it. At some point flowering boughs were strewn either on or below the couch, perhaps over the dead body itself.

Once everything was in the grave chamber, the onlookers withdrew and the carpenters set to work on the multilayered roof. Mound-builders then took over to complete their task, covering the primary turf tumulus with brown subsoil and yellow loess as they dug deeper and deeper for their material. The stone-built facade and the shallow artisans' pits were eventually engulfed in a structure 200 feet (60 meters) across and 20 feet (6 meters) high. The foot of this enormous mound was then edged with a curb of stones, reinforced by wooden posts, to prevent erosion.

By the time archaeologists arrived, the mound had been under the plow for centuries and survived only as a slight rise in the ground. The original height of 20 feet (6 meters) or more had been reduced to a mere 5 feet (1.5 meters). Thus we don't know whether any grave marker stood on the mound. Hochdorf, however, is only 3½ miles (6 kilometers) from Hirschlanden, another sixth-century B.C. burial mound, and Hirschlanden did have a grave marker, carved in stone, representing a naked man. The Hochdorf chieftain was in fact buried with the very equipment carved on the Hirschlanden statue: a neckring, a conical hat, and a dagger in the belt. The Hirschlanden figure is also ithyphallic and may be wearing a mask; it is difficult from the statue's present worn state to be sure on the latter point. The fixed, not-quite-human gaze certainly makes a troubling impression on the viewer. Might there not have been a similar grave marker at Hochdorf? If so, it was no doubt removed many centuries ago by a local farmer who was tired of having to steer his plow around it.

The Hirschlanden statue, found lying at the foot of a sixth-century burial mound a few miles south of Hochdorf in 1963–1964. Standing 5 feet (1.5 meters) tall (and hence roughly life-size), it depicts an ithyphallic man, naked save for a conical hat or helmet, a neckring, and a waistband into which a dagger is thrust. A similar figure may once have stood on top of the Hochdorf tumulus, though no trace of it survived.

Relatives and Retainers

The chamber was closed and the chieftain laid to rest, but this was not the end of activity at Hochdorf. Biel and his team found three other skeletons within the mound itself. The most curious was Grave 3, a burial near the center of the mound, only 6 feet (2 meters) west of the timber chamber. As found, it lay only 4 inches (10 centimeters) below the modern ground surface and had been heavily damaged by plowing. Originally, however, it must have been 13 feet (4 meters) or more below the top of the mound. Biel concluded that it can't have been dug into the finished monument, but must have been put there during the construction. It was a simply furnished grave with only a knife and a couple of brooches to attach a cloak. Who it was we don't know, though it was male—maybe a servant slain to accompany his master to the Otherworld? We can only speculate.

The other burials were toward the edges of the mound, and show the attraction of the dead ruler and of the monument under which he was buried. These people may have been relatives or retainers, remaining close to the chieftain in death just as they had in life. They were buried here as they died, during the years that followed their master's funeral. The best preserved of these was Grave 4, on the southern edge, and it was probably also the first of them, made

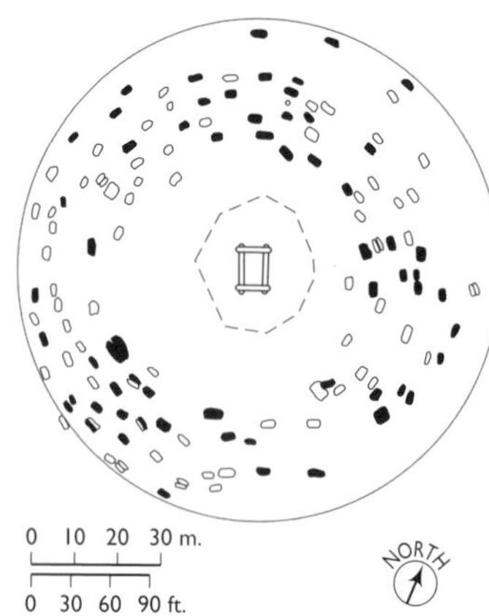

Plan of the Magdalenenberg, an enormous burial mound near Villingen in the Black Forest region of southern Germany. Larger (330 feet [100 meters] across) and slightly earlier (seventh century B.C.) than the Hochdorf tumulus, it contained at least 126 subsidiary burials arranged in concentric rings around a central timber grave chamber. Unlike Hochdorf, the timber chamber of the Magdalenenberg had been robbed in antiquity.

during the final stages of mound construction, a stone-lined pit just within the mound's stone kerb. Another skeleton lay on the northern edge of the tumulus, in a grave (Grave 2) dug into the stone-built entrance facade some years after the mound was finished. The body buried here was that of a young man with a pair of brooches at the shoulders to support his cloak, and a neck-ring and two iron spearheads. Nearby were found bronze objects from similar graves that had not survived the plow.

How many of these peripheral graves there had been we cannot hope to know, but the two that are left are probably only a fraction of the total. If the archaeologists had gotten there sooner, Hochdorf might have been like the slightly older (seventh century B.C.) Magdalenenberg tumulus, also in southern Germany. The Magdalenenberg is in fact one of the largest prehistoric burial mounds in Europe, measuring over 320 feet (100 meters) across and (originally) 26 feet (8 meters) high. When Konrad Spindler excavated there in the early 1970s, he found no fewer than 126 burials arranged in concentric rings around the foot of the mound. There were probably 140 or more before centuries of erosion took their toll. Unlike Hochdorf, however, the central timber grave chamber had been robbed in antiquity, and what was left was excavated early in the twentieth century. But it was large, measuring 25 by 16 feet (8 by 5 meters) and made of squared oak logs. The known finds from the Magdalenenberg are nothing as rich as those from Hochdorf, but the secondary burials are better preserved. Of course, the Magdalenenberg is much bigger, and if we were to assume the number of graves was simply proportional to the circumference of the mound, we would expect there to have been only sixty or so graves at Hochdorf. There may not even have been this many.

The peripheral burials at Hochdorf and the Magdalenenberg were not those of ordinary commoners. They weren't as richly furnished as the central grave by any means, but they had bronze ornaments and iron weapons that would have been beyond the reach of the poorer sections of society. At the Magdalenenberg, women and children were buried in these graves as well as men. The mounds became a cemetery for families related by ties of blood or service to the chieftain who lay in the richly furnished central grave.

The Hochdorf Settlement

So astonishing were the finds from the Hochdorf burial in 1978–1979 that the local authorities soon began to make plans for a museum near the site in which the objects could be displayed. The location they chose for this was 450 yards (400 meters) west of the burial mound. Here a further surprise lay in store, for when they began work on the new museum in 1989, they discovered the remains of a Celtic settlement, founded at around the time of the Hochdorf chieftain.

This proved to be no ordinary rural village, but a settlement of special importance, marked by rich finds including red-figure pottery imported from

Model reconstruction of the buildings of the sixth-century village discovered on the site of the Hochdorf museum. Of the buildings themselves only the post-holes and beam-slots survived, but the excavators recovered sufficient evidence to reconstruct their appearance and deduce their functions. They concluded that the largest building (right) was a dwelling. Next to it was a granary, raised on stilts to guard against rats and the damp. In another building (left) they found objects connected with weaving. In the foreground can be seen two smaller outbuildings.

Greece. Only leading members of Celtic society could have had access to such rarities, and it is tempting to speculate that here was the residence of the Hochdorf chieftain. The buildings themselves were fairly unremarkable—a mixture of storage sheds and workshops for the most part, though there was also a rectangular timber hall. Some of the workshops had looms for weaving, others had bronze-casting equipment, further emphasizing the special nature of this settlement. Perhaps we should imagine it as the Hochdorf chieftain's country retreat?

One particularly interesting conclusion came from the animal bones. Alongside the usual domestic species (cattle, pig, sheep, goat, and dog) were horses and hunted animals. The horses may well have been ridden, while the hunted animals were small species, notably roe deer and hare. They suggest that the landscape around Hochdorf was already deforested by this period, without extensive areas of woodland where larger game animals could be found.

Who Was the Hochdorf Chieftain?

So far we have been referring to the occupant of the central grave at Hochdorf as a chieftain. But who was he? What was his position in society, and how did he come to be buried with such rich accoutrements under such an enormous mound? To answer these questions we have to situate Hochdorf more clearly in both space and time. Let us begin with the time.

Hochdorf is far from being the only tomb of its kind, though it is far and away the richest and best preserved to have been excavated in recent years. Archaeologists assign it to the last phase of the Hallstatt period (Hallstatt D), which takes its name from the Hallstatt cemetery in central Austria. The Magdalenenberg belongs to the very beginning of the Hallstatt D period. The felling of the tree-trunks used to construct the central timber burial chamber at the Magdalenenberg has recently been dated by dendrochronology to 622 B.C. The Hochdorf burial is rather later than this. The best clue is provided by the Greek bronze cauldron. Classical scholars maintain this was made in a Greek city in southern Italy in around the 530s B.C., and from this reasoning, the Hochdorf burial must belong to about this time or a little later. But the excavator, Jörg Biel, is not convinced by the argument, and on the basis of broader parallels in the Hochdorf material prefers an earlier date for the burial, around 550 B.C. This places it some 70 years before the end of the Hallstatt D period, which falls at about 480 B.C.

Hallstatt D was a crucial period in the prehistory of southern Germany and eastern France. A whole series of chiefdoms developed in the region north and west of the Alps. The rulers controlled the key routes leading southward, connecting the Celtic world of central Europe with the Etruscan cities of northern Italy and the Greek colonies of southern Italy, Sicily, and southern France. The chiefs installed themselves in hilltop fortresses and grew rich on the profits of trade and the tribute they drew from their own subjects. The most vivid evidence of the trade is the Greek and Etruscan manufactures found at the hilltop fortresses and in the rich graves in which the chieftains were buried.

The foreign trade goods were probably flaunted by the chieftains before their subjects as evidence of their power and the wide reach of their contacts. The exotic imports set the chieftains apart from ordinary people, who did not have these contacts and could not afford these luxuries. The message was underlined by the costly furnishings the chieftains had made for themselves by local craftsmen, using valuable materials such as gold. Some of these were produced specifically for placing in the grave—the gold-decorated shoes from Hochdorf, for example, were in mint condition and had probably never been used in real life. The burial was designed to transmit a clear and unmistakable message: here was the leader of society, set apart from his subjects by his wealth and power, by the beautiful craftsmanship of his grave furnishings, and by the sheer size of his burial mound. In the decades that followed, relatives and retainers dutifully buried themselves around his tomb, while political power passed to his successors, who in due course had themselves buried in similar style somewhere nearby.

The Hochdorf chieftain and his dynasty controlled a broad swathe of territory in southern Germany. Only one major hilltop fortress of the Hallstatt D period is known in this region: the Hohenasperg, an isolated rocky outcrop rising high above the surrounding plain. Any prehistoric remains have been obliterated by the building of a medieval town and Renaissance fortress on top. In Hallstatt D times, however, it was a major center of power. We don't yet know how the Hohenasperg related to the wealthy settlement at Hochdorf, but it is certainly possible that the Hochdorf chieftain lived mainly at the Hohenasperg, in an impressive fortified residence similar to the one discovered by Wolfgang Kimmig and his colleagues at the Heuneburg on the River Danube.

Hochdorf is only 6 miles (10 kilometers) from the Hohenasperg, and the burial mound can be seen from the fortress. There are other rich Hallstatt burials in the area, some close to the foot of the Hohenasperg, others (generally of earlier date) rather more distant. They are evidence of a single nexus of power, perhaps members of the same ruling family. Like Hochdorf, they are (or were) large and imposing burial mounds with richly furnished chambers containing valuable imports from the Greek world. Some were male, others female, though we know little of the position of women in these systems of government. There is no reason to think they were downtrodden dependents, since some of the richest Hallstatt graves (notably that at Vix in Burgundy) contained female interments.

The latest of all the burial mounds in the Hohenasperg group is the Kleinaspergle, about a half-mile south of the hillfort. It belongs not to Hallstatt D but to the following La Tène period, around 450 B.C., and is the last gasp of a dying dynasty. By this time, the old trade routes had been broken and power had shifted irrevocably northward, to the middle Rhineland and the Marne. There, new La Tène dynasties emerged as the Hallstatt chiefdoms of southern Germany dissolved. The age of the Hochdorf chieftain was over, and the chieftain himself forgotten, until Biel rediscovered his final resting place twenty-five centuries later.

Location of Hochdorf and neighboring Early Iron Age burial mounds in relation to the "princely center" of the Hohenasperg. The burial mounds nearest to the hillfort (Kleinaspergle and Grafenbühl) seem to be later in date than the more distant mounds such as Römerhügel and Hochdorf, later even than the last clear evidence of Iron Age occupation at the Hohenasperg itself.

Further Reading

The best account of the Hochdorf grave is provided by the excavator, Jörg Biel, and is in German: *Der Keltenfürst von Hochdorf* (Stuttgart: Theiss, 1985). This contains numerous excellent illustrations of the grave and its contents. Biel has also written a shorter description for English readers: "The Late Hallstatt Chieftain's Grave at Hochdorf" in *Antiquity* 55 (1981), pp. 16–18. The specialist analysis of the cauldron deposit is reported by Udelgard Körber-Grohne in "Biologische Untersuchungen am keltischen Fürstengrab von Hochdorf, Kr. Ludwigsburg," *Archäologisches Korrespondenzblatt* 10 (1980), pp. 249–252. The general background to the Celtic Iron Age is given by John Collis in *The European Iron Age* (New York: Schocken Books, 1984), and more recently by Simon James in his excellent *The World of the Celts* (New York: Thames and Hudson, 1993). For relations between Celtic Europe and the Classical world, see Peter Wells, *Culture Contact and Culture Change* (New York: Cambridge University Press, 1980), and Barry Cunliffe, *Greeks, Romans and Barbarians* (New York: Methuen, 1988).

Further Viewing

The Keltenmuseum Hochdorf/Enz displays material related to the site's excavation.

CHAPTER

THIRTEEN

Maiden Castle

C. 4000 B.C.–A.D. 50

Neolithic enclosure to Iron Age hillfort

in southern England

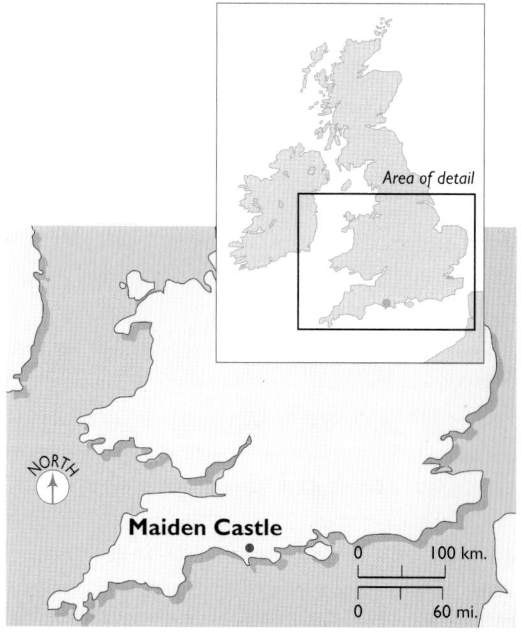

The chalklands of southern England provide an undulating landscape with rolling uplands divided into blocks by stream and river valleys. Many of the uplands escaped the impact of deep plowing until the present century, allowing time for antiquaries and archaeologists to notice the remarkable palimpsest of prehistoric mounds and earthworks that had survived in this area. There are entire field systems of prehistoric date, stretching acre after acre across the grass-covered slopes, revealed only as a pattern of criss-cross marks. There are Neolithic long mounds and Bronze Age round mounds. Far and away the most impressive, however, are the remains of the massive ramparts of Iron Age hillforts, and the greatest of these, without question, is Maiden Castle.

Maiden Castle is the largest hillfort in Britain, enclosing an area of 47 acres (19 hectares). In its final form, it was surrounded by ramparts up to 18 feet (5 meters) high arranged four deep, one inside the other, on the southern side of the hilltop, and three deep on the less exposed northern side. Today these appear as rounded, grass-grown humps, but when they were built they were formidable fighting platforms of dry-stone construction with steeply sloping outer faces. Manned by skilled defenders firing slingstones with fearsome accuracy, they were no mere decorative facade. Maiden Castle, indeed, was a key strongpoint, a center of local power and a symbol of the prestige and authority of the people by whom it was built.

The visitor today approaches Maiden Castle from the north, by the road leading south from the modern town of Dorchester. Dorchester was in fact a Roman creation, intentionally sited as the replacement to Maiden Castle. In more settled times under Roman rule, hilltop strongholds were no longer in vogue. They were difficult to reach, and new centers were established in the valley bottoms on the lower land where the major routeways ran.

So it is that the visitor traveling from Dorchester to Maiden Castle is in a very real sense going back in time, from the *pax Romana* to the more unsettled Iron Age, when prehistoric tribes and chiefdoms ruled southern Britain.

The Rediscovery of Maiden Castle

Maiden Castle is such a prominent feature of the landscape that it can never truly have been lost. The name itself is probably medieval, though it may incorporate the Celtic word "dun," a fortified place. There are in fact quite a number of "maiden castles" in England, virtually all of them Iron Age hillforts.

In terms of excavation, the story of Maiden Castle begins in 1934 when British archaeologist Mortimer (later Sir Mortimer) Wheeler began four seasons of summer fieldwork. Wheeler had a military background and was always fascinated by military sites. The spectacular defenses of Maiden Castle naturally exerted an irresistible attraction. The excavations were organized with military thoroughness on an impressive scale. Wheeler was keen to encourage visitors (an attitude relatively rare for those days) and even sold off duplicate

Aerial photograph of Mortimer Wheeler's excavations at Maiden Castle taken in 1937. The whiteness of the chalk subsoil makes the trenches stand out against the surface of green turf. In the foreground are the complex banks and ditches of the western entrance. The line of white marks extending back into the interior of the fort are small soundings across the Neolithic bank barrow. In the middle of the fort near the right-hand side is a cutting across the ditch of the smaller original hillfort. Finally, at the far end of the fort can be seen Wheeler's more extensive excavations in and around the eastern entrance.

(*facing page*) Phases of activity at Maiden Castle: (1) the causewayed enclosure c. 4000 B.C.; (2) the bank barrow c. 3350 B.C.; (3) Bronze Age barrows and land divisions; (4) the first hillfort, sixth century B.C.; (5) the enlarged hillfort, fourth century B.C.; (6) decline in the Late Iron Age; (7) disuse in the early Roman period, first to fourth century A.D.; and (8) Romano-British temple, late fourth century A.D.

finds (after they had been properly recorded) to help finance the work. He also took steps to make sure the results became known to a wider public through newspaper articles and cinema newsreels. This in turn attracted more visitors, putting Maiden Castle firmly on the tourist map and making Wheeler himself something of a media personality. But that wasn't the only reason for its fame. Wheeler's Maiden Castle excavation was also the largest of its day in the British Isles, and the techniques he employed were well in advance of their time.

Wheeler's aims were to investigate the defenses and to explore the interior, to see whether anything remained of the streets and houses that once must have occupied the hilltop. As it turned out, he did find traces of some houses, but the interior of the hillfort had been plowed in the Middle Ages and eroded over the centuries, so that most of the evidence had been obliterated. But he was able to show that the interior had been occupied during the Iron Age. Furthermore, Wheeler made other discoveries he had never expected, in particular the revelation that the eastern part of the hilltop had first been enclosed by ditches in the Neolithic period, to make one of the "causewayed camps" that are a key feature of the British Neolithic. Wheeler also discovered that the causewayed enclosure had been succeeded by a great linear mound or "bank barrow" toward the end of the Neolithic, and that when new occupation began at Maiden Castle some three thousand years later during the Iron Age, it began with a small hillfort occupying only the eastern half of the present enclosure. Finally, Wheeler was always intrigued by the links between archaeology and history. He had begun his archaeological career as a specialist in the Roman occupation of Britain, and was therefore delighted when just outside the eastern entrance of Maiden Castle he came across a group of burials, one with a Roman ballista bolt embedded in the spine. Were these the hastily buried remains of the last defenders of Maiden Castle, killed by the advancing Romans in A.D. 43?

WHEELER AND THE PUBLIC

Wheeler's excavations at Maiden Castle in the 1930s cost £5,363, a tiny figure by present day standards but a substantial outlay at the time. He raised most of the money (£3,307) from a printed appeal that was circulated in the spring of each year. He was also given a small grant (£790) by the Society of Antiquaries of London. The rest came from the sale of postcards and souvenirs, a resource that Wheeler was quick to appreciate:

> A well-stocked post-card stall is as popular as it is profitable. Picture post-cards of the site can be produced at a cost of little more than a halfpenny each and will sell readily at twopence each. Interim reports of the work, produced at fourpence each, will sell at one shilling each. . . . And trivial oddments such as beach-pebble slingstones, fragments of Roman tile, Roman oyster-shells, scraps of surface pottery, all marked in Indian ink with the name of the site, sell readily for a few pence each, and under proper control, are an entirely justifiable source of income.
>
> —R. E. M. Wheeler, *Maiden Castle, Dorset*

Wheeler's last summer of excavation at Maiden Castle was in 1937, and the hillfort lay untouched by archaeologists for the next fifty years. Then in 1985 a new program of investigation was begun, stimulated in part by the need to repair areas of Maiden Castle that were being damaged by natural erosion and the increasing numbers of visitors. White scars were appearing along the chalk ramparts as the turf cover slipped and bare patches were forming in the hillfort interior, especially near the site entrance. The need to rectify these problems provided an excellent opportunity for archaeologists to ask new questions of Maiden Castle, applying the most up-to-date tools and techniques. Many of these new techniques, such as radiocarbon dating and soil flotation for the recovery of seeds and organic remains, had not been available in Wheeler's day. The excavators also succeeded in discovering an area of the interior where Iron Age house foundations had survived. This was in the lee of the southwest rampart, where the ground is lower and the prehistoric remains have been buried under soil eroding downhill from the center of the hillfort. The excavations undertaken in this corner in 1985–1986 were limited in area, but they revealed traces of a whole series of Iron Age houses, built and rebuilt over several hundred years.

It cannot have been easy for the excavators, taking up the mantle of Sir Mortimer Wheeler on this famous site. But supported by English Heritage and directed on the ground by Niall Sharples, the new excavations have placed Maiden Castle once again at the heart of the British Iron Age.

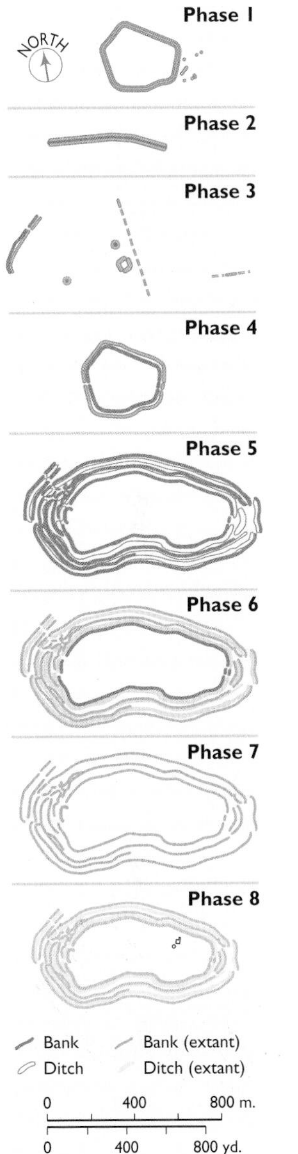

First Diggings on a Dorset Hilltop

As we have seen, Maiden Castle is a multiphase monument, not just an Iron Age hillfort but a Neolithic center as well. There are in fact two distinct Neolithic phases (causewayed enclosure and bank barrow) and several Iron Age phases as the hillfort was built and remodeled, not to mention sporadic activity in the intervening Bronze Age and during Roman and medieval times. Undoubtedly the simplest way of untangling this sequence is to describe the various stages in chronological order, beginning with the construction of the causewayed enclosure in around 4000 B.C.

The causewayed enclosure was made by digging a pair of concentric ditches, one inside the other, around the eastern part of the Maiden Castle hilltop. The complete plan isn't known, since the ditches lie almost exactly underneath the ditch and bank of the first Iron Age hillfort. This occupied only about half the area of the later hillfort we see today and was limited on the west by a bank and ditch running roughly north–south across the middle of the hilltop. Wheeler first came across the causewayed enclosure by accident when he was excavating a cutting through this north–south Iron Age defense.

The Maiden Castle causewayed enclosure is only one of several dozen similar constructions known throughout the British Isles. They became famous in the 1920s, through excavations on the Sussex Downs and at Windmill Hill near Avebury (*see* Chapter 6), but until the 1960s were thought to be peculiar to southern England. Then in the 1970s, as aerial photography became increasingly widely used, new causewayed enclosures came to light in the flatlands of eastern England and in the north. More recently still, Neolithic enclosures have been discovered in Scotland, Wales, and Northern Ireland.

Despite the new discoveries, there is still no agreement on what these enclosures were for. The name itself is significant. Archaeologists call them causewayed enclosures because of the frequent gaps in the ditches. It isn't a question of continuous ditches broken by an occasional entrance; causewayed enclosures have many such gaps, far more than would be expected if their purpose was defensive. The Maiden Castle causewayed enclosure wasn't then simply the Neolithic precursor to the Iron Age hillfort. The ditches were dug into the chalk in short segments, each one perhaps the work of a different community or family group. Their aim was to make an enclosure that wasn't defensive, but that marked out a special area for feasting or ceremonies. They wanted it to be clearly visible from a distance, hence the choice of a prominent hilltop. For this reason, too, they dug the ditches just below the crest of the hill, where they would have been most easily visible from below. The effect would have been all the more striking given the whiteness of the chalk beneath, and of the dug-out chalk piled in a low bank along the inner edges of the ditches.

If it wasn't defensive, what exactly went on within this Neolithic enclosure? To answer the question, we have only the clues provided by the remains excavated from the ditches and the area preserved beneath the later Neolithic bank barrow. There Wheeler found shallow pits and post-holes, suggesting that people had indeed lived within the enclosure during Neolithic times, but there was no trace of houses. There was, however, one deeper pit, containing broken pottery and limpets from the coast, some 5 miles (8 kilometers) to the south, and a grave with remains of two small children around age six or seven. Other burials (both children and adults) were found in the enclosure ditches. These support an alternative theory that the enclosures were places where rituals of the dead were carried out.

Sharples and his team discovered other important clues in the enclosure ditches. There were over 20,000 flint flakes, many of them from the manufacture of axes. Axe-making was probably a major activity in the enclosure. Other axes were made of hard stone, which must have been brought to Maiden Castle from Cornwall. There were also thousands of animal bones, more than half of them of cattle that had probably been butchered and eaten at the site. Finally, using up-to-date techniques, environmental specialists on Sharples's team found remains of cultivated cereals, weeds, and hazelnuts. The people who made the Maiden Castle enclosure were clearly farmers and stockbreeders, though they continued to collect wild foods. It is unlikely, however, that they lived at Maiden Castle all year round. The chalk-cut enclosure ditches were evidently intended to mark this out as a special place. The quantities of cattle bones trigger an image of feasting, perhaps on regular occasions, when people who spent most of their year in scattered communities in the surrounding region came together at the enclosure they had created to celebrate special festivals or to take part in important seasonal rituals. The Maiden Castle enclosure can be seen as a regional center, a tribal meeting place, though we shall probably never know exactly what went on there.

The Bank Barrow and the Bronze Age

After several centuries of use, the causewayed enclosure at Maiden Castle was abandoned. For fifty years or so, the ditches were left to silt up and were soon simply grass-filled depressions. Then, around 3350 B.C., people came back to Maiden Castle to build a new kind of monument—the bank barrow.

The bank barrow was another of Wheeler's unexpected discoveries. It is a linear mound flanked by shallow, parallel ditches cut into the chalk, around 60 feet (17.5 meters) apart and 5 feet (1.5 meters) deep. At the time it was built the bank barrow would have been another striking and highly visible feature, a great white ribbon of chalk running across the center of the hilltop. Today, after millennia of erosion, it can just be made out as a slight undulation in the ground surface. It can never have been more than five or six feet high at most. Wheeler explored the bank barrow with characteristic thoroughness, digging a whole series of trenches along the line of its northern ditch. As a result, we know that the barrow was 1,790 feet (546 meters) long, but it doesn't run in a straight line. There are in fact three distinct sections, each running on a slightly different alignment, though none of them is an exact straight line either. The separate sections are defined by breaks in the ditches alongside. Some archaeologists think that the short central section, only 210 feet (65 meters) long, was built first.

The Maiden Castle bank barrow is unique in the British Neolithic—or nearly so. Long burial mounds of about the same period are not uncommon, though very few approach even 300 feet (90 meters) in length. And they are burial mounds, with skeletal remains within or beneath them, whereas nothing like this has yet been discovered in the Maiden Castle bank barrow. The short central section of the bank barrow may have begun life as one of these ordinary long mounds, but the massive enlargement at either end turned it into something quite different. Perhaps the closest real parallels are the so-called cursus monuments, which consist of a pair of parallel banks and ditches running for considerable distances across the countryside. But if the bank barrow is bigger than an ordinary long mound, the cursus monuments are usually bigger again. The largest of them, the Dorset cursus, runs for almost 6 miles (9.6 kilometers) with ditches 300 feet (90 meters) apart. They are usually described as territorial markers or processional ways, and the Maiden Castle bank barrow might well have had a similar function. The people who built it were careful to place it not on the highest part of the Maiden Castle hilltop but on the "false crest" a little way downslope to the north, where it could be seen from far away.

Whatever its intended purpose, the bank barrow was abandoned soon after it was built. Left to itself for one thousand years or more, the Maiden Castle hilltop reverted to wilderness and eventually was covered by trees. We know this from the snail shells and rodent bones found in the upper infilling of the bank barrow ditches. This stage was brought to an end in the Early Bronze Age, shortly before 2000 B.C., when the hilltop was cleared of vegetation and turned over to cultivation. The reason was probably population growth or exhaustion of the soils in the lower-lying areas around Maiden Castle. There was increasing pressure to find new land to farm, and the Maiden Castle hilltop—along with other upland areas of southern England—was an obvious candidate. But it wasn't a total success. Once the hilltop was cleared, it was open to erosion and regular plowing simply accelerated the process. The soils were soon exhausted and Maiden Castle became grassland used only for grazing cattle and sheep. It has stayed that way (save for one later brief episode of plowing) down to the present day.

The First Hillfort

The most famous stage in the history of Maiden Castle, the construction of the hillfort, began in a modest way in the sixth century B.C. This was the Early Iron Age, a period when the new metal, iron, was coming into regular use. Cheaper than bronze, it led to technological changes that had profound repercussions on warfare, carpentry, and farming. But it was social rather than technological changes that led to the rise of Iron Age hillforts.

The key feature of hillforts is that they are defensive. They are built to protect individuals or communities against hostile attack. Hilltops provide an obvious natural advantage for defenders, and it was on hilltops that the Early Iron Age communities of southern Britain built their hillforts.

The sixth century B.C. was the great age of hillfort building. Apart from Maiden Castle itself, there are thirty hillforts of the period in the county of Dorset, the nearest being Poundbury in the western suburbs of Dorchester, a mere 1.5 miles (2.5 kilometers) from Maiden Castle. This dense concentration of fortifications suggests that these were far from peaceful times and that each local community was obliged to dig in on whatever high ground was available in its local territory. The work was probably directed by petty chieftains, and we may imagine a world in which bands of warriors mounted regular raids on the crops and cattle of their neighbors. In every area of southern Britain local farmers (warriors themselves in their spare time) sought to protect themselves and their belongings by joining together to build hillforts.

The first Maiden Castle hillfort was a relatively modest affair. It took in the eastern half of the hilltop—an area of 16 acres (6.4 hectares)—roughly the same as the causewayed enclosure over three thousand years before. The defensive perimeter was a single rampart of chalk blocks fronted by a massive, V-shaped ditch. The ditch was originally 18 feet (5.5 meters) deep, but soon afterward was deepened to 23 feet (7 meters) for still greater security. The rampart, of course, survives only as an eroded remnant, but we can guess that it must have been 10 feet (3 meters) high from the size of the ditch, since the stone for the rampart was taken from the ditch. Rampart and ditch together made a defensive circuit almost 35 feet (10.5 meters) high and 110 feet (33.5 meters) long. This was no mere stockade, but a serious obstacle to deter any attacker.

Entrances are the weakest point in any fortress, and in the first hillfort there were only two, one in the middle of the west side, the other in the middle of the east. The more important one was the eastern entrance, which had a double roadway. The rampart here had a vertical face held together by a framework of massive timbers. Soon afterward an outer rampart was added on either side of the eastern entrance, and these too had vertical timber-framed faces. This second rampart was made even more impressive than the first, since it wasn't just built of chalk blocks but had a facade of limestone blocks, brought to Maiden Castle from a quarry over 2 miles (3 kilometers) away. Remains of the limestone wall can still be seen at the eastern entrance today, though the original eastern defenses were largely buried beneath the massive new ramparts built when the hillfort was remodeled, probably in the fourth

The eastern entrance to Maiden Castle, showing the convoluted approach engineered by the Iron Age builders. With slingers stationed on the ramparts, any attempt to force the gate would have been a prolonged and dangerous affair. The serried lines of ramparts would also have presented an imposing impression of power.

Drawing of the section cut by Mortimer Wheeler in 1935 through the innermost rampart and ditch on the western side of Maiden Castle. Note the deep V-shaped ditch and the multiple phases of the rampart construction. The inner faces of ramparts 4 and 5 are visible as chalk walls; the outer faces present a smooth 45° incline. In their final form, ditch and rampart together gave a forbidding continuous slope rising more than 75 feet (23 meters) from the bottom of the ditch to the crest of the rampart. On the crest of the rampart were the sockets for a timber palisade.

WEST

MAIDEN CASTLE DORSET

SECTION THROUGH INNERMOST WESTERN DEFENC

(SITE 'E', 1935)

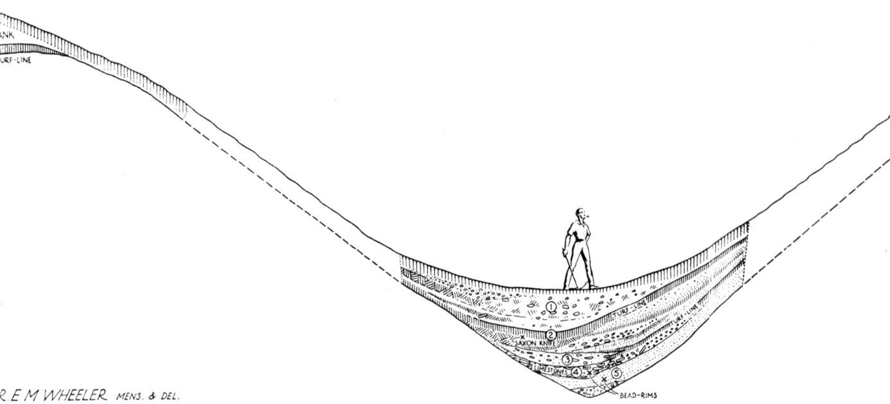

century. In its present form, Maiden Castle is mainly a creation of this Middle Iron Age remodeling.

Before we proceed to this later phase, however, something should be said of the settlement the first hillfort was built to defend. What was enclosed within the sixth century B.C. rampart? Unfortunately, neither Wheeler's excavations nor the more recent investigations have thrown much light on the Early Iron Age occupation. Wheeler did discover some storage pits cut in the chalk, however, and the footings of four-post wooden structures, which were probably raised granaries. It looks from this as if people were living within the hillfort, though their houses must have lain in an area that hasn't been excavated. Excavations at other Dorset hillforts of the period have revealed clear evidence of round houses within the defenses, and we can imagine the same pattern of occupation at Maiden Castle too.

Defenses in Depth: The Middle Iron Age Hillfort

Maiden Castle's greatest moment probably came in the Middle Iron Age, when the hillfort was extended to over three times its original size. The defenses now enclosed an area of 43 acres (17 hectares), making it the largest hillfort in Britain. The full significance of this expansion only becomes clear when we discover what was happening at the hillforts nearest to Maiden Castle at this time. The story there is very different. The nearest of all, Poundbury and

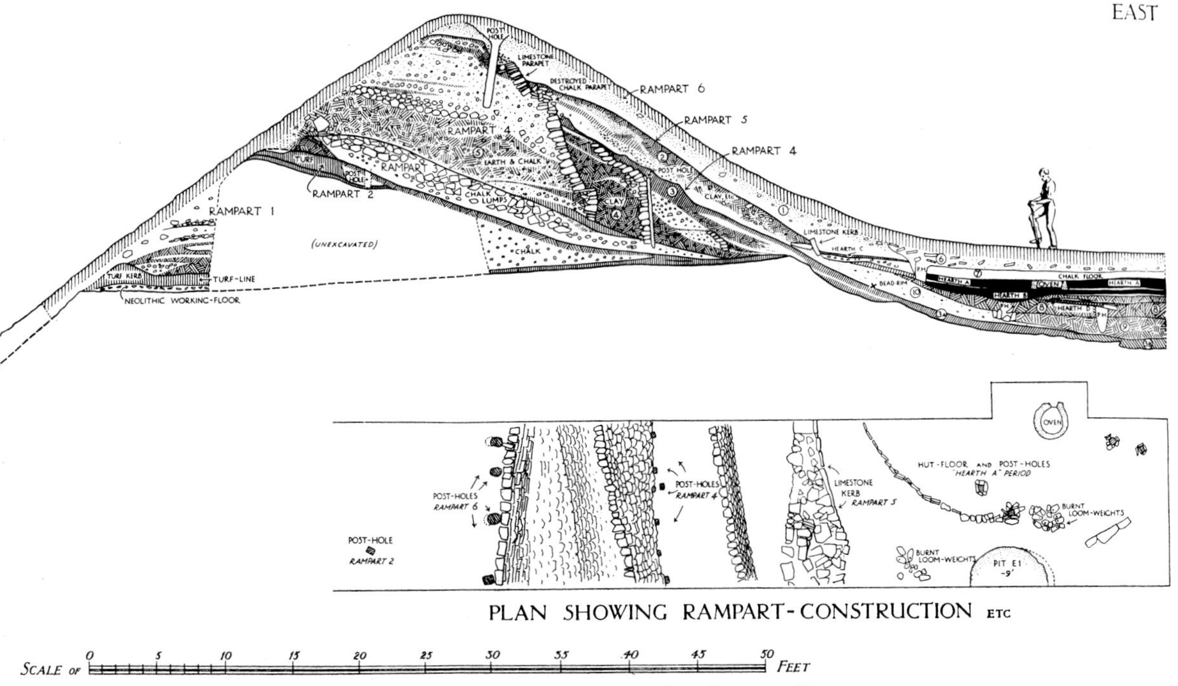

Chalbury, were abandoned, leaving Maiden Castle the dominant hillfort in the whole of southern Dorset. What seems to have happened is that a protracted struggle for preeminence among several local groups ended in victory for the people of Maiden Castle, who then set about enlarging and strengthening their hillfort with the aid of the additional manpower and resources now available to them. Henceforth, Maiden Castle was a center not just of local but of regional significance.

The initial enlargement of the hillfort was achieved by extending the single rampart and ditch of the Early Iron Age hillfort around the rest of the hilltop. This event can be placed early in the Middle Iron Age, probably in the fourth century B.C. The really impressive phase of Maiden Castle belongs in the years that followed, as the defenses were progressively elaborated.

The inhabitants began by raising the height of the rampart to 11.5 feet (3.5 meters), but that was only a modest first step. The major change to the appearance of Maiden Castle came when they began to add additional lines of rampart immediately outside the original perimeter. Along the south side they added four ramparts; on the north, where the hillside was steeper, only three. Between the new lines of rampart were ditches that served the double purpose of strengthening the defenses and also providing a quarry for the chalk needed to build the ramparts. The final stage was a further enhancement of the inner rampart, to a height of almost 20 feet (6 meters). When Wheeler dug trenches through this in the 1930s, he found that it had been stiffened

A hoard of slingstones discovered during the recent excavations at Maiden Castle. Water-worn pebbles such as these are available locally, but the people of Maiden Castle may have had to go as far as Chesil Beach on the south coast of England to collect the large numbers they needed for slingstones.

by a system of internal stone revetments to prevent the chalk and rubble fill from slipping and collapsing. This final phase was thus structurally more sophisticated than the earlier dump rampart. It posed the builders another problem, too, since by now the hillfort was ringed by multiple lines of defense. There was no scope for taking new building material from the ditch at the foot of the inner rampart, since that would have undermined the second rampart beyond. Instead, the builders took the material from within the rampart, creating a shallow quarry hollow that can still be seen in places just inside the inner rampart.

The entrances naturally were not unaffected by these radical changes. There were now two entrances: the original eastern entrance of the Early Iron Age hillfort remained in use, and a new entrance was built at the western end of the enlarged hillfort. By the time the builders of Maiden Castle had finished with them, these were the most elaborate defensive structures ever created in prehistoric Britain. In both cases, a whole series of outworks was created, barring direct access to the main gate in the inner rampart and forcing any would-be attackers to twist and turn as they advanced. In the case of the eastern entrance, the final approach took the form of a winding corridor over 240 feet (73 meters) long, overlooked all the way by outworks and ramparts. The western entrance was even more elaborate. These arrangements remain impressive today, even in their eroded and grass-covered state. How much more daunting must they have been in their original condition, with steep outer faces topped by breastworks manned by defenders, and bridges and gates barring access at strategic points.

The principle, like that of the multiple ramparts, was defense in depth. Wheeler, with his army background, was quite convinced that military considerations lay behind this design. He believed that defense in depth was a response to the use of the slingstone in warfare. The argument is that the outer defenses were built to keep attackers at a distance, making it difficult for their slingstones to reach defenders on the inner rampart. The defenders, on the other hand, would have gravity to help them in firing downslope. It would have been easier for them to kill attackers at a distance. We know for a fact that slingstones were used at Maiden Castle. Archaeologists have found thousands of them in the excavations both in the 1930s and the 1980s. The rounded pebbles were probably collected on Chesil Beach, on the south coast of Dorset, and brought specially to Maiden Castle. They were stored there in large hoards ready for use in times of need.

Wheeler's military explanation is persuasive, but it may not be the whole truth. Were the extra ramparts and elaborate defenses at Maiden Castle really designed for strategic reasons? Or were they intended more for show, to advertise the power and prestige of this major regional center and the people who controlled it? The two lines of reasoning are not incompatible, of course, but visitors today are impressed by Maiden Castle, and we can only imagine its impact in the Middle Iron Age, when the hillfort was at its peak.

Reconstruction of the houses recently excavated in the southwest corner of the hillfort, before (*below, left*) and after (*below, right*) the third century reorganization. If the early arrangement of four houses facing onto a yard suggests a family cluster, the later arrangement, with houses in an orderly line, may be the work of a powerful central authority.

Within the Ramparts

So much for the defenses. What were they there to protect? We have already remarked how Wheeler in his 1930s excavations was disappointed at how little survived within the ramparts, but he did succeed in recovering some traces

in a trench that he dug in the eastern half of the site. There were remains of Iron Age occupations spanning several centuries, including two streets running in from the eastern entrance of the hillfort. He also found storage pits cut into the chalk and traces of several circular houses, but it wasn't possible to divide them into separate phases. Even so, these findings suggested that during the Middle Iron Age the interior of Maiden Castle was densely occupied.

This impression has been confirmed by the recent excavations, which looked in detail at an area in the southwestern corner of the fort where the deposits were deeper and better preserved. Wheeler had found traces of round houses here as well, but he hadn't separated them into phases. Sharples, by contrast, using up-to-date techniques and approaches, identified four major periods of occupation and was able to show how the area had changed over time. In the first phase there were four four-post structures. These are more of the raised granaries already present in the Early Iron Age fort. The second phase was much more interesting, with remains of three round houses facing onto a cobbled yard. This might have been the residence of an individual family. The houses had low walls of wattle and daub and a high, conical thatched roof, though little survived save the central hearth and the drainage gully, which ran under the eaves. The next or third phase saw more houses of this type, but now these were arranged in a row, and one had a stone-built wall. It shows that at some time during the third century B.C., the internal layout of Maiden Castle was changed. We shouldn't read too much into this change—the excavation covered only a tiny area of the hillfort interior—but it could be significant. Was it the ruler of Maiden Castle who ordered the reorganization, breaking down the family clusters of round houses and replacing them with orderly, regimented rows?

The End of Maiden Castle

The final phase in the southwest sector was one of decline. The orderly row of round houses was succeeded by a disorganized scatter of pits and a single house, and then abandoned altogether. The defenses, too, seem to have been neglected; ramparts eroded and silt collected in the V-shaped ditches. After its Middle Iron Age period of glory, Maiden Castle in the Late Iron Age seems to have fallen into rapid disuse.

The exception to this is the area of the eastern entrance, which became a small industrial complex producing iron manufactures. Wheeler discovered a cluster of round houses here, spreading out from the eastern entrance and partly built over the filled-in ditches of the entrance outworks. He also discovered a cemetery, groups of graves scattered among the earthworks of the disused entrance. One group of graves in particular drew Wheeler's attention. It lay just outside the main gate through the inner rampart and comprised burials of fifty-two individuals. Of these, fourteen bore clear signs of violent death. Most dramatic of all was the skeleton of a young man with a Roman

Skeleton from the "war cemetery" at Maiden Castle, a young man with a Roman ballista bolt embedded in the spine. This graphic evidence of violent death inspired Mortimer Wheeler to write in vivid terms of the capture of Maiden Castle by the invading Romans and the slaughter of the native defenders.

ballista bolt embedded in the spine. Another had had a spear punched through the skull; still others had skulls hacked by sword cuts.

Wheeler called these burials the "war cemetery" and saw them as the graves of the last defenders of Maiden Castle, who had died fighting the Romans. He even wrote an imaginary account of the final battle: the Roman attackers laying down a barrage of ballista fire as they advanced on the east gate, setting light to the huts recently built within the entrance and butchering men, women, and children. Alas, this dramatic reconstruction has now been thrown into doubt. The mutilated men in the war cemetery may have died fighting the Romans, but not necessarily at Maiden Castle. An alternative view puts these burials in the first century A.D. and sees them as fatalities in Boudicca's abortive rebellion against Roman rule in A.D. 60–61. They were buried in regular graves, with offerings of food and other equipment, alongside compatriots who showed no signs of violence and may have died ordinary natural deaths. Furthermore, there is no evidence that the round houses were burned, though there is a lot of charcoal from the iron-working establishment.

Yet the Romans did fight their way across southern England. We have this information from the historian Suetonius, who tells us that in A.D. 43 the future emperor Vespasian commanded a legion in this sector that fought thirty battles, captured twenty "oppida," and conquered the Isle of Wight. The word "oppidum" means a town or fortified center, and one of the twenty could have been Maiden Castle. It would have been a natural place to regroup to resist an invader, even though the defenses themselves, after centuries of neglect, can hardly have been in a serviceable condition.

Whatever the event, with the invasion of A.D. 43 Maiden Castle passed into Roman control. For a while, they may even have stationed a military detachment on the hilltop to deter the locals from thoughts of rebellion. Once peace was secure, the Romans set about establishing a new order on the landscape, and in around A.D.70 they founded the town of Durnovaria (Dorchester) nearby as the regional capital of the local tribe. Maiden Castle was finally abandoned as fortress and settlement. The last significant building event came toward the end of the fourth century, when the advance of Christianity drove the old pagan religion out of the towns. At about that time, a small square temple was built in the northeastern corner of the hillfort. It survived for over a century but finally collapsed, leaving the great Iron Age hillfort of Maiden Castle to the sheep and cattle that have grazed on it down to the present day.

Further Reading

The full report on the recent excavations at Maiden Castle is by Niall Sharples, *Maiden Castle: Excavation and Field Survey 1985–6* (London: English Heritage, 1991). Sharples has also provided a shorter, more popular account, which integrates his new findings with Wheeler's earlier work: *Maiden Castle* (London: Batsford, 1991). Mortimer Wheeler's own excavation report is now a classic and still well worth consulting: R. E. M. Wheeler, *Maiden Castle, Dorset* (London: Society of Antiquaries, 1943). For an authoritative survey of the British Iron Age as a whole, setting Maiden Castle in context, see Barry Cunliffe, *Iron Age Communities in Britain,* 3rd ed. (New York: Routledge, 1991).

Further Viewing

The finds from Maiden Castle are housed in the Dorset County Museum in Dorchester.

CHAPTER

FOURTEEN

Entremont

c. 190–120 B.C.

Native township

in southern France

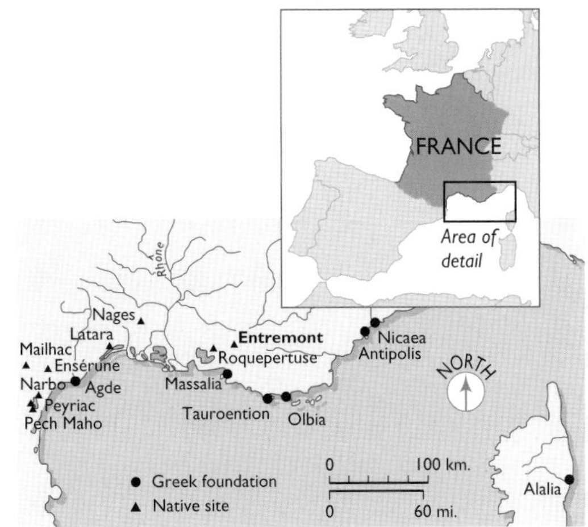

No visitor touring Provence today can fail to be impressed by the striking testimony of Roman rule: the lofty arches of the Pont du Gard, the well-preserved temple of the Maison Carrée, or the amphitheatre at Arles where open-air performances are still held every summer. They may well come away with the idea that Provence was backward and undeveloped before the Romans arrived. Yet in a sense the Romans simply brought to fulfillment developments stretching back several centuries. The native peoples of Provence had already built their own grid-plan towns and developed their own unique sculptural tradition two hundred and more years before. The best place to see these is at Entremont, a hilltop settlement near the popular tourist destination of Aix-en-Provence.

Entremont was a stone-built town with regular grid-plan streets and buildings. The general opinion is that it was established early in the second century B.C., but there is fourth century material from the site, and it is just possible that Entremont has a longer history than is currently realized. Whichever date is correct, to understand the origins of Entremont in its regional context we need to go back still further, to the foundation of the Greek colony at Massalia (modern Marseille) in c. 600 B.C. In founding their colony the Greeks also carved out a territory for themselves in the lowlands around the Rhone

Plan of Entremont showing the division into upper and lower town, each with its defensive wall, and the location of the hypostyle hall in the space between two of the towers of the inner wall.

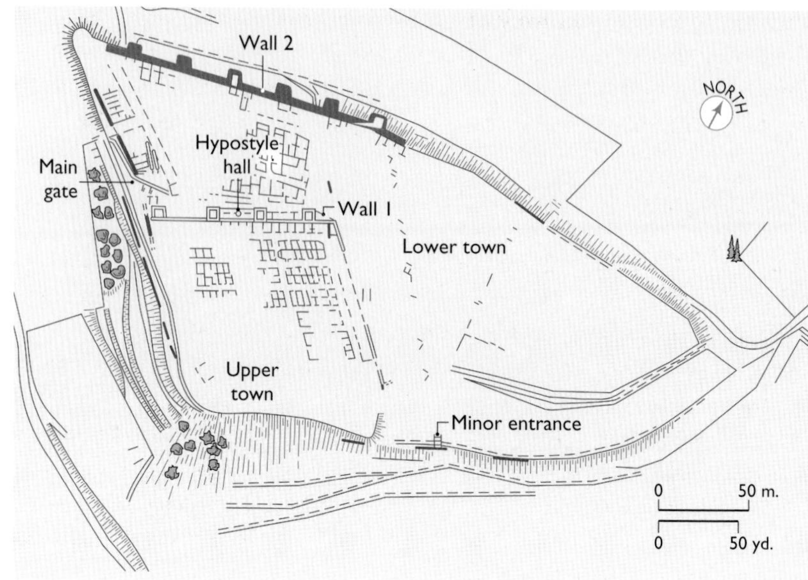

delta. The natives may not have welcomed them with open arms, but both sides soon came to realize the advantages they could gain from peaceful coexistence, for the site of Massalia wasn't chosen at random. The Rhone valley corridor gave the Greeks access to central France. At the same time, Massalia was a port city, linked by maritime trade routes with the rest of the Mediterranean. Hence, Mediterranean goods could be traded northward via Massalia to the native peoples of France. They in turn provided raw materials, which the Massaliotes could export throughout the Mediterranean—in return for a healthy profit, of course.

Massalia grew prosperous on the proceeds of this trade. So did the native peoples of the region, the so-called Ligurians or Celto-Ligurians, who supplied many of the raw materials. The whole coastal region became an interactive zone, where native peoples and traditions came into contact with Greek colonists. The Greeks introduced luxuries such as wine and tableware, which were avidly snapped up by native elites. The Celto-Ligurians soon began to build more substantial settlements, which incorporated features of Greek inspiration such as mud-brick.

Entremont came relatively late into the picture, but it is the best surviving example of a native hilltop settlement, owing something to Greek influence but a great deal also to its own inhabitants, the people known as the Salluvians. "Salluvii" (or "Salyes" in its Greek form) is the name given by Classical writers to the Celto-Ligurian people of the Entremont region. They were the leaders of an important federation of tribes occupying most of modern Provence, between the mouth of the River Rhone and the Alps. This, at least, was the situation in the second century B.C., when the Greek writer Posidonius described the federation and its division into ten sectors or peoples. The federation had a combined army under Salluvian command, and the Salluvians themselves were ruled by a king who stood at the head of the whole edifice. Entremont is probably the "polis" or city of the Celto-Ligurians referred to by Roman historians, the purpose-built capital of this new federation.

A Divided City

A glance at the plan of Entremont shows that it is made up of two separate parts. The smaller of these occupied a parallelogram of land, just under 3 acres (1 hectare) in extent, in the southwest corner of the site. We know its precise size because it was surrounded by a fortification wall with square towers on the northern side and probably along the east side, too. To the south and west there was less need for artificial defenses since the steeply sloping plateau edge provided good natural protection. The wall here was thinner and had no towers. To the north and east of this first settlement is a broad swathe of buildings filling the rest of the site, up to the solid defensive wall with rounded towers—the second settlement.

Thus Entremont as we see it today consists of one fortified enclosure within another. The excavator, Fernand Benoit, had two explanations for this. First, that the smaller enclosure might be a citadel or "upper town." Since Entremont was the capital of the Salluvians, it may have been the quarter where the kings and princes of the tribe lived. Ordinary people were

View along one of the streets in the "upper town" at Entremont. The repetitive standardization of house plans is particularly visible on the left-hand side, where each house has an identically placed street door leading into a ground floor room of the same size and shape. What survive today are only the stone foundations; originally these buildings had upper floors of mudbrick (as shown in the reconstruction drawing on p. 204).

relegated to the "lower town" round about. The square-towered wall would then have marked the division between the privileged families and the rest.

Benoît's second explanation, the one generally accepted today, was not that Entremont was divided into "elite" and "commoner" zones, but that the "upper town" was the small initial settlement, and the "lower town" a massive expansion as more and more people came to live at Entremont. The lower town in fact represents the growth of Entremont from a small settlement to a major regional center, quadrupling in size in only a matter of decades. It tells of the rapid rise to power of the Salluvians in the first half of the second century B.C.

The dating of these developments rests on the pottery. Here the most useful vessels are not the locally produced pots but those imported from Italy. The key vessels for dating the origins of Entremont are the so-called Campanian A wares, manufactured mainly in the cities of Campania, the region of Naples and Pompeii to the south of Rome. The upper town of Entremont was built after the earliest Campanian A had gone out of circulation. Leaving aside the problem of the fourth century pottery mentioned above, the Campanian A wares suggest a date for the upper town of Entremont somewhere in the early second century B.C.

How much time passed before the lower town was added? The interval can only have been short, since there is little perceptible change in the types and styles of pottery or other artifacts. It was probably a matter of a few decades at most. Thus if the first settlement was founded c. 190 B.C., the second may have followed around 150 B.C.

Defending the Settlement

The natural place to begin an account of Entremont is the defenses. As we have seen, both upper town and lower town had dry-stone walls with towers at intervals. In the early wall, the towers are solid and square, each side measuring about 20 feet (6 meters). The wall itself is some 5 feet (1.5 meters) thick, but since it was later demolished we know little more about it. The second phase wall was twice as thick and is much better preserved, standing to a height of 15 feet (4.5 meters) in places, and originally much higher. It, too, is of dry-stone construction and may have had an upper part of mud-brick. (This was by no means a poor provincial imitation: most Classical cities of fifth century Greece had defenses of mud-brick on a stone base or foundation.) The towers of this second wall are slightly larger than those of the first, projecting 30 feet (9 meters) beyond the wall. They also have rounded corners, an innovation intended to remove the weakness presented by a sharp angle, which could be chipped away by an attacker.

Details of the second wall show how skilled the builders of Entremont were at their job. They began by cutting a foundation trench into the bedrock. Then the outer faces of the wall were built of large, squarish blocks. Small stones were carefully packed into the crevices between the blocks for greater stability. The builders then poured earth and rubble into the space between the faces to give the wall a solid core. This second wall was a major undertaking, built to give security to the inhabitants. But it was also a statement in stone of the new-found power of the Salluvians.

One feature that hasn't yet been found is the main gate. Archaeologists have discovered a minor entrance on the southern side of Entremont, opening onto the steeply sloping ground outside. It is even provided with an access stairway, part stone-built, part rock-cut, but only wide enough for pedestrians. The main gate was probably on the western edge of the site. Here some of the streets just inside the perimeter have been rutted by cart wheels. Since most of the streets at Entremont don't have such wheel ruts (and were too narrow for easy access by carts), it seems that this part of the site saw more wheeled traffic than other areas. It was probably close to the main gate. The approach road may well have climbed up the slope below the western wall, exposing any would-be attackers to defenders stationed on the wall top. It was a safer (if less convenient) arrangement than making the main gate in the north wall, where the slope was less steep.

Within the Defenses

What we see at Entremont today are the stone foundations of buildings. We know that some of the houses, possibly most or even all of them, had an upper floor. Upper floors were of unbaked mud-brick, plastered over to protect them from the elements. The only visible sign of them are the stairway foundations along the street facades of some houses; to reach the upper floors you clearly had to go outside first. We have little evidence for the roofs, but there were no terracotta tiles, so roofs were probably of clay or beaten earth on a timber frame. Southern France isn't exactly an arid zone, but it is dry enough for this kind of roof to have worked.

The early buildings of the upper town at Entremont were simple blocks or terraces with single rooms of roughly equal size, 10 feet (3 meters) wide and 16 to 20 feet (5 to 6 meters) deep. Each room had a doorway onto one of the streets and could have been an independent family unit. Alternatively, a single family may have occupied a number of rooms, not to mention any possible upper floor. In either case, what is striking about these buildings is the regularity of their construction. Grid-plan city layouts had long been known in the Classical world of Greece and Rome. The builders of Entremont would have known of at least one good example close at hand: the Greek colony of Massalia (Marseilles) only 20 miles (30 kilometers) to the south.

In detail, however, the residential blocks of Entremont are totally different from those of any Greek city. Indeed, they are more like barrack blocks than houses. Entremont was a planned settlement; it didn't develop organically from an existing village. Such a rigid plan must be the work of a power-

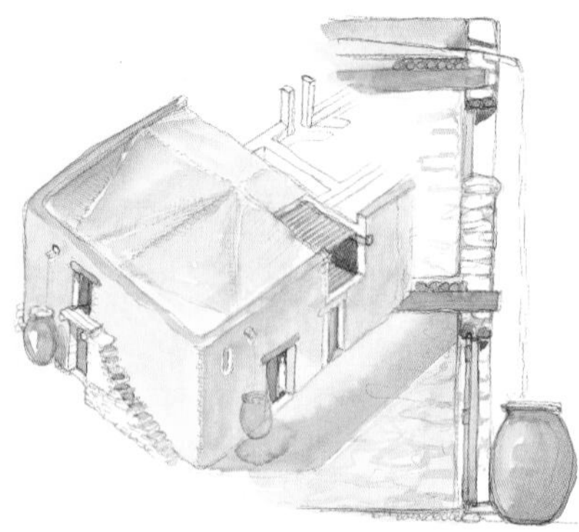

Reconstruction of the end of a residential block in the upper town. An external stair leads to the upper floor. The large pottery vessel (known as a *dolium*) standing next to the lower door collected rainwater draining off the roof. Other water would have had to be brought to Entremont from sources outside the walls.

ful central authority, perhaps a council of elders. But these small regimented housing blocks give little sign of distinctions in rank or status. How, then, were they owned or allocated? And did the rulers of Entremont live elsewhere, in parts of the settlement that have not yet been excavated?

We might also question how much the Entremont layout really owes to Greek connections. It is easy to jump to the wrong conclusions. Grid-plan layouts are known in several areas of Europe at earlier periods; Biskupin in Poland is one notable example that owes nothing to Mediterranean inspiration. Grid-plan layouts are perhaps a natural feature of any new settlement that is planted on a virgin site through a coordinated scheme.

Grid-plan layout at Entremont is not confined to the upper town. The lower town, too, has a formal arrangement of criss-cross streets, though the houses themselves are less standardized. Some of them, indeed, became rambling multiroomed structures with courtyards open to the sky. They didn't only house families, either, but also livestock and workshops. In many respects, Entremont became a more natural, more organic settlement as it moved into this second phase. The houses of the upper town were also modified in this phase to take account of changing needs. And it is the second phase of Entremont that provides evidence of daily life and the preoccupations of the ordinary inhabitants.

Daily Life at Entremont

Archaeologists working at Entremont since the Second World War have discovered enormous quantities of pottery and other debris. Sometimes, these finds show us exactly what went on in a particular building, such as production of olive oil. Olive oil was much in demand among the Greeks and Romans, who used it both for cooking and lighting. The people of Entremont may well have developed a taste for it too. They planted olive groves on the hillsides around their town, extracted the oil in olive presses at Entremont, and sold it to the Greek merchants of Massalia. Several olive presses have been identified by archaeologists from the stone weights and trays. The weights were attached to the timber levers used to press the olives, which were placed on the stone trays for the purpose. These trays had a groove and a spout in which the pressed oil was collected and funneled away.

Another activity well represented at Entremont is metalworking, above all of iron and lead. One building had three arched furnace openings at ground level, side by side. An unused sheet of lead found in one of the openings suggested this was a lead foundry. A courtyard with over five hundred bronze fragments and eight hundred glass beads (some of them miscast) must have been the scene of industrial activity. Tools and other iron objects were abundant everywhere: nails for wood-working; iron keys for locks; axes, knives, and chains; and agricultural items. Among the last were pruning hooks for olives or vines. Most families in the settlement probably took an active part in agriculture, even if some of them drew most of their livelihood from craft

Olive pressing tray with funnel and spout to collect and channel the oil. Production of olive oil was an important activity at Entremont, and numerous stone weights and trays for pressing the olives have been found.

production. Others might have been merchants; one room had a great pile of broken amphorae by its street door, suggesting it was an office involved with imports or exports.

Workshops, storerooms, and oil presses seem to have taken up an increasing amount of space in Entremont during its relatively short life. So far as we can tell, these activities were all situated at ground level, in the lower floors of the buildings. Livestock, too, were probably kept in some of these ground floor rooms. Entremont, for all its pretensions, remained an essentially rural community.

Municipal Endeavors

We have seen how walls and street plan give evidence of centralized organization at Entremont, but what of the public buildings that such a settlement must have possessed? Here we are on difficult ground, not least because important discoveries are still no doubt to be made in the parts of the site that haven't yet been excavated. Two features, however, do deserve special mention: the central roadway (variously called "Road VI" or sometimes the "Sacred Way") and the so-called hypostyle hall.

The Sacred Way is wider than the other roads (up to 30 feet [10 meters] rather than the 10–13 feet [3–4 meters] that is the norm) and had a central raised band paved with stone blocks surfaced by earth and fine gravel. It runs eastward across the site from somewhere near where the main gate must have been. The name "Sacred Way" suggests a processional way, but it may simply have been Entremont's Main Street, the raised central section for wheeled vehicles and the lower bands on either side for pedestrians. As ancient roads go it wasn't especially grand. But it did lead past the "hypostyle hall."

Reconstruction of the hypostyle hall at Entremont. The ground floor was a columned hall open to the street, but on the upper story was a grand room with a decorated floor of baked clay set with dice-shaped pieces of black and white limestone. In its original state, human skulls (or embalmed heads) were displayed within this building or along its street frontage, attached to the timbers by iron nails.

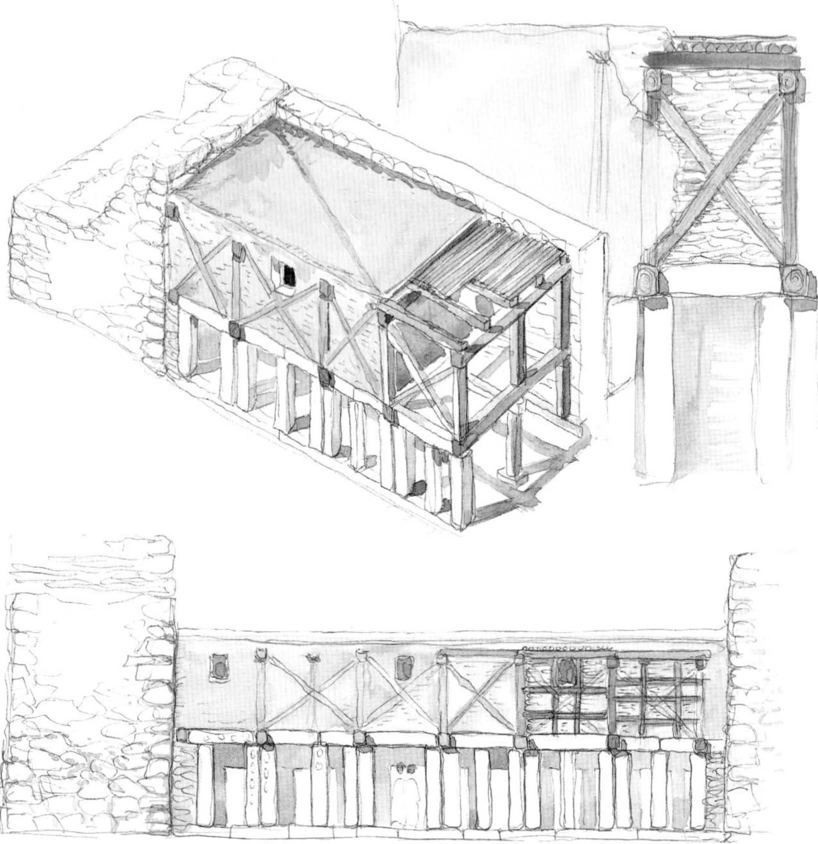

(*facing page*) Stone pillar 8.5 feet (2.6 meters) high carved with twelve human faces representing severed heads. When found, this pillar was lying on its side, facing the street in the front kerb of the "hypostyle hall." Originally, however, it must have been part of a standing structure. French archaeologist Fernand Benoît suggested that it was one of the side-supports of a doorway or portico. A stone lintel found nearby may have been part of the same original structure and had carved faces alternating with hollows for human skulls.

This pillared hall is the only grand building so far discovered at Entremont. It was built in the space between the foundations of two towers of the first phase wall. This gave it an impressive length of 70 feet (21 meters), though it was only 18 feet (5.5 meters) deep, and at ground-floor level it was open-fronted toward the street. Along the street front a kerb of carefully cut stones had been laid, supporting a row of timber piers that created a kind of portico. Many of the kerbstones were reused from some earlier grand structure; one of them was a carved pillar. Halfway back within the building was a line of stone bases for wooden piers to support the floor of the room above. Judging from fallen fragments, this upper-story room was one of the grandest at Entremont, with colored geometric patterns set into the floor, well-worn through frequent use. The most interesting aspect of this hypostyle hall, however, lay in the quite different kind of decoration displayed along its street frontage. Nearby, archaeologists discovered twenty skulls, the remains of embalmed human heads. Three of the skulls even retained holes left by the iron nails hammered through them to fix them to the timber supports of the hypostyle hall.

Whose were these heads? Prominent citizens, sacrificed individuals, or slaughtered enemies? For answers we must turn to the sculptures of Entremont, which provide graphic evidence of a grisly cult of head worship.

Skull Cults and Severed Heads

It was in 1817 that Entremont first came to public notice, when a group of carved relief slabs were found reused on the site. Two showed severed human heads; the third a horseman with trophy skull swinging below his bridle. The discovery was a revelation. In 1943, many more sculptures were unearthed in the Sacred Way by German troops building barrack blocks. More were found in excavations from the 1940s to 1960s, and more recently in the 1980s. With the opening of the new Musée Granet at Aix in 1987, it is now possible to see the collection of sculptures in a modern setting, the ideal complement to visiting the ruins of Entremont itself.

Two of the famous sculptures come from the hypostyle hall, but they had clearly been reused and neither was in its original location. One was a broken fragment of a limestone lintel with an alternating row of head-sized hollows and schematically carved faces. The hollows presumably held mummified heads of the kind already mentioned. The second sculpture from the hypostyle hall was a square-sectioned pillar carved with no fewer than twelve schematic faces. The style of these two pieces is so similar that they must belong together, one as an upright, the other as a lintel, in a building that preceded the hypostyle hall. The kerb also has a third sculpture, a snake carving in low relief on the fourth kerbstone from the left. This too may have been reused in this position.

The other sculptures were found in the vicinity of the hypostyle hall but had apparently come from other buildings. Pride of place goes to five male heads (some wearing helmets) and five headless torsos, each slightly larger than life-size and carved in the same fine limestone. Each of the torsos depicts a warrior clad in body armor. One example is marked with a dense pattern of dots, the others are plain save for a decorative braid across the chest and a medallion (in one case a human face) just above. Originally they would all have been painted, so whether the dot pattern indicates a different kind of material or whether the dots were normally rendered in paint, we can't be sure. There is no agreement either on what the body armor was made of. Some who have studied it think in terms of chain mail or metal plates; others (perhaps more convincingly) of burnished leather. Bronze is a third (though rather expensive) possibility. One of the statues bears traces of blue paint on the body armor, a color normally used to represent silver or iron.

The grisly nature of these statues becomes clear when we add in the other fragments found with them. There are hands and feet, though most of the statues were seated. More revealingly, there are severed heads—carvings of human heads with closed eyes. In one case a group of five heads belongs together, while a sixth nestles against the inside right knee of a seated figure. The heads were evidently propped between the legs of the seated warrior figures or held on their knees. We may imagine such an ensemble when it was complete: a seated statue with helmeted head, clad in body armor and

Detail of one of the five headless torsos from Entremont. The dotted decoration may represent chain mail, though leather has also been suggested. In the center of the chest is an ornament representing rivets surrounded by rings; the larger central roundel might originally have been in the form of a severed human head (better preserved on another of the Entremont torsos). Traces of red and blue paint have been found on some of these statues, showing that originally they were brightly colored.

wearing a necklet or torc, hands resting on a group of six severed human heads propped between the knees. Not all of the Entremont statues were like this, but there was certainly more than one of the type, and it was a shocking, not to say frightening image.

They weren't, however, the only sculptures from Entremont, nor was the seated warrior the only pose. Fragments survive of horses and horsemen and of apparently female statues. There are also several plinths with sandaled feet, showing that some of the statues stood upright. But it is naturally the severed heads that grip the modern imagination most strongly.

There may well be Classical influences in all this. Large-scale sculpture is rare in prehistoric Europe, and details such as the tight curls in the hair of some

STRABO ON THE SEVERED HEAD CULT

Again . . . there is also that custom, barbarous and exotic, which attends most of the northern tribes—I mean the fact that when they depart from the battle they hang the heads of their enemies from the necks of their horses, and when they have brought them home, nail the spectacle to the entrances of their homes. At any rate, Posidonius [a Greek writer of the second century B.C.] says that he himself saw this spectacle in many places, and that, although at first he loathed it, afterward, through familiarity with it, he could bear it calmly. The heads of enemies of high repute, however, they used to embalm in cedar-oil and exhibit to strangers, and they would not deign to give them back even for a ransom of an equal weight of gold.

—From Strabo, *Geography* IV.4.5

In his *Geography,* Greek writer Strabo described the customs of the Gallic peoples of pre-Roman France in general, but his account fits closely the evidence of a severed head cult that archaeologists have unearthed at Entremont. Furthermore ,Posidonius, whom he quotes as a source, is known to have spent some time at the nearby Greek town of Massalia, from whence he might easily have visited the lands of the Celto-Ligurians.

of the figures could be taken directly from Greek or Roman models. The body armor, too, resembles Greek and Roman forms. But whatever the borrowings, the meaning and symbolism of the Entremont statues are pure Celto-Ligurian. Similar sculptures are known from other sites, above all the shrine at nearby Roquepertuse. The severed head was clearly a crucial part of Celto-Ligurian symbolism.

What can we say of this grisly cult? First, the head is often seen as a source of power and that many societies have displayed heads of their ancestors or cut off heads of their enemies with pride. Second, the Entremont sculptures do seem to fit with what Classical authors tell us about the peoples of southern France. Strabo in particular, writing in the first century B.C., tells us how before the Romans conquered them, native warriors used to cut off the heads of the enemies they killed in combat and carry them home, where they preserved them by embalming and fixed them to the doors of their houses. This is exactly what we suspect at Entremont. According to François Salviat, the leading authority on these sculptures, the seated warriors were not statues of gods (they have no symbols of divinity) but of famous warriors, chiefs, or aristocrats who were portrayed with the evidence of their status and success—the heads of the men they had killed. Salviat envisages them displayed in a public building—a monument to civic pride and aristocratic prowess—fronting on to the Sacred Way, close to where they were found.

The Fall of Entremont

The fragmentary condition of the Entremont statues shows that the final destruction of the settlement was thorough and decisive. There can be no doubt that Entremont came to a violent end.

Fernand Benoît, excavator of Entremont, was convinced that the Romans must have been the culprits. The most likely occasion was in 124 B.C., when the Roman consul Marcus Fulvius Flaccus marched an army into Provence in support of Massalia. The Greek colony had a track record as one of Rome's staunchest allies. The Salluvians, the people of Entremont, may have traded with the Massaliotes, but relations between Greeks and natives were frequently tense. In 124 B.C., we are told, the Salluvians were putting pressure on Massaliote territory, and in response to the Massaliotes' pleas for help the Romans marched in. Flaccus was victorious, but not decisively so, since the following year the Romans had to send another army under the new consul Caius Sextius Calvinus. He succeeded in capturing the "city" of the local inhabitants, probably a direct reference to Entremont.

Reconstruction of one of the Entremont statues, showing the kneeling warrior with hands resting on a cluster of severed human heads.

The Roman account gives an idea of the settlement's size. We are told that a certain Crato, leader of the pro-Roman faction within the walls, was able to secure the freedom of nine hundred of the residents, implying that many more must have been taken into slavery. The king of the Salluvians, Teutomalius, fled with his supporters to the territory of the Allobroges, who also entered the fray. It was after that tribe, too, had been defeated by the Romans in 121 B.C. that southern France became a Roman province, giving its name to the modern region "Provence."

That the Romans attacked Entremont is clear from the finds of Roman missiles among the ruins. But there is also evidence that the settlement was destroyed on two separate occasions, and that people were still living there early in the first century B.C. The end may only have come in 90 B.C. when the Ligurians rebelled against Rome and had once again to be suppressed.

The chief beneficiaries of Entremont's fall were probably the Massaliotes, who were given control of the whole area. For several decades, the Roman presence was confined to a permanent Roman legionary base at Aquae Sextiae (Aix-en-Provence), on lower ground 1.5 miles (2.5 kilometers) southeast of Entremont. In around 50 B.C., however, Julius Caesar made Aquae Sextiae a city in its own right. Aquae Sextiae remained an important regional center, the lineal successor to Entremont, throughout the Roman period. It is there today, in the Musée Granet, that the sculptures from Entremont can be seen.

Further Reading

Up-to-date information on Entremont is given in the catalogue edited by Denis Coutagne, *Archéologie d'Entremont au Musée Granet* (Aix-en-Provence: Musée Granet, 1987). For an earlier description, in English, see Fernand Benoît, "The Celtic Oppidum of Entremont, Provence," in Rupert Bruce-Mitfored (ed.), *Recent Archaeological Excavations in Europe* (Boston: Routledge and Kegan Paul, 1975), pp. 227–259. A more recent summary account is given on pp. 130–134 of James Bromwich's *The Roman Remains of Southern France: A Guidebook* (New York: Routledge, 1993). For traces of paint on these and other statues from pre-Roman southern France, see Alix Barbet "Roquepertuse et la polychromie en Gaule méridionale a l'époque préromaine" in *Documents d'Archéologie Méridionale* 14 (1991), 53–81. The interaction between Greek colonists and local peoples in different parts of Europe is expertly covered by Barry Cunliffe in *Greeks, Romans and Barbarians* (New York: Methuen, 1988). For Celtic religious beliefs, including the severed head cult, see Miranda Green, *The Gods of the Celts* (Totowa, NJ: Barnes and Noble, 1986).

Further Viewing

The remarkable sculptures from Entremont together with other finds from the site are displayed in three special basement rooms at the Musée Granet, Aix-en-Provence.

CHAPTER

FIFTEEN

Borremose

c. 300–100 B.C.

A Danish peat bog

and its prehistoric settlement

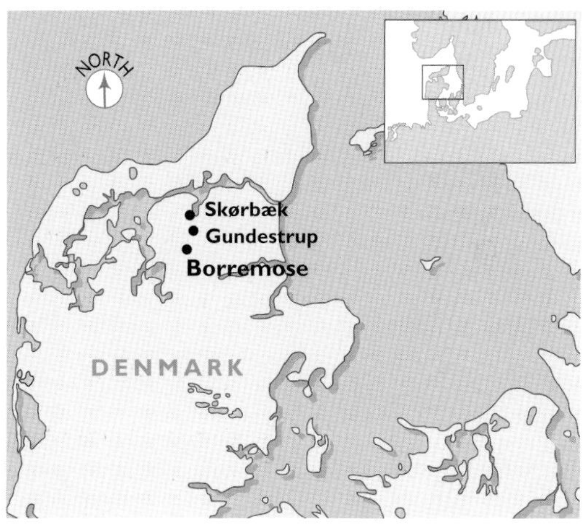

Borremose is the name of a raised bog in northern Jutland, the mainland peninsula of Denmark. Not a prepossessing location, one might think, for great archaeological discoveries. Yet here, within a relatively narrow compass, archaeologists have found some of the most interesting remains of prehistoric date ever to be unearthed in Europe. First and foremost is the Gundestrup cauldron, a splendid silver vessel found just to the north of Borremose fen. Then from the fen itself have come three of the famous "bog bodies," bodies preserved down the centuries by the tanning action of the acid bog. Finally, and still visible today, there is the Borremose settlement, a defended village of 300–100 B.C.

Although scarcely visible from a distance—just a low bump in the fen—the Borremose settlement has been described as the most imposing Iron Age site in Denmark. Together with Gundestrup and the bog bodies, it belongs more precisely to the period known in Danish archaeology as the "late pre-Roman Iron Age." This may seem a curious label, given that the Roman legions never reached northern Europe, and Jutland and the Danish islands always remained outside their control. But Roman objects did arrive in Denmark, as gifts, trade goods, or war booty, and Danish archaeologists have accordingly divided their Iron Age into pre-Roman (500–1 B.C.); Roman, contemporary with the Roman occupation of northwestern Europe (A.D. 1–400); and Germanic (A.D. 400–800). The latter leads in turn into the famous Viking age, and the beginnings of historical Denmark.

Borremose itself is one of the largest raised bogs in Denmark. The Iron Age settlement lies in its southernmost part, around 300 feet (less than 100 meters) from the dry land. It sits on an island, a low mound of glacial moraine, the debris of sand and gravel left by the retreating glaciers some 10,000 years ago. The surrounding bog would have been useless to the inhabitants in agri-

IRON AGE FARMERS

The inhabitants of Borremose depended for food on the raising of livestock (especially cattle) and the growing of cultivated plants. The main crop was barley, followed by wheat and oats, the latter (originally a weed of cereal fields) becoming increasingly important as time went by. In addition to cereals the Iron Age farmers also grew flax (for clothing) and beans. We know something of how the cultivation was managed from the remains of field systems—patchwork-type layouts of small rectangular fields marked by low banks of earth and stones. The banks may originally have been topped by hedges, which would have served as windbreaks, especially valuable given the light, sandy nature of many Danish soils. One of the best examples—a 150-acre (60-hectare) complex of Iron Age fields with attached farmstead—can be seen a few miles north of Borremose at Skørbaek hede. The fields were worked by wooden plows pulled by pairs of oxen. Some of the wooden plows have actually survived, preserved when they were discarded or deposited (perhaps as offerings to the gods) in the Danish lakes or bogs. One of the most complete examples is the Donnerupland ard (an ard being a simple type of plow). This has a triangular, pointed share (the cutting head) but no mouldboard, so that the plow would have broken up the ground but had no means of turning the earth.

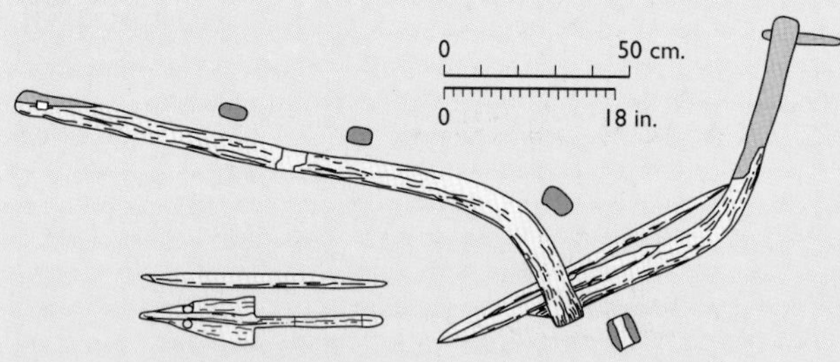

Remains of an Iron Age ard found at Donnerupland in eastern Jutland. Pulled by horses or oxen, the triangular share would have broken up the ground, but there was no mouldboard to turn over the earth. By turning the share from side to side, however, it was possible to aerate the soil and remove weeds. Although not as effective as the mouldboard plow, this was nonetheless a complex piece of carpentry, made of several pieces of wood jointed together. Iron Age plows often used different types of wood for the different parts, matching the qualities of the timber to the functions of the separate elements (e.g., hard wood for the beam and cutting share, softer wood for the stilt or handle).

Cattle were the principal livestock animal for these Danish Iron Age farmers. They were a major source of wealth for individual households, and were used as plow animals, for meat, and for milk. The typical Iron Age house in northern Europe is specifically designed to accommodate cattle stalls in its eastern section. At Borremose, there were no traces of the individual stalls, but at contemporary Grøntoft, a small village in western Jutland, the houses could be divided into three groups on the basis of the number of cattle stalls they contained: the five wealthiest households had from eight to eighteen head of cattle; two in the middle range had space for only three or four cattle; while three of the houses had no cattle stalls at all. The cattle would have been kept indoors during the winter months, but put out to pasture in the spring and summer. The stalling of cattle would have allowed milking to continue during the winter, but would have been very labor-demanding, involving the large-scale collection and storage of hay and other winter fodder. Probably only milk cows and a few breeding bulls were over-wintered in this way, the surplus males being killed for meat in the autumn as the nights began to draw in.

Aerial view of the Borremose settlement, showing the outlines of the houses within the rampart and the causeway crossing the peat bog to link the site with the drier land adjacent.

cultural terms, though a very effective defense. They chose a site that was well protected, in an inaccessible location, but near enough to their fields to allow easy everyday access. We may imagine them setting out each morning with their ox carts and livestock, heading for the farmland on the low, well-drained hills round about. Some of the fields survive as patterns of small rectangular enclosures, marked by low banks.

The History of Borremose

The discovery of the Borremose settlement goes back to 1929 when local workers were draining the southern part of the fen. They cut through a stone-paved road, which was evidently of great antiquity. The local museum was called out to advise, and they in turn called in experts from the National Museum in Copenhagen. It was at once apparent that this was a stone causeway leading to the small island within the bog, but it was only in 1935, after a gap of several years, that archaeologists began systematic exploration of the settlement on the island.

The visitor to Borremose today still approaches the site across the same causeway that served the original Iron Age inhabitants. It spans 160 feet (50 meters) of bog to provide all-weather access from dry land to the southeast corner of the enclosure. The causeway measures 10 feet (3 meters) wide with an edging of large flat stones and a paving of smaller stones and pebbles between, wide and solid enough for the wooden-wheeled wagons that we know were in use at this time.

The causeway enters the settlement through a simple gap in the bank and ditch. There is nothing to be seen of the original arrangements, but we may

Excavations in progress at Borremose. The cobbled main street is clearly visible. To its left, separated by an area of cobbling, is the faint outline of one of the rectangular houses. What we see is the house floor; the turf walls left virtually no trace.

imagine a stout timber gateway closed by a solid two-leafed gate. The main ditch runs right around the site and would originally have been filled with water. The excavators estimated it had been 20 feet (6 meters) wide and 7 feet (2 meters) deep, and the material dug out from it was piled on the inner edge to form an earthwork bank. This cannot have been the only defense, and there must also have been a timber palisade along the crest of the bank. The bank itself would once have been much higher than it is today; much of the material has slid back into the ditch.

The modest fortification was of course greatly enhanced by its location. The settlement was surrounded by marshland, dangerous to cross before modern drainage lowered the water table. But the Iron Age builders didn't rely only on that. The archaeologists dug a series of trenches into the bog in order to investigate the site's surroundings. There they found evidence that the peat had been intentionally cut away during the Iron Age to create a lake around the site.

The defenses of Borremose give a strong impression of a warlike society anxiously seeking to protect itself against hostile neighbors. But before jumping to any conclusions, we must bear in mind that it is the only defensive site of the period that has yet come to light in Denmark.

A Mistake and a Reassessment

One of the main obstacles to understanding Borremose is the fact that the original excavations were never fully published. This means that despite its evident importance, many questions remain about what the visitor sees today and about the accuracy of the reconstructions that have been put forward by archaeologists. But recent work has enabled some earlier misconceptions to be set straight.

The most crucial is the phasing. The original excavators thought that there had been two distinct phases in the history of the Borremose site. In the first of these, it had been a marshland fortress, a refuge rather than a settlement. The builders had constructed the enclosure by digging the ditch and building the rampart and palisade. According to this view, they had also created the lake by digging away the upper layers of peat around the island. But they hadn't built any houses. The houses, they argued, came only in the second phase when the ditches were filled in and the site took on a non-defensive character.

We now know that this is wrong. A careful study of the pottery (that essential tool for dating a site) has shown that houses and defenses belong to much the same period. Or more accurately, that Borremose was built as an enclosed settlement, a group of houses surrounded by defenses, and remained a defensive site during the two hundred years it was occupied, as new houses were built to replace old. The lake, indeed, probably belongs to a late stage in the settlement's history, not to some early "defensive" phase. Thus the impression given by the site today—of house foundations within an enclosure—is essentially correct.

Houses and Community

The archaeologists who excavated at Borremose in the 1930s and 1940s found all or part of at least thirty-two longhouses. In some cases a new house had been built over an earlier one, and only twenty-three or so have been marked

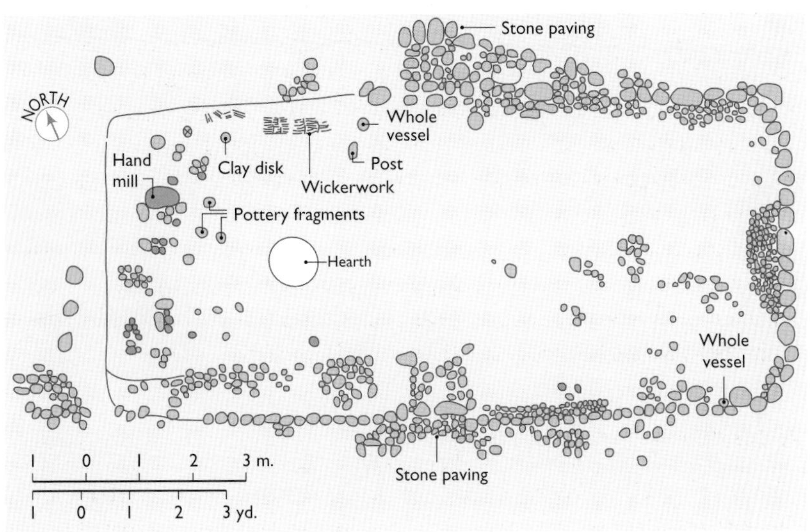

Plan of House VIII at Borremose. The locations of the doors in the middle of the longer sides are indicated by areas of rough stone paving. A fragment of charred wickerwork is the only trace of the material that once lined the inner face of the turf walling. Domestic activity was concentrated in the western end of the house, around the hearth; the eastern end was almost devoid of artifacts and may have served as a cattle byre.

out in the turf. The walls we see today are entirely modern, though the original house walls were probably of turf and they follow closely the outlines of houses that were excavated.

In areas where stone is rare or absent, prehistoric communities usually built in timber, and remains of structures survive as post-holes cut into the ground, which show where the timber posts were removed or have rotted. In northern Europe, however, turf provided an alternative building material, one with excellent insulating and draft-proofing qualities. For the archaeologist, it has the serious disadvantage that once a turf wall has decayed, it is very difficult to detect its remains. At Borremose, the outer turf walls were not found, and it was the houses' floors of clay or earth that showed where they had stood. They followed a fairly standard plan—rectangular buildings oriented east–west, with a hearth in the middle of the western end. The eastern end had an earth floor, the western end a clay floor. This together with the position of the hearth (and the overall size of the houses, which averaged over 40 feet [12 meters] long) supports the idea that the household lived in the western end, with the eastern end devoted to stalls where the cattle could be kept in winter. Most other houses in Iron Age Denmark followed this plan, and in some cases (as for example at Grøntoft in west Jutland) traces of the individual cattle stalls have been discovered. We can reconstruct the appearance of the Borremose houses on the basis of remains from these other sites.

The houses had a door in the middle of each of the long sides. We know this because the builders laid out a small paved area in front of the doors. Stones were also laid around the edge of the house floor where the turf walls once sat, to form a kind of footing or kerb. The roof was supported by internal rows of timber posts. It was probably steeply pitched to withstand the winter snow-

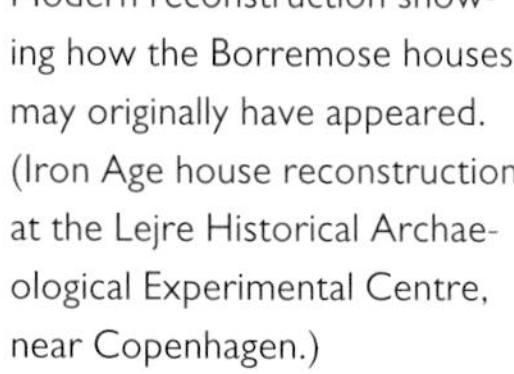

Modern reconstruction showing how the Borremose houses may originally have appeared. (Iron Age house reconstruction at the Lejre Historical Archaeological Experimental Centre, near Copenhagen.)

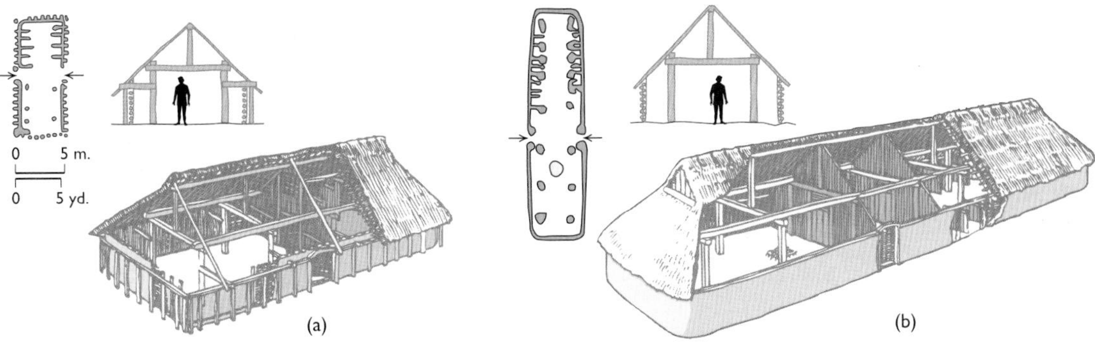

Reconstructions of Danish Iron Age houses from Grøntoft (a) and Hodde (b), showing lines of internal posts and partitions and the heavy thatched roofs. Rows of cattle stalls occupy the eastern ends. These reconstructions provide a good idea of how the Borremose houses might originally have looked.

fall and may have come down close to the ground. The turf walls might have been only three feet or so in height. The householders nonetheless took care to tidy up their inner faces, lining them with wickerwork.

What about the community at Borremose? We don't know how many people lived there at any one time, since we don't know which houses were in contemporary use, but in its heyday it may well have had over one hundred inhabitants. The enclosure itself, though, is of no great size, only 260 by 500 feet (80 by 150 meters) across. The fact that all the houses are oriented in the same direction shows that there was some order in their construction. The stone-paved road connecting with the access causeway wound its way to the middle of the site and then stopped at what may have been a small open space. But we lack the kind of detail found at other Danish settlements of the period, where post-holes reveal a pattern of internal fence lines dividing the settlement space into yards and enclosures. At these sites each enclosure represents a single farmstead, with two or more buildings. Borremose, too, was probably a cluster of farmsteads, clubbing together for protection, rather than a village of individual houses.

Before leaving the site, a word must be said about the elongated trough or depression that the visitor sees in the northwestern corner of the settlement. This was an oval pond that can be interpreted in one of two ways. The more straightforward explanation is that here the animals, which were herded within the enclosure, could find drinking water. The alternative possibility, however, is that this was a ritual pond, the sort of watery location in which the people of the time so often placed offerings to the gods.

But if it is ritual we are interested in, we must look beyond the Borremose settlement to the surrounding bog. Here have been found no fewer than three of the well-preserved bog bodies for which Denmark is so famous. In time, they straddle the period from the Danish Late Bronze Age to the Early Iron Age, a few centuries before the Borremose settlers built their houses on the island. But these particular bog bodies are part of a longer pattern that goes back into the Neolithic and on down to recent times. The key question is how they met their fate: were they convicts or sacrifices, merely hapless individuals who lost their footing and drowned, or were they murdered and cast into the bog?

The Borremose Bog Bodies

The first of the Borremose bog bodies was found in 1946, not far from the Iron Age settlement. Danish police were alerted, but this wasn't the first such discovery in a Danish bog and responsibility for the investigation soon passed to S. Vestergaard Nielsen, the curator of the local museum at Års. He carefully dug out the body, still encased in a block of peat, and packaged it up for transport to the National Museum in Copenhagen. There it underwent specialist analysis, which showed it to be the body of a man who had died over two thousand years ago—according to radiocarbon dating, around 840 B.C.

Most bodies once buried in the ground decay to bones within a matter of years (and in especially acidic soils not even the bones survive). Bodies that lie in peat bogs, however, can be amazingly well preserved, since the acid from the sphagnum moss, dissolved in the waters of the bog, both inhibits microbial decay and tans the skin, making it impervious and sometimes conserving even the internal organs. Occasionally the stomach contents have survived well enough for analysis, and hardy individuals on television programs have tasted the reconstructed "last meals" of Iron Age corpses. These have been notably unappealing to the modern palate, and indeed contain such a mixture of crops and weeds that archaeologists guess these individuals hadn't lived altogether ordinary lives before they died.

The Borremose man, like so many bog bodies, had died a violent death. The back of his skull had been smashed in and his upper right leg had been broken. It wasn't these injuries that caused his demise, however, since around his neck was a hemp rope. Investigators concluded he had been either hanged or strangled. There was another curious feature: the body was entirely naked, but a pair of sheepskin capes had been carefully rolled up and placed at his feet. This is hardly the action of highway robbers.

The following year, a second bog body was found in Borremose, two-thirds of a mile away. This was the body of a woman who had been placed face-down on a birch-bark sheet. The skull was crushed so severely that the brain was exposed, but the lower part of the naked body had been covered by a blanket and other cloths. Radiocarbon dating suggests that this happened around 475 B.C., making it the most recent of the three Borremose bodies. Nearby were the bones of a newborn baby.

The third and final Borremose body was discovered in 1948, a quarter of a mile south of the first. This was the body of a woman between twenty and thirty-five years old, radiocarbon dated to 770 B.C. Like the previous find, the skull was severely crushed, as if somebody had bludgeoned the face with a wooden club. Yet careful analysis of the body suggested it may very well have happened after death, and we don't really know how this individual died. The neck was too poorly preserved to say whether she had been strangled. But she did seem to have been scalped, the shoulder-length hair still attached to the loose flap of skin lying next to the head. She, too, went naked to the grave, though a woollen skirt had been placed over the body.

Archaeologists have long debated what these bodies might mean. They have combed the writings of Roman historians on the Germans, notably Tacitus, for clues as to how these unfortunates met their ends. Were they set upon on a dark night, dragged ignominiously to a shameful execution, or bludgeoned to death in honor of the gods? Execution seems, on balance, the most likely explanation. Whatever the true story, the remains throw remarkable if gruesome light on the people of Iron Age Denmark, bringing us face to face with real individuals.

The Thracian Cauldron from Gundestrup

Two miles (3 kilometers) north of Borremose lies another raised bog, the Raevemose (Fox fen), smaller in size but the site of a discovery even more remarkable than the Borremose bog bodies. Here, on 28 May 1891, a local farmworker digging for peat came upon the Gundestrup cauldron. The spot is marked today by a stone, as well it might be, for the Gundestrup cauldron has with justice been called "the single most discussed artefact from European prehistory" (*Antiquity,* 1987).

The visitor can see the cauldron today in the National Museum in Copenhagen, or view an excellent replica in the local West Himmerland museum at Års, near the findspot. It is made of silver, with a bowl-shaped base and horizontal sides decorated with figured scenes, hammered up from the back in relief. Closer inspection shows that some of the figures had gilding to pick out details of hair or ornaments. The eyes, which today are hollow, must once have been filled with colored glass.

This was not how the Gundestrup cauldron appeared when it was first discovered. It is made not from a single sheet of silver, but from a whole series of plates—five long rectangular plates, seven smaller rectangular plates, a circular "base plate," and two tubular rim fragments, which had been dismantled and stacked in the bowl-shaped base. It wasn't until it was taken to the Copenhagen Museum that it was reconstructed in the form we see today. And the arguments have been numerous as to whether that reconstruction is correct, whether the individual plates, for example, have been assembled in the correct order.

We know from numerous other finds that the people of Iron Age Denmark frequently deposited objects in lakes and peat bogs as offerings to the gods. It would be natural to regard the Gundestrup cauldron as one of these. But analysis of the peat around the cauldron showed that this had been dry ground in the Iron Age; the raised bog had grown up around it at a later date. It must, then, have been hidden in long grass or undergrowth—perhaps not an offering at all, but simply a possession that the owner never returned to claim.

The most remarkable feature of the Gundestrup cauldron is its weird decoration. The seven small plates around the outside and five larger plates around the inside have relief scenes skillfully hammered up from the back. What they

The silver cauldron found at Gundestrup, north of Borremose, in 1891. Richly decorated with mythological scenes, this cauldron is now thought to have been manufactured in southeast Europe and to have reached Denmark by trade or as war-booty.

represent isn't at all clear, though they seem to show mythological characters and deities. On one of the inner plates, for example, a human figure with deer antlers sits cross-legged, yoga-fashion, holding a metal torc in one hand and grasping the head of a snake in the other. On another plate, two registers of soldiers appear—cavalry above, footsoldiers beneath—while at the end of the file an overlife-sized figure thrusts a hapless individual head downward into a pot or cauldron. The whole set may represent a single legend or mythological story, now long forgotten.

When and where was this remarkable cauldron made? The "when" turns out to be easier than the "where," for although its date can be fixed at around 100 B.C. (or perhaps a little earlier), the origin of the cauldron is clouded in uncertainty. Most people now think it was made not in Denmark but by the Thracians, a people who during the last few centuries B.C. occupied part of modern Romania and Bulgaria. The Thracians were expert workers of sheet metal, and close parallels to elements of the Gundestrup cauldron have been found there. Nor does the iconography of the cauldron's scenes tie in with what we know of pagan Germanic beliefs. The yogalike pose of one of the figures, and the spoke wheel held aloft by another, may indicate links with even more easterly religious traditions, reaching across the steppes perhaps to Afghanistan and India. This exotic background makes it difficult to explain how it came to end up in a Danish bog. The simple, prosaic hypothesis is that it reached Denmark by trade. But there is also a theory that it was brought back as booty by the Cimbri, a Danish (Germanic) war-band who fought and plundered their way across Europe in the late second century B.C. They attacked the Danube lands in 118 B.C. and may have looted the cauldron in that same campaign. To add weight to the theory, Classical writers tell us the

BOG BODIES AND PREHISTORIC RITUALS

In the writings of Roman authors, the whole of the territory east of the Rhine, including modern Denmark, was occupied by peoples whom they referred to as "Germani" or Germans. The most famous account is by Tacitus, a Roman historian of the early second century A.D. One of his themes is the virtue and nobility of the Germans, which he contrasts with the corruption and vice of contemporary Rome. Despite this political coloring, Tacitus's account does contain information useful to archaeologists. In one passage, for example, he describes the punishment meted out for certain offenses: "Traitors and deserters are hanged on trees; cowards, shirkers, and those guilty of "unnatural vice" are pressed down under a wicker hurdle into the bog." The "unnatural vice" referred to here may include both homosexuality and promiscuity. The punishment of adulterous wives is described separately: "A guilty wife is summarily punished by her husband. He shaves off her hair, strips her naked, and in the presence of kinsmen turns her out of his house and flogs her all through the village." We are not told that adulterous wives are killed, but Danish archaeologist Elisabeth Munksgaard has remarked how many of the bog bodies are naked and have close-cropped hair. This may have been a mark of disgrace and could indicate that these were people executed for particular types of offenses.

Bog bodies have been unearthed in Denmark since at least the eighteenth century and probably long before. They have also been found in peat bogs elsewhere in northwestern Europe, notably in Germany, the Netherlands, and the British Isles. The recorded total comes to around seven hundred. One of the most famous to be found in recent years is Lindow man, a well-preserved bog body unearthed in northwest England in 1984. According to the specialists who studied the body, this individual had been knocked unconscious by two blows to the head, then killed by having his throat slit and his neck broken by a garrotte. Some of the Danish bog bodies, too—such as the famous Grauballe man—had apparently had their throats cut.

The "Borremose man" bog body, discovered near the Iron Age settlement in 1946. Note the rope still in position around the neck; the man had probably been killed by hanging or strangulation.

British archaeologist Stephen Briggs has recently made the provocative suggestion that archaeologists have entirely misread the evidence and that most (if not all) of these bog finds are the bodies of people who died by misadventure rather than execution or sacrifice. Briggs points out that the horrific injuries were very possibly inflicted long after death, perhaps during peat cutting or even through clumsy attempts to extract the corpse from the bog. Many of the bog bodies have neck injuries of one kind or another, and he argues these are the result, too, of failed attempts to drag the bodies clear, usually after death. In some cases a rope or halter may have been flung around the neck of a living person not to strangle them but during their final moments in a last desperate attempt to save them. This would explain why the ropes were found still in place around the necks. Some of the slit throats, Briggs argues, might also have been caused by ropes cutting into the soft tissue during rescue or recovery. Other clues point in the same direction: the branches or sticks often found near to the bodies (held out to the drowning person by would-be rescuers?); the inherent danger of the locations, where the supposed executioners, too, would have been risking death while they disposed of the victim; and the fact that bog bodies span a broad chronological range, from the Neolithic to modern times. All these make us rethink the theory of Iron Age bog bodies as ritual. Yet it is hard to escape from the idea that some, at least, were sacrifices or criminals, put to violent death before being disposed of in the bogs.

Cimbri came from Jutland. Furthermore, modern etymologists claim that their name is preserved in "Himmerland," the very region in which Gundestrup and Borremose are located.

A Moment in Time

Standing within the ramparts of Borremose, looking north across the level fenland, we can try to put together once again the landscape of the Iron Age: the raised bog around the settlement, providing security from attack; further away, the area in the middle of the bog where they disposed of the bodies; the small square fields on the low hills to either side, from which the people derived their food; and in the distance, beyond a slight rise, the Raevemose bog, once also dry, where the Gundestrup cauldron was hidden, perhaps by a local warrior returning to his homeland after long years abroad. We may also imagine the changing seasons—the bog bleak and windswept in winter, blooming with broom and aromatic bog-myrtle every spring; the hills breaking into new life as farmers returned to till their fields and lead their cattle out to pasture across the stone-built causeway after the hard winter cold. It was a pattern of life that endured barely changed for many centuries, but that is brought vividly into focus in the final centuries B.C. by the Borremose settlement, the gruesome bog bodies, and the great silver cauldron.

Further Reading

The published accounts of the early excavations at Borremose are scanty but Jes Martens has recently reviewed the site and its associated finds in "Borremose Reconsidered: The Date and Development of a Fortified Settlement of the Early Iron Age," *Journal of Danish Archaeology* 7 (1988), pp. 159–181. For the broader background, see Malcolm Todd, *The Northern Barbarians 100 BC–AD 300*, 2nd ed. (Oxford: Blackwell, 1987), and Lotte Hedeager, *Iron-Age Societies: From Tribe to State in Northern Europe, 500 BC to AD 700* (Cambridge, MA: Blackwell, 1992). The discovery of the Borremose bog bodies is described by P. V. Glob in *The Bog People: Iron Age Man Preserved* (Ithaca, NY: Cornell University Press, 1969), to be supplemented now (as regards the general study of bog bodies) by R. C. Turner and R. G. Scaife, eds., *Bog Bodies: New Discoveries and New Perspectives* (London: British Museum Press, 1995). For the Gundestrup cauldron, see the stimulating article by Anders Bergquist and Timothy Taylor, "The Origin of the Gundestrup Cauldron," *Antiquity* 61 (1987), pp. 10–24.

Further Viewing

Finds from Borremose, including the Borremose bog body and the Gundestrup cauldron, are in the National Museum (Nationalmuseet) at Copenhagen.

Picture Credits

Alexander Keiller Museum, Avebury: 92; R. Ambard/Centre Camille Jullian: 209; Arquivo Nacional de Fotografia/Instituto Portugues de Museus: 53, 55; Ashmolean Museum/Oxford: 185; N. Aujoulat, CNP-Ministère de la Culture: 35, 37; J. S. Barros/Arquivo Nacional de Fotografia/Instituto Portugues de Museus: 48, 52; Martin Beddal/Arquivo Nacional de Fotografia/Instituto Portugues de Museus: 47; Tadeusz Biniewski, Warsaw: 165 (top); Biskupin Museum Archives: 162, 165 (bottom), 167; Otto Braasch/Landesdenkmalamt Baden-Württemberg: 178; British Library: 93; Dr. Aubrey Burl: 58, 61; S. Cassen/CNRS: 66 (top); © 1997 by Centro Camuno di Studi Preistorici, Capo di Ponte, Italy: 146, 149, 150, 152 (all), 154, 155, 156, 157; CNRS/Centre Camille Jullian: 201, 205, 207, 208; Photograph by Henry de Lumley: 25; Dept. of Arts, Heritage, Gaeltacht and the Islands, Ireland: 116, 120, 121, 125; *Der Keltenfürst von Hochdorf*, by Jörg Biel/Konrad Theiss Verlag, Stuttgart: 173 (top), 175 (bottom); © English Heritage Photographic Library: 88, 90, 135, 137; J. M. Gassend, Institute De Recherche Sur L'Architecture Antique, Aix-en-Provence: 204, 206; Jean-Claude Golvin, Paris: 67; Historic Scotland: 101, 102, 104, 106; Historisk Arkæologisk Forsøgscenter, Lejre, Denmark: 216; Courtesy Keltenmuseum Hochdorf/Enz: 173 (bottom), 174 (all), 175 (top), 181; Malta Tourist board, London: 75 (bottom), 82; Eric Mose: 24, 26; Musee d'Archeologie du Morbihan-vannes: 66 (bottom); National Monuments Record/RCHME, © Crown Copyright: 194; Nationalmuseet, Copenhagen: 213, 214, 220, 221; National Museum of Archaeology, Valletta, Malta: 74, 75 (top),79; © S. Piggot/National Monuments Record Centre/RCHME: 89; Drawing by Henri Puech: 23; RCHME © Crown Copyright: 91, 144, 191; Andrzej Ring, Warsaw: 164, 168, 169 (all); Photo RMN-Jean Schormans: 42 (bottom); Photo Dominique Sacchi, Carcassone, France: 51; Chris Scarre: 64, 77, 78, 100, 112, 118, 179; Miranda Schonfield/© English Heritage Photographic Library: 195 (all); Society of Antiquaries of London: 192–193, 197; Sygma: 147; Javier Trueba/Contact Press Images: 22; David Trump: 81; Photo Jean Vertut: 30, 42 (top), 43; Wessex Archaeology: 141; Wiltshire Archaeological and Natural History Society: 142, 143.

Index

Note: Page numbers in italics indicate illustrations.

SKARA BRAE
BORREMOSE
NEWGRANGE
AVEBURY
STONEHENGE
MAIDEN CASTLE
BISKUPIN
CARNAC
HOCHDORF
LASCAUX
VALCAMONICA
CÔA VALLEY
ENTREMONT
TERRA AMATA
TARXIEN
Côa Valley
Lascaux
380,000 years ago
20,000 B.C.
18,000 B.C.
16,000 B.C.
14,000 B.C.
Terra Amata